The Covering

By: Lillian Nowlin-Hunt

That I may publish with the voice of thanksgiving, and tell of all thy wondrous works. Psalm 26:7

The Covering by Lillian Nowlin-Hunt

© 2013 Lillian Hunt. All rights reserved.

No part of this book may be reproduced in any written, electronic, recording, or photocopying without written permission of the publisher or author. The exception would be in the case of brief quotations embodied in the critical articles or reviews and pages where permission is specifically granted by the publisher or author.

Cover Illustration Copyright © 2013 by Lillian Hunt
Cover design by Kevin Berry
Editing by Nakeia Daniels of The Writers Fellowship Group Inc.
Author photograph by Pam Deal of iDEAL Photography
Lyrics "I'm Still Holding On" used by permission of Rev. Luther Barnes

Books may be purchased by contacting the publisher and author at: thecovering@hotmail.com.

Library of Congress Cataloging-in-Publication Data

ISBN: 978-0-9899462-0-9

10 9 8 7 6 5 4 3 2 1

UNITED BOOK PRESS, INC.

Baltimore, Maryland

PRINTED IN THE UNITED STATES OF AMERICA

DEDICATION

This book "The Covering" is dedicated to the one God inspired me to write it for, **You**!

It is because of **You** this book was created, and although I may not know **You**, God does and He had **You** in mind as every word was written, every emotion exposed, and every story told. This was all done specifically to reach **You**.

Acknowledgements

First and foremost, I would like to thank my Heavenly Father for entrusting me to be obedient to His instructions. It is because of Him I am here today. It is because of Him that I was able to write this memoir.

I cannot express the depth of my gratitude to my husband and children for patiently allowing me to follow through with the directives I received from the Lord. It has been your prayers and confidence in me that gave me strength to carry this project out to the end. God couldn't have placed me within a better household providing me with the greatest covering and offspring I could ever imagine.

To my mother, father, brother and sisters I love you all and thank you so much for letting me get it out, and for trusting that I would uphold the utmost integrity and love throughout this process. I have been blessed with a family that I love dearly and for that I am grateful.

As always, I can never thank my mother and father-in-law enough for birthing my covering. You raised him to be a man that provides for, loves, and protects his home. It is because of your nurturing with the help of the Lord that my husband is the awesome God fearing man that he is today. Also thank you for birthing such an extraordinary daughter for me to have as a sister-in-law.

I must take this opportunity to appreciate my beloved aunt Dr. Joanne Gabbin. Your guidance and mentoring has been priceless. I look up to you and I am honored to have you in my life. You truly are a phenomenal woman who was willing to invest in me. I am proud to have you as my aunt, and I hope I have made you proud as well.

I am extremely thankful for my cousin Kevin Berry, who in my time of need came through for me designing the book layout and cover. I appreciate your gift and look forward to doing more work with you. Love you always.

To Pam Deal of iDEAL Photography, my hair stylist Tiearra Wright, and my sweet cousin and make-up artist Crystal Boadu. Thank you all so much for making my photo-shoot a success. Thank you Harriett Wilson for your words of encouragement and support, they kept me running towards the finish line. You are an exceptional sister-friend for life.

A huge thank you goes out to one and to all who have directly or indirectly helped with this endeavor from the beginning to the end.

Lastly to my editor Nakeia Daniels and The Writers Fellowship Group Inc. who took my words, thoughts, ideas and concepts and made them jump off the page. I adore your passion for writing. Thank you for knowing just what to say at just the right time. Your resilience kept me focused.

Contents

Foreword

Introduction

Chapter 1   Daddy

Chapter 2   Choices

Chapter 3   Missing

Chapter 4   Lost

Chapter 5   New World Changes

Chapter 6   False Security

Chapter 7   Hope

Chapter 8   Soul Ties

Chapter 9   Independent Woman

Chapter 10   The Move

Chapter 11   A New Life

Chapter 12   Transition

Chapter 13   Deception

Chapter 14   Forgiveness

Chapter 15   A Storm

Chapter 16   Engaged

Chapter 17   The Wedding

Reflections

Foreword

What can be said about a woman of God that He has not already declared? What words can be shared about a daughter of Zion that God Himself has not already spoken in the earth?

"Who can find a virtuous woman? For her price is far above rubies. The heart of her husband doth safely trust her, so that he shall have no need of spoil...she is like the merchants ship, she bringeth her food from afar...she girdeth her loins with strength and strengtheneth her arms..she stretcheth out her hand to the poor; yea, she stretcheth forth her hand to the needy...she openeth her mouth with wisdom and in her tongue is the law of kindness...her children rise up and call her blessed, her husband also, and he praiseth her...favor is deceitful and beauty is vain, but a woman that feareth the Lord, she shall be praised."
Proverbs 31[excerpt]

Each line of this beautifully poetic scripture and more could be used to describe the author of this book. As someone who has known her for years, Lillian Nowlin-Hunt is indeed a virtuous woman. What amazes me about her life is that it resembles a rose. But not just any rose, a rose grown in the middle of a desert whose petals the fierce sand storms have blown away. And when it seemed the rose was bare and uncovered, destitute and destined to be scorched by the blazing sun, God sent rain, yes, rain, in the middle of the desert and began the miracle of her restoring her health and gathering all her precious petals back to Him. As the potter did with his clay, God took her limp, lifeless petals, rearranged them to His liking, and presented her radiant, stunning, and purified for the entire world to see.

Many view her rose today in astonishment and wonder, while others assume how she came to be the strong woman she is. Lillian wrote *The Covering* to make her life plain; to testify of the blessings of God, to tell her story free of filtration, safety nets and reservations. She embodies the woman who Proverbs juxtaposes to a merchant's ship, bringing food from afar. Lillian has come a mighty long way, carrying with her a unique and precious sustenance, not only for herself, but for the world to feast on.

Lillian has chosen to expose her real, unadulterated life in order to bring hope to those in pain, joy to those in sorrow, and deliverance to those bound by their yesterdays. Who better to write such a work? Who better to tell a prisoner shackled by one bad decision after another how to walk in liberty? That is exactly what God did for her. He set her free because she trusted in Him. That is what God will do for you when you read this book with a heart open to the love, forgiveness, and redemptive blood of Jesus Christ.

I pray that every word, every story, and every chapter will illuminate the power of God to save and set your heart, mind and soul free. I pray that you allow the covering of The Master to shroud your life with His love. I pray that you allow the testimony of a little girl from Rochester, N.Y. who grew into a virtuous woman of God to change your life as it did mine.

Nakeia L. Daniels
President and Founder
The Writers Fellowship Group
Riverside, CA

Introduction

Onlookers have the luxury of dissecting your life with no strings attached. They can - if they desire, express strong thoughts and opinions about the choices you've made with little insight or intellect of your inner world. Effortlessly the journey of your existence is scrutinized with enumerated observations of how you've handled significant life experiences. You are rated by the results of these circumstances (whether good or bad) leaving others to have what would seem like solid, concrete opinions of who you are.

Have you ever wondered why many onlookers are hesitant to disclose their own encounters in life? Could it be that doing so would expose the reality that they are just as flawed as you and I? The truth is we're all flawed; we've all sinned and fallen short of God's wondrous glory. For a while I've noticed a breakdown between those who are Christians and those who we were commanded to share Christ with and I think it grieves the heart of God.

All of my life my one desire was to have people who were genuinely interested in helping, not debating about my choices. Living is hard enough. It's even harder when you have the expectations of passing and failing all the while feeling as if you are placed under a microscope for close review at every turn. I wanted to share my story with anyone who will read it. I wanted to tell of God's goodness, even when I was not good to Him. I wanted to use my story to encourage anyone that with God, nothing is impossible. This book is a memoir about my life. God told me to write it and I obeyed.

Traditionally the first male who comes into a female's life is her father. Daddy is there to love to his little princess and shield her as no one else can. A little girl should sleep soundly at night because her father is there to protect her. A daddy should be there to comfort his daughter from bad dreams to bad decisions because he is her earthly covering. Of course every female doesn't have the luxury of having daddy there from the beginning, and over time we realize the importance of the father in a child's life – especially to their daughter.

I wasn't my father's princess, I was his Oreo cookie. This was a name I was given at a young age. It was a label (I grew to understand as I matured); a name that had an immense impact on how I would view myself for years. My relationship with my dad or lack thereof caused the grown-up princess (or in my case the adult-sized Oreo cookie) to seek attention, validation and love from questionable men. Often women wonder how they got in their bad situation or relationship and are desperate to get out. Some women believe that the misfortune and mistreatment they receive is what they deserve.

God created us in His image and likeness, which denotes that what is done on earth, should reflect what is done in heaven. That means everyone needs a covering. Although unsure of what a covering is we know we need it; we know there is a void in our souls and we search frantically throughout life for it from birth. Coming across diverse challenges we discover a world filled with deception misleading us to believe in false safety. The optimal design of a covering is to give you real security, to make you understand that you are protected, complete, hidden, relevant, emotionally and spiritually connected with your mind, body and soul.

My memoir consists of real events that have taken place in my life. They are not just real to me, but also to many women far and wide who live with their silence. We feel that we are the only ones dealing with tough times in life and make wrong decisions, but we are not alone. I have chosen to be courageous; to be transparent with my life to help someone else. While some choose to be onlookers, I choose to use my life as a platform and be a partaker in your encouragement. I choose to expose my scars and use my life as a resource for you to reflect upon.

This book was written to be a source of truth and support for individuals who think that their life is full of horrible mistakes and that those mistakes define them. These moments in our lives are just that – moments and with every moment a time and season is developed. These times and seasons create a way of life that becomes our journey, our reality and our story. Every story doesn't have the happy ending that we dream about, yet it is ours. In the end we all come to realize God had a plan in mind, He knows you by name, and will provide The Covering that you need if you let Him.

Lillian Nowlin-Hunt
Author
Baltimore, MD

Chapter 1

Daddy

"I'm not having any children! I don't like kids, and I don't EVER want to have any!" I said. *"Be careful of what you say Lillian, you'll end up with a whole crew of children."* Thanks Mommy...

*****

So now I am an Oreo Cookie – Black on the outside White on the inside. Why am I considered White when I speak proper English? I got teased so much that I intentionally diminished my vocabulary to stop the teasing.

> Note to self: Lillian, joining after school clubs and focusing dutifully on your studies will only make the teasing worse for you so try not to do either of those things, ok? You're smart, but don't let it show. It intimidates people. Got it? Good.

There was never a real plan for me to succeed in this life so why try, right? It's easier to be mean and rude. No one expects anything from a child like that. Her forecast is nothing but doom and gloom.

Daddy

I was never going to meet anyone's expectations anyway so no need to waste time on dreams that come from the inside – the *White* side. Just be tough on the outside – the *Black* side where you don't have to meet any standards. You can say what you want and no one will correct you because they think you don't know any better. Pronounce words improperly and be corrected to make the educated folk feel superior as if they are helping you out when all along the inside of you – the *White* side knows far more than anyone will ever know.

This was the life of an Oreo Cookie. My daddy gave me that name.

I am the middle child of four children. In most families you can easily see what position each child holds. However, there is always something about the middle child that is difficult to figure out. My brother Douglas Jr. (Patrick) is the only boy and the oldest child, so he holds two positions: being the only boy (coveted position, I might add) *and* being the first born. My sister Pamela Irene comes next. She holds the title of the oldest daughter – the first born baby girl. Then there's me. *Hmmmm, first born boy position – taken. First born girl position – taken. Where does that leave me? Oh yeah, I'm the baby!* Yes, baby girl Lillian Mary Nowlin. How about that? Holding a position and a title. Not too bad for my first few days on earth.

> Note to self: Lillian, We come into this world without knowing that we're already in a dog

> fight for positions! Make that a lesson learned, darling.

Unfortunately I didn't hold my initial position long, and by no fault of my own. It was not lost due to my incompetence, fiscal irresponsibility, or issues with my style of management. Nothing quite as dramatic. I lost my position by way of natural causes.

When a mommy and daddy love each other very much…

Just a few years after I was born, our family welcomed home my baby sister. Another beautiful little girl named Melody Marie, my one and only baby sister. Now that she is the baby of the family, booting me out of my spot by no fault of her own, what title do I have? What position do I hold? I'm not the first born, not the first girl, not the last – who ever remembers the non-title holder? I'm already scrambling to make a name for myself so I won't be forgotten; so someone will remember that I exist. It's not easy being a kid trying to understand where you fit in, unsure who has time for you, and all the while wondering if your mere existence even matters to anyone because you don't really have a place – proverbially stuck in the middle.

*****

"Oh Daddy, can we go to Carvel Ice Cream and get some ice cream sandwiches?" Whether summer or winter Carvel ice cream tasted the same. Delicious. This was one of Daddy's favorites and we loved it too. Daddy took the time out to get ice cream for us and make sure there were vanilla and chocolate sandwiches to choose

Daddy

from. I always wanted vanilla – too much chocolate puts me in tune with my outside – my Black side, because as I said, I'm the Oreo cookie. Daddy got us ice cream sandwiches and Mommy had a soft cone. It was always fun to sit outside of Carvel's and enjoy our creamy treat while listening to my parents lovingly chat with each other.

We listened to daddy's CB scanner to see what was happening on our side of the city. We heard about a local showdown and Daddy jumped in the car and drove us by to see the police in action. Fun times for sure. Especially since Daddy drove a sky-blue Dodge Plymouth. Police would mistake him for a detective and we would be able to drive up close to the scene. Daddy sure knew how to make a night interesting.

All that excitement made me tired. Going to bed after a night like that would seem easy, except when the sound of a door bell stirs you and instantaneously you smell an aroma that would wake you up no matter how deep your slumber; a fresh pizza with everything on it no anchovies. Daddy would order pizza after all four of us children had gone to sleep. Sometimes if you listened to Mommy and Daddy's conversation you would know when they were going to order pizza. It was a childproof secret-parent-code they would use to throw us off their scent but I decoded their cryptograms. I would go upstairs and begin my plan. The strategy was very simple. Occupy myself doing something boring that no one else wanted to do so they'd fall asleep as I remained awake – quietly so my parents wouldn't know.

Daddy

Once everyone was sleep and the pizza ordered, there was nothing left for me to do but keep quiet, not making a sound so my parents would think I was asleep as well. The concentration it took to hold that still caused me to get sleepy, but I was determined to complete my mission. The doorbell ringing would wake me up if I fell asleep, and I would prepare for the next step. Easing out of the bed gently to not wake any of my siblings, I quietly begin tiptoeing down the steps very slowly so that the stairs would not make that creaking noise as I step down on them, carefully, one by one. I made it down and prepared my eyes to look tired and sad, put on my sleepiest voice and said to my parents "I can't sleep, I'm hungry". Any Daddy that is a true parent knows he would never want to send a child to bed hungry. What would I get for all my troubles? A slice of pizza! Mission accomplished. To this day pizza is one of my favorite foods. It has to be made right, not this commercial pizza but a family owned special NY recipe pizza.

There is a point of time in one's life where weight gain is prominent, and the children notice the change. For us, tying daddy's shoes became a regular task. His belly sat out so far that bending over to tie his own shoes was not something he could comfortably do. Daddy kept his shoes shined, so no matter how old they were they didn't look that way. He made sure we knew how to shine his shoes well. There were white rags with black polish stains on them tucked away in different areas around the house and we knew that they were used for shining daddy's shoes only. I hated tying his shoes or putting his socks on for him. After a while I thought, maybe we shouldn't be eating those large pizzas so late at night.

Mommy started baking daddy's chicken. She would have one of us season it and place it in the oven because daddy was trying to lose weight. Mommy wanted to lose weight too so now they both drank Slim Fast drinks in a can. Strawberry, chocolate and vanilla drinks – but do they work? We couldn't tell. Daddy would ride a bike. He would find bikes that were being thrown away and fix the chain on them so that we could have a bike to ride too, and we would all go out and ride our bikes together. All those exercise ideas were great but inconsistent. No one lost a pound.

As a child I saw boneless, skinless baked chicken breast in our kitchen often. Eating baked foods seemed to be how everyone thought losing weight would happen, as if by osmosis. But when it came down to some folks, I thought they were supposed to be big. My mother, father and grandmother were all portly. Being overweight wasn't something I was concerned with. I didn't know what all the fuss was about. You were either slender or plump and my family was plump. End of story. Or so I thought.

Everything has to have an opposite. For every mountain there is a valley, after every dark night comes the luminous morning light, for every act of hatred, there are acts of love to confound the world and bring us to our knees. If that's the case, what's the big deal about being fat and losing weight? It's not that serious, is it? Maybe it is serious. Maybe daddy's shortness of breath and exasperation at menial tasks was more serious than I understood at the time. At the age of adolescence I could never imagine being overweight. But if my parents were overweight would that mean that I would be like them when I got older? If my parents suffered and struggled through life, would that mean I would suffer and struggle too?

*****

My given name is Lillian Mary, derived from my paternal grandmother's name - Mary Katherine, and my maternal grandmother's name – Lillie Mae. I love my grandmothers and carry them with me wherever I go. My maternal grandmother's full name is Lillie Mae Brumfield. Grandma Mary was very slender and full of energy; she could run circles around us children. Grandma Lillie liked to take her time doing things like baking cookies in the kitchen, and while my first name came from hers, I didn't want those big arms. Every woman in our family seemed to acquire those big arms. Mommy has big arms and is short; short and chubby like Grandma a.k.a 'Chaney' and I love it. She looks like a mom, not a sister or best friend.

Everyone always said how I strongly favor my mom, but I have my dad's complexion. I want to be light skinned like my mom with the beautiful thin hair she has. Her hair is soft and easy to comb – it never gets thick needing to be straightened with a straightening comb like mine. She can bind it up into a bun in the back with little curls hanging on the side with a wavy bang in the front. Hailing from

Mississippi the Brumfield clan were known to have Cherokee Indians in their ancestry. At least that's what they said.

Being the parents of four children obviously had its challenges, but there were advantages. With three girls and one boy my parents had free labor times four. Yes, there was a dishwasher, but the dishes were washed by hand. We all had chores no matter our age. From feeding the dog to cleaning the bathrooms, housekeeping was something all four of us could have specialized in. My daddy never had to take his dress shirts to the cleaners. Mommy made sure the shirts were cleaned and we ironed and starched his shirts so well you would never see a wrinkle. Learning how to sew with a needle and thread, washing and folding clothes neatly, and learning how to clean collard greens and snap peas to freeze for later were all learned at an early age.

We would get collard greens and string beans from the fields and from gardens and pile them in the sink for cleaning, sorting, bagging and freezing. We got happy when Mommy would have cans of string beans because we didn't have to do anything but eat those after she cooked them. A lot of food like apples, plums, cherries, collard greens and string beans came from farms or from gardens. No matter who the kind person was that gave them to us, it was our job to make sure they were clean. We had to clean chicken too. Pulling hairs and fat off the chicken and looking at all that blood would cause me to rethink whether I wanted to eat it. After one whiff of that chicken frying in Crisco lard my thoughts would change. I still love me some fried chicken.

*****

There was a vent in the floor of the room that Pam and I stayed in. We used to sweep all of the trash from up under our beds and in our rooms down into that vent and close it. It made cleaning the room so easy we never had to take a dustpan and pick up trash. All we had to do was sweep the trash into the vent. Mommy never knew that's where we put the trash. Until one time in the winter when it was very cold, and the vent needed to be opened. When she opened it and looked down at all the trash we hid down in there, we knew we were in trouble. She explained to us that putting paper and trash down in the vent could cause a fire and we could all burn up. We no longer put trash in the vent. Well, not big pieces of paper anyway. Having a clean house with clean bedrooms was mom's priority. Since it was her priority it was made our priority as well. A clean house was important. We never knew who would have to stay at our home as visitors unexpectedly.

*****

What was going on with Daddy? He was always ready to beat us with the belt. Well if the belt got lost we wouldn't get a whipping right? Wrong. Daddy would go down the street and into neighbors yards and hand pick specific branches off trees to make switches. All of our neighborhood friends knew when one of us or all of us was getting ready to get a whipping. When we did something really bad

Daddy

or the switch looked a little flimsy he would braid a few together. Getting out of line was not an option in our house. If we did, we would suffer the consequences. Even the dog had to be obedient – if dogs could speak I imagine Snowball would have a lot to say.

Daddy made sure our life wasn't full of chores, but we had our share. Part of our chores was taking care of the house pet. We had many dogs: Mickey, King, Queeny, Bullet, and the last was Snowball, our all white full-blooded German shepherd. Snowball was a house pet; she had been so well taken care of we didn't think she would make it in the outside world. After a while Daddy said he was tired of Snowball and we couldn't afford to keep her anymore. He took Snowball in the car and drove far out into the suburbs. Once out there he put her out the car and pulled off.

When daddy came home we were all sad that a member of our family was gone forever. Bittersweet feelings erupted in the house. We were happy we didn't have to clean up after Snowball anymore. Daddy was happy too because he no longer had to buy dog food. What we didn't consider were all the things we would miss about her now that she was gone. What about walking her in the neighborhood and everyone being scared of her? What about feeding her chicken bones with hot sauce all over them? What about her running in the yard from one side to the other excited to play with us? We wanted our dog back.

A day or so went by with no family pet to play with. Things didn't seem the same. The doorbell rang and looking out the window there was no one there. Opening the front door there was no one in the driveway. The doorbell rang again. We raced to the back door assuming our visitor didn't think to come to the front of the house. We opened the back door and there she was. It was Snowball! Snowball found her way back home and rang the doorbell for us to let her in. There you have it. She may not have been able to talk, but she showed how smart she was by finding her way back home and ringing the doorbell like she was a human. Daddy could do nothing but laugh and we were able to keep her – she knew where she belonged!

Mommy and the rest of us were fine with having a dog for a pet, but any other pet or animals in the house was unacceptable. In every home there may be some ants, or few spiders, but when it came down to a rodent that was a whole other story. Dad and Mom were so young with four children, people often wanted to give us things. There was an elderly woman at the church we attended who had a bag of clothes to give to us. Although my mother did not want to take the bag of clothes, she expressed her gratitude and took them anyway. It was a big black garbage bag and we brought it home not knowing what a bad idea that would turn out to be. Once the bag got into the house and my mom went through it, she saw that not only were their clothes in the bag, but there were also roaches. Mommy tried to kill all of the roaches but they were crawling everywhere. This was the beginning of the infestation of roaches in our home. Rapidly the house became infested. They were everywhere. Daddy

Daddy

was furious. He went out and bought something called Combat that was supposed to kill them right away.

I would sit and watch the roaches go in a hole on one side of the small Combat structure and out a hole on the other side but they didn't die. Daddy then bought some white powder called Borax and poured it down along the edges of the wall. Not long afterwards we saw powder-covered roaches roaming around the house. It was irritating in the beginning because it looked like those roaches just would not die. Daddy went even further with a liquid spray around the house to kill them. Roaches everywhere with no sign of them dying off.

There was a ritual we would do when coming into the house. We didn't just come into the house and go to our rooms or sit down and relax. When we would come in the house at night after being at church we would come in through the back door. Coming through the back door meant we entered the house through the kitchen. Dad would wait until everyone came into the house and then he would turn on the lights. The light switch was on the right hand side of the wall next to the door, but no one would dare turn the lights on until everyone made it into the house. We knew once the lights came on we didn't have time to waste.

As the back door shut and the light switch was turned on we began stomping in every area throughout the kitchen on the floor to kill roaches. Looking on the floor we see the roaches running everywhere. Daddy would do a count, one, two, three, and then

Daddy

turned on the light and we would begin stomping. We were stomping on little roaches, big roaches, baby roaches, pregnant roaches, male roaches, female roaches, all kinds of roaches everywhere. All of us would try to kill as many as possible. Leaving no survivors we tried to kill every roach before they could run from the light and scatter. Once we killed all the roaches possible, the dead roaches would be swept up and thrown away. The kitchen floor would then have to be mopped with bleach.

No matter how long it took or how annoying it was, my mother refused to have a nasty home and with or without roaches this was going to be a clean house. We learned that roaches like to live and breed in wet gloomy areas. That meant we couldn't leave dishes in the sink or put dishes in the cabinets without drying them off. No matter if the dishes were clean or not, when it was time to eat or cook, the dishes were washed and rinsed again in the event that roaches crawled on them while sitting in the cabinets. Condiments had to be closed tightly and wiped down clean. The water in the iron used to make steam had to be cleaned out, because if left in there too long the roaches would use the iron as a new breeding space.

It took no time for those roaches to come out of that bag and infest our entire house, but it took a very long time for the roaches to be removed. After a long while the roaches were gone but the effect lingered on. It did not matter who was giving us things the rule was to shake everything out before they came in the house. Who knew from one bag with roaches in it an entire house could be affected. We

Daddy

never said a word to the woman who gave us the bag of clothes but any bag of clothes that she gave after was immediately thrown in the trash once leaving the church.

    The same woman loved my dad so much she wanted to cook dinner for him one Sunday. She lived out in the country on a gloomy dirt road. Her house was a small rancher, and Mommy really didn't want to go. The invitation kept coming over and over and over again so finally my parents gave in and we went to her home for Sunday dinner. On the drive there Mom and Dad gave us the typical parent speech: do not touch anything, do not ask for anything, speak when spoken to otherwise I won't hesitate to beat your behind. While being so hungry after service on Sunday afternoon ready to eat dinner, we had no intentions of touching or doing anything but getting a good meal.

    When we got to the home we had to sit in the living room and wait for dinner to be ready. The living room was small with patterned sofas covered in plastic. There was an old huge floor model TV that we all gathered around to watch, but none of us wanted to sit on the floor. The carpet on the floor was light in shade, a tan and pepper multi-color type of carpet. No one wanted to sit on the floor because it was hard to distinguish if the dark-shaded areas on the floor were indeed the color scheme or little baby roaches. The only way we could tell the difference is by staring down at the carpet and waiting to see if anything moved.

Daddy

There was one wall in the living room that was covered with mirror tiles. As I was looking at myself in the mirror, I saw a black spot. The black spot was interesting to me because it began to move. I focused in on it to realize that it was a roach. After seeing the roach on the mirror I began to look around the house. On the carpeted floor there was another black spot, but the black spot wasn't a stain, they were baby roaches. After being told not to make a move by our parents, we were looking at each other wondering how Mom and Dad will get us out of this one. All I could think about was whether there were roaches in the food. As adult conversations were going on, the children continued inspecting ourselves to ensure no roaches crawled on us.

We try not to pay attention to the roaches on the mirror wall or on the floor and concentrated on the television. Just then a roach begin to cross the screen of the TV. In total shock with our mouths wide open someone yelled, Roach! At that very same time we were being called to the kitchen because dinner was ready. Needless to say I did not have an appetite that day. No matter how hungry we were, I don't think any of us really ate the food that day.

I always thought so highly of Mom and Dad for still being so kind and continuing to thank the woman for her hospitality and feeding us even though we didn't eat the food. They made it seem as if they had such a wonderful time at her home when the whole time all we were thinking about where those roaches. Dad knew how to make someone feel like their kind gestures, no matter how small, were worth a million dollars. But when we got in our car we were all shaking our clothing to make sure we weren't taking anything with us that we did not bring. No matter what pest problems this elderly woman had, she was a nice woman. A woman that we had much respect for, because for as many kind people there were in our church, there was definitely a portion of mean folk as well.

*****

> ```
> Note to self: This Oreo Cookie has plans for her
> life, and it doesn't include these mean old
> church folk!
> ```

Church is all I know because that was what we did the most: go to church. Daddy being an Elder was always preaching. That meant we were always at church, and we were going to sing his sermonic selection *God Has Smiled On Me*. I hate singing. Big Sister has the voice so why should I sing. So many different churches Daddy preached at. Revival after revival and invitation after invitation with his wife and children right by his side. I could hear him preaching in my sleep.

"Jesus – AhHaw, Is the Answer – AhHaw".

With all that loud preaching falling asleep wasn't easy to do during service at times. Who are all these women that would hug on us and kiss on us smiling in my daddy's face saying "Oh Elder Nowlin, you so crazy" as Dad makes a joke. Why is it that these women like to make meals for my family and cater to my daddy? Daddy's preaching must really take an effect on women because they seem to flock to him once service is over. Getting nice gifts wasn't so

Daddy

bad, but all the whispers and hearing other children repeat what their parents were talking about mentioning your family didn't feel good at all.

The preacher with a wandering eye.

Daddy taught me it doesn't matter if you are religious or not. If you give a man the impression that you are interested in doing any and everything with him – even if he is married he will take you up on the offer – if he is a preacher or not. Watching women hover around a man because of a gift God has given him is distasteful to witness. Who wants a woman that will easily give herself to you without hesitation, thought or a care in the world? Only a man who has yet to realize his worth will link up with a woman who has yet to recognize hers.

What about Mom? Mom made sure we all looked good and represented Daddy well. Why is it that women are so attracted to preachers?

Note to self: I will NEVER marry a preacher.

I don't want to be held accountable for what I would do to a woman for disrespecting me because she wants my husband. Mommy stood strong, she held on. In my opinion Mommy was crazy.

I would sneak into my parent's bedroom and into my mother's closet when she was not home. I would put on my mommy's high heel shoes and start shouting like I got 'the spirit' while looking in the mirror. As I look at my reflection, I realize how much I want to be just like her when I grow up. She loves her husband and her children – family means everything to her. Taking care of our home is a priority and no matter what is said or done, she remained the battery that our family operated on.

Little girls shouldn't be in men's faces. You are to speak when spoken to. Sit next to your mother and don't say a word or you will be pinched. Everyone only sees the tears running down your face never noticing that your skin has been twisted to the point it is now wrinkled and red. My mother was a gifted pincher. Her pinches could be felt for days. If we made the wrong move while being pinched we were subject to have a bump raised where the skin was being twisted together. She would talk so softly to us without raising her voice. In a whisper she would chastise us with the features in her face remaining happy. Never a look of anger across her face, she would pinch us as if she was just rubbing our arm - never breaking a sweat, but hurting worse than a belt to our behind. The soreness of my arm would feel as if I just left the pediatricians office getting an immunization. My arm was so red I wanted to cover it with a band aid.

It's Sunday. Daddy made sure we were in church. No matter what happened we were going to be in church. Daddy challenged us to learn the Lord's Prayer. Whoever could say it correctly would get some money. Daddy knew how to motivate us, and Mommy was right there supporting him and raising us the best they both could. I got my hair straightened the night before. Mommy always knows how to let that heat get really close to your neck. "Be still or you will get burned," she would say. Many times I think I was burned on purpose. I cut the hair closest to my ears on each side so that she didn't have to put the hot comb so close, but all that did was make her put it closer because now my edges were shorter.

> Note to self: Don't cut your edges before you get your hair straightened. It will only make matters worse.

Up early for Sunday school. Do we have to go? Absolutely. We go to church all day long on Sundays. Sunday school with Sister Hopkins is a blast. She is a fun Sunday school teacher – just don't make her upset. I want to keep my Sunday school card because it has a picture on it that tells the Bible story that we learned for that Sunday. So interesting to see a picture of the story she is telling us and believing every word that comes out of her mouth. Oh, I love Sunday school. Not just because of Sister Hopkins and the card class, but because I get to sit next to Johnnie. Johnnie and I are going to get married soon. It didn't matter that we were little kids – we were going to be together forever. Johnnie asked me did I like him yes or no. I had to circle my answer and give the note back to Tina for her to give it to him. Will you be my girlfriend yes or no? Oh, yes Johnnie! We are in love. Why won't Daddy let Johnnie be my boyfriend? Doesn't he know that puppy love is not just cute it's real? Well Johnnie's aunt Michelle made me a ring out of a paper clip and we picked some wild flowers from the field next to the church. This wedding is going to happen no matter what Daddy says. Johnnie is my best friend, always has been and always will be.

Daddy

After Sunday Morning worship we stayed at the church for dinner. Redeem Church of God In Christ in Williamson, New York where the very fine pastor is Elder William Jones. Mommy and Daddy would do anything for that man – truth is he would do anything for them too. Why does Elder Jones always feel the need to pray for me every time he sees me? Whenever I fall asleep in church he calls my name out in the middle of his sermon to wake me up. He never calls out my other besties Tina or Dyna, just me. Get this. Do that. Say this. Grab that. He sat in the pulpit and we would sometimes catch him picking his nose.

Lillian can't do this. Lillian don't do that. Lillian, Lillian, Lillian. I wondered – is my name the easiest to remember? Is that why he called my name so many times? No matter how old I got he never let up on me. What made that man feel that he had to show me that type of love and attention? I didn't have a grandfather – he was the closest thing to being one to me, but in the end he was so much more.

Superintendent William Jones, the husband of Willie Pearl Jones, the father of so many, and the spiritual leader to so many more. Friday night was pastoral teaching, after service we couldn't wait to hear the words "I went fishing today". We knew what that meant, we were on our way to Pastor Jones' house and we were going to eat fish and grits. The adults would be in the kitchen holding adult conversations, and the children would be in the living room sitting in front of the television with it turned down low on the Fox channel watching Arsenio Hall. We had to keep the television down low because of the musical guests that would be on the show. We could get through the comedy jokes in the beginning and the naming of the dog pound, but we had to be careful when the musical guest came on. It seemed like just at that time when the guests would be on stage to sing an adult will come in the room and ask the question "What are y'all watching in here?"

A little white church in the middle of nowhere. Sitting off the side of the highway – route 104, surrounded by so many open fields gave us a place to run around between services. We would play in the dirt parking lot or race around the church until we got tired. Six in the evening was the time for Young People Willing Workers (YPWW) group session. After that was the evening service. Ugh! Service lasted all day. It's okay because Johnnie and Tina were there and sometimes Dyna would be there too. We knew how to make the most boring church services fun.

Having my daddy around, although I was unaware at the time, was priceless. The fear and respect I had for him goes without saying. So many were against the way Daddy disciplined us, always telling us how wrong Daddy was for treating us the way that he did. You don't have to be such a stern and strict parent for your children to be obedient and do the right things, some would say. He handled his children the way that he did because he was responsible for us. God gave us to him and expected for him to show us the right way to live. Anything less than that was unacceptable.

Daddy

Daddy is who all little girls look to as their first love. The man who protects you from all your fears, and treats you as you should be treated; making you feel special even with more than one daughter. Daddy makes his little girl feel like she is his favorite – the one that has all his love and attention. Daddy anoints your head with oil with those ashy, hard hands. Daddy is the man that sets your expectations for the future. Daddy is the provider, the head of the household, the decision maker. You never see weakness in Daddy – nothing but power and strength. Daddy may not have all the money in the world and may not supply all your wants, but Daddy supplies your needs. More than getting all that we wanted, we had our Daddy in the house. I got to see my Daddy every day, not just on weekends. I know who my Daddy is and look a lot like him.

From the discipline to the fun – being a daddy is not an easy job. There was no employee manual that came with having children – so we all say. But there is one book that is referred to multiple times throughout this life – The Holy Bible. In there is the guide to being a good husband and wife. In there is the guide to being a parent and being a good child. Everything you can think of in life, the Bible is the guide to your success. Daddy knew this and Daddy followed the teachings of the Bible. He was a husband to his wife and a father to his children. Being the head of our household meant blessings flowed through him and so would curses. God spoke to him on how to run this house and we followed in obedience with respect and the fear of God. Daddy is our covering. Daddy is my Covering.

CHAPTER 2

CHOICES

When I was in school I loved to read. As a child I read books that were full of adventure and knowledge and history. Who wouldn't want to read a book? I was hooked. I couldn't imagine life without books. Then one day everything changed. I will never forget the day I stopped reading books for good.

"Alright class. This year we will have a reading competition," Ms. Haskins explained. "For those of you who do not have books to read at home please take this catalog home to your parents and bring it back with the correct amount of money to purchase the books you would like to read." She continued. "Any of you who may already have these books please look for books that you do not have. For every book you read you need to complete a summary, including what your book was about and what you most enjoyed about the book. There will be different levels of prizes for every book that you read."

The more Ms. Haskins explained this reading competition the more excited I became. I was the prize charger at the racetrack gate chomping at the bit. I planned on getting all the prizes. I didn't want

Choices

to ask my parents for the money to purchase any new books out of the Scholastic catalog, but I loved taking the catalog home and circling the books that I would have gotten if we had extra money. Each book advertised in the catalog had a description of what the book was about with a picture of the book beside it. I salivated reading the summary of each book, feeling the slick, shiny paperback cover, or the expensive hardcover in my hand, sniffing the pages in my mind, only to be jolted by the reality that I was unable to purchase any of the books I wanted. I definitely wouldn't want to ask my parents to purchase me a book when we were struggling to obtain our general needs.

    Ms. Haskins was a heavy set White woman with short brown hair. She loved her students, all the little Black and White children that filled the chairs in her room. Heather was one of my best friends and she was White. Heather like me, loved to read too. The only difference was Heather was always able to purchase books and I wasn't. She would let me borrow her books once she was finished, but this always left me behind and not on the same competition level as everyone else.

    Once we read our 15th book we were rewarded a special lunch with Ms. Haskins. She was always taking the class on fun field trips and nature walks around the school. Whoever read enough books would be able to go. It didn't look like I would be done in time since I didn't have my own books to read, and had to wait to read Heather's. I had read about 4 books maybe 5 but I couldn't read them fast enough to keep up with the kids who had their own books. Even my Black friends who couldn't afford books were passing me. I was flabbergasted. I wondered how my Black friends were able to read more books than me when I never saw them read any books. They were racking in the prizes and were very close to getting the highly coveted Lunch Prize. After I inquired my friend enlightened me to the scheme. Instead of actually reading the books they read the summary on the catalog, changed a few words around, wrote it out and turned it in and, ta-da! No one would ever know they didn't actually read the book.

This was easy. I went from reading books to summarizing them and was able to turn in more summaries right away. I was so excited to receive the prizes for each summary I turned in. I didn't stop there. I had the goal in mind to get all 15 books. I was going to be able to go out to eat with my favorite teacher. I turned in 5 more summaries that I had written from old scholastic catalogs I had at home. This was the easiest reading I had ever done. I proudly turned in my summaries and saw the excitement on Ms. Haskins face. She was so proud of all of us working so hard to read all of these books and gladly looked forward to taking us out to eat.

I couldn't wait to get home and tell my mom how I was able to finish enough reading summaries and turned them in within enough time to attend the outing with some of the other classmates. My mom was so proud of me and was glad I had taken the time to finish something I had started. As anxious as I was to get my coveted

Choices

prize, it felt dishonest taking credit for something that I didn't actually do. I wanted to confess and say that I had cheated, but all that would do is get me in trouble. Part of me was excited and the other part was sad. No matter what happened I would know that I didn't deserve the prize. Nothing, not even a special lunch could change that. Nevertheless, the excitement took over and the sadness was buried inside. The Oreo cookie knew she had done wrong. The part of me that I was told was the White me wanted to actually read those books and enjoy them page for page. The part of me I was told was the Black me didn't care as long as I was able to go with my friends out to eat. This is what I was taught. This is what was expected of me. I didn't believe that anyone seriously counted me in the group of children that would read all 15 books just to go out to eat.

> Note to self: Black children don't read books. We find anything to do except read a book. Haven't you heard? If you want to hide something from a Black person, put it in a book. Reading is for smart folks. Don't you know that Girl?

The next day in class we were all excited talking about the outing as we walked into the room. When we came to the doorway all the lights were off in the classroom. The only light in the class were the sunbeams shining through the long row of windows. Ms. Haskins didn't greet us in the doorway as usual. She was sitting at her desk and looked up at us as we took our seats. I sat down and looked at Ms. Haskins face; the face that always had a wonderful smile with the tooth that had a silver ring around it, didn't look the same. Everyone began to mumble, wondering what had happened to her. Did someone in her family die? Did this mean we weren't going out for lunch?

Ms. Haskins stood up, walked to the door to shut it. She turned the lights on and began a lesson. She wasn't her ordinary self and we all knew that there was something wrong. In my household when things go wrong for someone we would pray, so that is what I did. I began to pray for Ms. Haskins. Whatever is wrong, I prayed God please help her to be happy again.

We made it through the morning lessons and it was time for lunch. As we were getting ready to go Ms. Haskins called my name and a few of my other friends and asked us to stay behind for a moment. Yes! Finally! This was the moment I had been waiting for. We were preparing to discuss the extravagant details such as where we were going to eat, and when we were planning to ditch the rest of the losers. After all the other children left the classroom, Ms. Haskins asked us all to come up to her desk. I looked at her face and got worried – whatever she wanted to say to us wasn't going to be good news. I was disappointed because whatever personal situation had her sad was going to cause us to not be able to go out.

"Girls, I want to talk to you about this reading competition," she stated. "You all have great potential in life and as your teacher it is my job to pull it out of you." she said softly, speaking in a calm voice. "I do what I do because I am a proud teacher who takes delight

Choices

in teaching you everything you need to know to get to the next grade." She continued. Ms. Haskins got up from her desk and began to walk around with the ruler in her hand patting it. "I like to do things differently to show you all just how much I care about you, but I never want to be taken advantage of. Being mistreated doesn't feel good and no one wants to feel bad. Participating in this book competition was a time to show yourselves just how intelligent you are. I was particularly curious about some of the book selections that you chose to read. As I read your summaries, they seemed to sound the same and the wording looked familiar." She said. Bam! She slammed the ruler down on a desk startling us all. She walked back over to her desk and began lifting up old scholastic catalogs throwing them in the air. Catalog after catalog has your summaries on them, she said. "Every book you all have claimed to read looks like the author chose to summarize the books in the same way as you."

Ms. Haskins asked us why, why would we do this? Tears rolled down her face. "All I wanted to do was give you a fair chance in life. I wanted to push you beyond your limits. You will never get anywhere in life cheating and that is what you girls have done." She said definitively. We had been caught and there was nothing we could do about it. I had never felt so low and worthless. How in the world did she find out? Would she tell our parents? *I don't want to get a beating for this. I am so scared right now.* My mind raced from one extreme to another. There was no way out of this, we had to come clean and tell the truth right? After all, it was just some books that we didn't read. This really isn't a big deal is it?

No matter how tough I tried to be with my friends, my inside couldn't take it and I wanted to make things right. I had to come clean and be honest about the books I did read. After all, I loved to read and I would have been better off just reading the books instead of taking the easy way out, even if I didn't win the big prize. To see the disappointment in Ms. Haskins face was disheartening. I told myself I never wanted to get into reading books again. Ever. She believed in me and I let her down. It seemed as though I would never be able to repair that, so I chose never to be interested in reading books again.

This was around the time I embraced what was considered my Black side, my outside, the tough I-don't-give-a-care-side the, so-what-I-was-caught-side; the embarrassed side, the I-refuse-to-let-anyone-see-that-I-feel-horrible-about-all-of-this-side. Yes, before I would show a sign of weakness, I would rather hide the hurt and the disappointment in myself and never engage in book reading again. *I don't need books anyway.*

*****

In life there are times when we must make choices. While making these selections it was important to understand that we would live with their outcome, whether good or bad. There are times when choices are forced or rushed, even provoked, leaving you feeling that you have no time to contemplate your options.

Choices

Choices, choices, choices.

They're everywhere. Interestingly, as a child I felt that children didn't have choices. For instance, we don't choose our parents. We don't choose where we live. We don't choose what we are going to eat or drink – at least not in my house. We don't even get to choose what people think of us no matter how much we try. We don't choose our race. We don't choose socio-economic status. We don't choose our siblings, how many we would have or their gender. In my case I didn't choose to have most of my belongings be hand-me-downs.

As I grew older, I realized the choices I made in the present would affect my future. Not only the choices I made, but the choices made by the people around me. I am thankful I was surrounded by my best friends who, like me, struggled with choices.

*****

Don't mess with me, my siblings or my best friends. This Oreo cookie has a mean streak and she has lock-jaw. Anyone that I care about, I care about whole-heartedly. Personifying my nickname, I see things only in Black and White. No gray areas for me. Either I like you or I don't. Either I trust you or I don't. Either I want to be your friend or I don't. Mama would say to me and my brother and sisters, "Ya'll don't have no friends! You only have your brother and sisters!" We were four-deep and if you added all the cousins (our first best friends before we discovered people outside the family) there really wasn't room for anyone else. But somehow we made room.

Choices

My older sister has always been smaller than me, so everyone thinks I am older than her. I feel it is my job to protect her, and I do. No one can say or do anything to my sisters without having to deal with me. Fighting was never a problem. I had plenty of reasons to hit on something and didn't mind if that something just so happened to be a bully.

By this time I had become more comfortable with my gloomier side. Every now and then a blade under the tongue, Vaseline on my face and a big bulky key chain consisting of a leather cord – one of many boondoggles, locks and maybe one key, was used as my weapon. My motto became Action now, Lip service later – never wasting any time asking questions or getting clarity on a situation. Fear wasn't an option, but in all actuality that is what drove me. I never wanted to be viewed as weak. I had to continue to show I was willing to fight anyone, curse anyone out, and by any means necessary walk away the winner, all out of fear. Fear that my Black skin would be rejected and then who would I be, where would I belong? I wasn't White but I was teased as though I were if I didn't act tough enough. I couldn't retreat to my inside, what was called my White side. In my environment my inner man; who I truly am would never be accepted. If I exposed myself I would be left without an identity.

This Oreo cookie has talent. Getting good grades in school wasn't hard for me. I pretended to struggle so I could get attention. I didn't want to be too smart, because the expectations would raise and

Choices

I might not be able to meet them. No one believes in my intelligence anyway, I tell myself. Who am I kidding? It's not easy being an Oreo cookie. Around my White friends I can talk intelligently, but around my Black friends I couldn't. After all, no one likes to be picked on or called Miss Know-it-all.

*****

I wanted to learn how to play the piano. My mom saw this in me because we had a piano in our living room and I was always drawn to it. Sometimes Daddy would get on the piano and play fast, shouting music or sing a song. I would look at him and laugh and say I want to learn how to play. Mom signed me up for piano lessons at school. Playing the piano was fun, but it wasn't like the other children's instruments. They could carry their instrument on the bus so everyone would know they were talented. I couldn't carry a piano, so who is going to give me the attention I wanted? Maybe playing the piano isn't such a good idea after all. My mother would send me to school with a sealed white envelope with $2.25 inside to give to my piano teacher. My teacher would meet me at the piano that sometimes would be rolled out of the music room into the hallway where we would begin practicing. I had a thin music book with pages of songs, full of notes for me to learn.

My fingers are short, but I can reach the keys. I heard music in my head and words that sounded perfect with each note. I made up songs in my sleep. This music was taking over me. I started having dreams of singing songs I had never heard before. We sounded melodic and beautiful. The music was breathtaking and the words were perfect. When I awoke from the dream, the song was gone, the music was gone and I couldn't remember the rhythm, nor could I remember the bridge, but I felt the music. I knew it was there. How could I get it out of my dreams; out of my head and into reality?

Choices...

I made the choice not to give the piano a fair chance. Everyone already knows that I am an Oreo, playing the piano only added to the scrutiny. No matter how bad I wanted to play, I couldn't be a pianist *and* a tom-boy in my neighborhood. I had to make a choice.

At church I wanted to sing but only if I could sing with the Youth Choir, not the Sunshine Band. Everyone else got to sing in the Youth Choir. Why not me? I felt like my voice was as strong as anyone else in the choir and thought they could use my talent, but the choir president said I was too young. I knew if I got a chance to sing with the youth choir it would be great. I wanted to be a part of something in the church. I wanted to be with my friends. I wanted to make our choir sound one voice better than before. Each year I kept getting the same response. I was too young. Had this woman heard me sing, I wondered. It didn't feel good to be left out.

Finally, I was old enough to sing in the Youth Choir. I was ready to go to the rehearsals and have fun with the other youth. Then the bomb dropped. No more Youth Choir, just the Sunshine Band and the Young Adult Choir. I was not a young adult so that put me back

Choices

with the Sunshine Band. After all the years I waited in anticipation to sing in the Youth Choir and have an opportunity to shine – that moment would never be. Holding resentment inside and never wanting to sing in a choir again is how I chose to respond; although, that didn't last for long.

I told everyone that I hated to sing. The truth is I loved to sing – to myself. Singing was a part of me. It was inside of me. What's inside of you will always be revealed, whether you want it to or not. Singing was my outlet. When I sang I felt free. I could close my eyes and it would feel as though I was in another world. Let's make our own group. We would call ourselves the Little Lights. We'll sing, "We are the little lights and we're marching for glory, and we're marching for glory". We'll get matching outfits and we will be the best sounding group in the world. Okay, everyone in the group couldn't sing quite as well as others, but putting us all together we would ROCK! Effie, Fifi, Tina, Pam and me. Elder Jones was so proud of us, and he loved to hear us sing. Suddenly we were requested to sing all over the place.

Banquets and birthday parties we were the guest singers. We would sing, "I believe the children are the future. Teach them well and let them lead the way…" a song made popular by Whitney Houston. *The Greatest Love of All* was one of the first songs we sang as a group.

We loved to go to musicals and hear the different groups and then practice to sound better than anyone else. Daddy would take us

Choices

to the musicals. Rumor had it that one of the best singers in Rochester had her eyes on my daddy and maybe he had his eyes on her too. My friends kept telling me that there were a lot of women that were after my daddy. But my dad was married so what did they plan on doing? There's one woman in particular that always speaks to my dad in a very friendly way. She was at all of the musicals and could sing very well. She was one of the best singers in Rochester. We went to a musical one night and I looked down at her stomach. Wow she's pregnant, and everyone made the accusation that it may be my daddy's baby. Months later at another church service there she was again and she has had the baby. Taking a good look at this baby, she looked like my big sister Pam.

I didn't want to believe that my daddy wasn't being faithful to my mother. Why would he do such a thing? Year after year there was a new rumor and a new woman. Was all of this true? Who would make up such terrible things? I made the choice to act like this was not real. Then the letter something like this came:

> Sister Nowlin,
>
> I am in love with your husband. He and I are in a relationship and I want to be with him. We have been keeping this from you for a while, but I can't stay silent any longer. Please divorce him so that we can be together. You are the only thing holding us back from this relationship we both want.

Who would write such a letter? And why is it that my mother is crying more now than I have ever seen before. This can't be any of my friend's mothers. Don't tell me my friends know that my dad has inappropriate relationships with their mothers. We were too young to comprehend all of this. I wanted to pretend like this wasn't happening but I couldn't. My mother was surrounded by women who made advances on my father, or my father made advances towards them. Who were these women that were after my father? Are these the same women who bought us gifts and gave us candy while they grinned in my daddy's face, and feigned friendship with my mom?

I just wanted to be a kid. I wanted to go and spend the night at my best friend's house, drink soda pop, chew gum and talk about boys. Or we could go spend the night at Blonnie's house and have some fun eating all the candy we could stand staying up all night long. Not knowing that this fun was going to come to an abrupt end. We went from spending every other weekend at Blonnie's to barely being able to speak to her in church. What happened? Too young to know or understand, too young to care.

It seems as though the more I hear that my father is being unfaithful to my mother, the more our fun weekends of sleepovers are rejected. My best friend and I can only talk on the phone, and that is when Daddy isn't being mean and blocking us from talking. My dad started being mean to my best friend Tina and I couldn't understand why. He knew we always wanted to be together and have fun. That's what best friends are for. Tina and I would have to sneak to talk. The more my dad tried to separate us, the closer we became.

The older I got, the more I felt there was a lot of something missing. I wanted to be loved. I wished my daddy loved me. I realized that his love was missing. I realized that what I wanted was to feel the love I felt when I was smaller, younger, when I saw him as my hero, my provider, my covering. He seems to only love to beat us now. What happened to the love?

I'm older now and I have a monthly cycle which is changing my hormones and everything else. My mom gave me a book to read about having my menstrual cycle. My body is developing and emotions are flowing. I guess I want a boyfriend. Everyone else has one. Not Johnnie though. He's my best friend and my boyfriend, but only at church. There is a high school senior who is a cute guy that loves to make me smile. He is the cutest guy I've ever seen, but he is so much older than me. I can't believe that he is actually interested in me.

Before Mom or Dad would come home from work, I would call him on the phone just to hear him call me "Sweetness". We would discuss how much we liked each other and he began asking me was I ready to take the relationship to another level. He asked me was I a virgin and I told him no. I made up stories about guys that I had been with and he believed me. It was all a big lie, but I thought that since he was older than me he may not be interested in me anymore if he knew that I was sexually inexperienced. He wanted me to skip school so that he and I could spend time together. He even had a home-boy that he hung with that was interested in one of my girlfriends from school, so we made it a double date. He was very gentle with me and he was the first guy that I was willing to give access to my heart and more. I made the choice. I knew it was too good to be true – an older fine looking guy is my boyfriend and my boyfriend only? I was right. It was too good to be true.

After spending so much time with him and giving him all of me, I saw him downtown with another girl. I was on the bus getting ready to get off at the next stop when I spotted him. It was a summer day and he had on a nice shorts outfit with a thick gold herringbone necklace on. He walked with his head high holding hands with this beautiful girl. She was so pretty and it immediately crushed me because I thought she was prettier than me, older than me, and she won him over me. He was my first; the one to take my innocence and the first to move on to someone closer to his age. She was prettier, had longer hair, pretty skin, and she dressed nice too. He didn't think twice about cheating on me, and definitely didn't care to tell me that our relationship was over before moving on.

Daddy never talked to me about boys and what to expect, so I had no choice but to be hurt and keep the hurt to myself. I couldn't believe what had taken place in my life in such a short span of time. To make matters worse, I had no protector to share this with. Daddy wasn't alert and around enough to see that I was hurting. Daddy didn't notice that there was a change in my demeanor. I started to resent him for not being there and seeming not to even care.

*****

Choices

The arguments between Mommy and Daddy were scary. What were they arguing about? Why couldn't Daddy just be the nice daddy he had always been? Why did things have to change? I didn't like the way my mom was being treated. I wanted my dad to stop treating her badly. The more my mom cried the more anger filled my heart.

I was just a child that barely understood being a child, and there was no possible way I would understand adults or an adult relationship. I am not the one married and I don't know what it takes to be married. I don't know if it is hard or if it is easy. I see that every day may not be a good day, and there will be hard times, but being a child all I know is my parents are my parents and there is no questioning that. I don't understand adult love and what it means to be loved in an adult way. Happily ever after is all I know, every one of my favorite shows and cartoons ends that way and that is what I feel marriage between my mom and dad should be as well.

The light bill needs to be paid and Daddy won't pay it. We need food in the house and Daddy won't go get it. Why aren't we being provided for like we use to be? What happened to my covering? The attention is no longer on us, nurturing the children has taken a back seat to fulfilling personal needs. I no longer have respect for a man that will preach one thing in church and come home and treat his family the opposite.

The sweet home as I knew it was falling apart. Where can I go for safety? Who can I turn to for love and comfort? Definitely not my daddy. Not anymore. He's not home. Mommy is trying to do all she can so she's not home either – she is working late nights.

The more my father disrespects my mother the more I feel he deserves no respect. The more it seems my mother is the only one who cares for me the more bitter I become towards my father. Where is he when we need him? I have listened to my father tell lies, and then go and preach in church. How can you preach the word of God and immediately turn and do wrong? I decided I will no longer accepted instruction from someone who was a hypocrite. Either live what you preach or don't preach to me. This was the beginning of the standoff between me and my Dad. He could no longer demand anything from me without there being some push-back. From then on everything he said to me was questioned, because I knew there had to be motive behind whatever he was doing. Whatever his reasoning was I realized it was not for my benefit therefore he deserved no respect and he got none.

I'm just a child who wants to go to the amusement park with my best friend. But the answer I get is no, with no explanation and no justification as to why. I was angry, bitter, and hurt. It became a routine to question my father. I begin to understand that I couldn't go places out of fear I would see things that I was not supposed to see, or hear things I was not supposed to hear. As I stood toe to toe with my father full of frustration and disappointment in him, I told him I will tell Mommy everything I knew about him, and everything he was doing to her. He said to me, "Go right ahead. I don't care." Right then

Choices

I knew the man I thought would always be there for me to protect me and my sisters and protect my mom had lost his way.

In church they say the devil gets into people and makes them do things that they wouldn't normally do, and that was the only logical excuse I had for my father. I took my pillow and begin cutting it with a knife angry at the fact of knowing the devil had gotten into my father. But with every stab I resolved that this wouldn't be the end for us. I refused to let my family be destroyed. We needed to be together. When my father saw the cut up pillow he made a big deal out of it as if his life had been in danger. He told my mother it would be either me or him but someone had to go. I knew my mom wanted to make their marriage work. I knew she wanted everything to go back to normal with her husband. I knew she needed him and wanted to remain in a relationship with him to keep the family together. That left only one option. I had to go.

Where could I go? The only other place I ever wanted to live was with my grandmother Lillie Mae Brumfield. Grandma always knew what to say to me to make me feel special. I could talk to her about anything and she would listen attentively. She always had time to encourage me, making me feel like I mattered. Why did she have to die? Why did she have to leave me and not be around to watch me grow into a woman carrying her name? She requested that I sing at her funeral so I did. The way she took special interest in my gift to sing made me believe in myself. No one was prepared for her passing, but she died and I had to accept that she was gone. Daddy didn't seem to care much about what I was feeling, that meant grieving was not an option, and without grandma's house as a place of refuge I was left short on choices.

The hurt, rejection and confusion of being put out of a house by a man who doesn't want to be there; I didn't have words to express it. My uncle Terry and my aunt Niecy were right there to take me in. Uncle Terry was kind and caring towards me. But by then I was damaged. I wondered why he cared. What was his motive? I would babysit for them all of the time so it was no big deal for me to come and stay with them. By now I am in high school. I have a job and I no longer live with my parents. This is my life.

Maybe that was it – my aunt and uncle didn't need to find a babysitter anymore and could go out whenever they wanted to and have a good time knowing that their children would be in good hands if I lived with them. No – that wasn't it. We partied right there in the house – card parties with multiple tables of Spades going on. Music rocking, dancing and drinking, and the children were right upstairs. All I had to do was go up every now and then to make sure they were okay. Fun times for sure. It was my hustle to make sure whoever came to the parties had a good time. While they were having a good time I would make sure that any lost or misplaced money would become mine. Yes, people would get so drunk they had no clear sense of how much money they would give to me or would leave behind tipping me for making good drinks. Sometimes they would drop money on the floor and I would ease my way over to it and pocket it.

No matter what was going on Uncle Terry always had something to say about any guy friend I called myself being in a relationship with. Uncle Terry always tells me don't be stupid Lillian. He gave me input on relationships from a man's point of view. He and I along with Aunt Niecy would have heated debates on relationships, where he would give me wise advice that I needed to take heed to. He cared about me and my wellbeing. He didn't want me to be caught up in a relationship with a boy and get myself hurt. How about that? An uncle I felt was way more concerned about me than my own father.

Uncle Terry would always call Aunt Niecy by her first name Charlotte, so instead of calling her Aunt Niecy I would call her Char. Char and I were more than aunt and niece. We were close confidants and she looked out for me as a big sister would. We both took pride in being a buck o' five, 105 pounds; nothing like being a Brumfield and having the Brumfield shape and swag. Char and I would wear each other's clothes and I finally had someone to talk to about boys. Char and Uncle Terry were both cigarette smokers who tried time after time to quit with no success. I looked up to the both of them. They had four children: two boys and two girls. I looked at their children as my little sisters and brothers. I loved them with all my heart; Jehna, Terry (aka TT), Kayla, and Corey. They were the best second set of siblings anyone could ask for.

Choices

Finally I was the oldest, the first, the one with a title and a position. Uncle Terry took the time to treat me like a daughter. Giving me attention and taking care of me. He would sit and hold conversations with me asking open ended questions that would make me have to think. He knew I was a hard-head, but he loved me anyway. He was there with every boyfriend and every break up. He kept letting me know that no matter what happened with these clowns I called boyfriends that he would always be there, and he was. I was thankful that God didn't leave me uncovered. With an absent daddy my uncle became my covering.

CHAPTER 3

MISSING

How do you deal with the loss of a father's love? For a daughter the love of her father means everything. Her father's love is her foundation; it is the base that every meaningful relationship is built upon. After my father's indiscretions I wondered if I was to blame for his behavior. I wondered if I had done something to cause it. Was I to blame for everything falling apart? I reasoned within my pubescent self that if I had been more aware of what was called my White side, maybe I could have kept his attention. Maybe, just maybe, he would have been so proud of me, my good grades and perfect behavior that he wouldn't have time for inappropriate relationships.

Maybe I should've been more aggressive with my outside, my Black side. Should I have done more misbehaving, getting into more fights at school? Surely frequent visits to the principal's office would have garnered more attention from him, keeping him busy for years. I could have been defiant in our home, keeping him busy disciplining me. If he was too busy raising me there would be no time to look at another woman. What did I do to deserve this? I wondered if there were other girls going through the same things I was feeling; confused about their place in their family, about their place in the church, their place in the world. Then again, I'm just a little girl – too young and confused to understand. Why can't my dad be who he's always been, the head of the household, our protector, our provider, our covering? My pride won't allow me to show my pain to anyone, least of all to him. It only allows me to show disgust and disappointment. I reason that if I'm no longer a priority to him, then he's no longer a priority to me.

> Note to self: You've been abandoned by your father, the man who was supposed to love you all your life and unconditionally. You want to cry, scream, kick and rage. But, who will listen? Who will care? Instead of wasting your time showing all those emotions, pick up a few of your broken pieces and look for love somewhere else.

I have more guy friends than girl friends in high school. These guys are like my brothers. We all look out for each other and can be close without any sexual associations. I always thought it was strange that these guys looked at me as a sister instead of a potential girlfriend. One of them finally explained to me why. Of course if given the opportunity any one of them would love to get to second base with me, he clarified. But what caused them to think twice was my family of crazy uncles and cousins. They were even more cautious because of the poor choices I made in boyfriends that had criminal histories, not to mention my willingness to break the law and cause havoc at any given time.

I had gone into a rebellious stage of my life with no fear or worry about any of the consequences of my actions. I am hurting in every part of my being, and it seems as if the only way I can relieve myself from hurt is to bring pain to someone else. I reasoned that if someone you love is hurt because of my actions, so what? I'm dying inside too. So what I robbed you and your prize possessions have been taken. I have been robbed too of a relationship that I need, my dad is my prize possession and the love he used to show me has been taken. So what you have been disrespected, spit on or insulted by me. Whoever stood in my path had to feel the pain and misery that I was feeling and this was the only way I knew how to express myself. It is true that hurting people, hurt people. I am a living, breathing witness.

My friends told me that my relationships weren't healthy. They warned me that the dangerous environments and behavior of the groups I frequented were going to land me in prison for a long time. Because I didn't listen to my friends, there was nothing they could do about it. Why didn't I listen?

*****

I'm looking for a man, someone to fill the void of my missing father; someone that is going to make me forget what has gone on in my heart, and in my home. Now that I know what it feels like to be with a man sexually, I accept that feeling instead of admitting to myself that I miss feeling my father's love. That will be my trade off.

Missing

Being in high school is a time when teenagers express themselves sexually anyway, right? My dad is dark-skinned so it's only natural that I have a dark-skinned boyfriend. Although I lived with my uncle and aunt, I could never forget the first rebellious acts of a dangerous boyfriend when I was still at home living with my parents.

Joseph had the cutest dark chocolate skin. He was smooth and sexy. As muscular and attractive as he was I wondered why he would be interested in me. I thought it was because of my schoolmates Tarchia and Meghan. They introduced me to Joseph because they knew him from middle school. I had never met him before, but he sure looked good to me. Is this going to be my man? Yes. Yes I want to be your girl, and yes I want you to rock my world. My hormones were doing somersaults and cartwheels. But Joseph was a gentleman first, and then a thug. I was even more attracted to his hard-yet-soft mannerisms, knowing that he sold drugs and was a hustler and a fighter, but he had a gentle side too. He had respect for women and children - as much as a drug dealer could anyway, and he looked after his little brothers and sister all the time.

That's what I thought I wanted; a guy that was a hustler and knew the streets, but had some respect for his mom too which meant he might show some level of respect to me as well. In my circle of friends you had to have a bad boy that was from the street. Nobody wanted a nerd or church-boy. I needed someone with action, someone who knew how to get in and out of trouble. Joseph was that one. The bear hugs and French kisses made me desire him much more. I would never forget the night I received a call from my drill team coach telling me about Joseph. She was a bit nervous and concerned about me at the same time. She said she was calling to tell me that Joseph had been stabbed. I felt helpless knowing that my parents weren't going to care about my feelings for him. I cried the entire night wishing I could be at the hospital with him. My dad wasn't going to let me see him because I wasn't supposed to have a boyfriend in the first place – I'm a church girl.

I imagined the disgrace; the preacher's daughter had a thug for a boyfriend, and now she was in the hospital at his bedside. Watching on the news the next day and reading in the morning paper I learned, with a sigh of relief, that he had survived the stabbing, but was in critical condition at Genesee hospital. Any opportunity I had to sneak up to the hospital to be with Joseph I would. Sitting on the side of his bed, holding his hand and rubbing his head as he lay there in pain was the least I could do as his girlfriend. His brothers treated me like their sister and kept me informed of his condition when I couldn't come to the hospital. He would call me every night so we could talk on the phone, telling me he loved me. He was even honest enough to tell me that his ex-girlfriend had visited him, and assuring me there was nothing to worry about.

I was elated when he got out of the hospital. In a strange and crazy way this made me more attracted to him. After all the tears and the fear of losing Joseph, I felt a connection with him. It was something different; something new.

This was the first guy that I really felt love for. I cared about him and had real concern for his well being. I waited for the perfect opportunity to give him my body - my most prized possession, because he made me feel safe; something I hadn't felt in a while. Joseph made me feel as though he could protect me from anything and everything – even my father. He was a gentleman, showing me the utmost respect. Many opportunities arose for us to become sexually active with each other, but Joseph treated me like a delicate butterfly and refused to lay down with me in any random location just because he could. He told me I was too special to do something like that. This made me want him even more because I knew he wasn't just after my body, but truly wanted a friendship with me. Joseph and I didn't sleep together. We would never become intimate.

I could call Joseph and tell him all about my dad, and he would talk to me about his mom. Joseph sat and listened to how cruel my father had been to me. He became upset when I told him about my father; how he put his hands on me, beating me with belts and switches. Joseph saw the bruises my father left on me after one particular beating. I don't even remember what lead to that punishment. When I told him I couldn't live with my father any longer Joseph loved me enough to arrange for me to run away. Where could I go? How would I survive?

We were only in high school and neither one of us was ready or able to take care of ourselves. I knew that I could no longer take the beatings and hypocritical behavior of my father. I could not force myself to get back on the school bus and make that trip home. I knew this would destroy my mom, but I couldn't stand to stick around and hear another negative thing about what my father is doing or is no longer doing to our home. His love for us seemed to be gone, and I had nothing but bitterness for him. Regardless of my frustration I had to remain there and respect him, stay in the home and be obedient to him even when I know he was doing wrong and pretending to be right. When Joseph would call the house my dad wouldn't let me speak to him. I felt like my dad didn't want to be the man in my life, and he didn't want me to have another either.

I decided I'd had enough and ran away to my "big brother" T-Jay's house. T-Jay is my brother-from-another-mother. We went to high school together. There was nothing he wouldn't do for me. T-Jay's mom Mil, short for Mildred, treated me kindly and welcomed me into her home. Even at T-Jay's with space and privacy Joseph still respected me and did not attempt to sleep with me. My mom was worried about me because I wrote a letter and sent it home from school explaining why I would never come back home again. I could no longer take the way my father treated me. I could no longer accept his coarse behavior towards me. Home was no longer a place that I wanted to be.

T-Jay's mom said that I could live with them and that was my plan. T-Jay was Joseph's first cousin so I would be with the family of the boy I loved; the boy who took interest in me, the one who wanted to protect and provide for me. My puppy-love covering. Joseph would always ask me if my father was my stepdad. He would tell me that a real dad would not treat his daughter the way my father treated me. He felt that only guys who were stepfathers would act like that. I began to wonder if my dad was really my dad. That turned out to be a waste of time. I looked just like him.

I couldn't bear breaking my mom's heart. I knew no matter how bad I wanted to stay with Mil, I needed to go home. I needed to let my mom see my face and know that I was alright. It was amazing to me that the thoughts going through people's mind at this time was that I was running away because I wanted to be grown. *Did you hear about Lillian? Her fast-tailed self is running around with some boy. Can you believe her?* That was actually the farthest thing from my mind. I was running for my life. I was pushed away by the man who should have held me close. I was the victim, but some painted the picture of me as the villain. Those accusations did nothing but push me more and more towards Joseph.

Going back home after running away was one of the hardest things to do, but with Joseph by my side and T-Jay and Mil in my corner I felt it was the right thing to do for my mother's sake. Mil took the harsh words my father had to say to her over the phone. After all that was said to her, she still had my back and was willing to look out for me again if need be. I can never forget how supportive Mil was and all that she did and was willing to do for me. Mil and T-Jay showed me they cared. They showed me that they were concerned and blood or no blood, we bonded together as family forever.

No one believed that Joseph and his family had nothing but love, respect and concern for me. My dad did everything in his power to keep me away from Joseph, but it didn't work. My best friend Tina lived in the country closer to the church we went to. She would come into the city to hang out with me once she got her license. She picked me up one day so that I could go and see Joseph at a place called *770*, his hangout spot on North Street. The only problem with Tina taking me over to see Joseph was that her parent's car had their last name on the license plate and North Street is one of the main streets on the east side. We laughed when people said they saw the car on North Street not knowing that it was where we had no business being. It was funny and scary at the same time because of course, we never wanted to get caught in that area.

Tina came to pick me up one day to do our usual stop to *770*. My dad wasn't home, so I was able to leave the house without his knowing that I was with Tina. For some reason he didn't want me hanging out with her either. Tina and I began driving and who did we come across? My dad. Tina began speeding up Hudson Avenue going down Joseph Avenue and in circles going everywhere but to *770*. We couldn't let my dad know where we were going, and we weren't sure whether he had seen us. When we looked behind us, he wasn't there anymore and we let out a sigh of relief. Just as we began going through the light to go and see Joseph, Tina sees my dad again in the

Missing

rearview mirror. She starts speeding down Clifford Avenue and turns into someone's driveway as if that was where we intended to go. Daddy drove right past us and Tina and I couldn't believe we had dodged that bullet. He didn't see us - well, at least we didn't think he did. Finally we were able go and see Joseph.

I guess the utmost respect that Joseph had for me was the same reason he cheated on me. Tina and I drove by the house he *worked* at because she had started dating one of his friends. I had been so excited to see him just so he could give me one of those big bear hugs. He didn't have a regular phone number I could contact him on, so whenever I got to see him it was good. When Tina and I pulled up to the house there he was; the love of my life on the porch with another girl sitting on his lap. He couldn't even look at me, and for the first time I was speechless. I was done with him.

Since he was not getting any sex from me, he decided to get it somewhere else. I was hurt. I knew our relationship had to end. It didn't end right, so there would always be some closure that needed to take place. When I went to live with my aunt and uncle I didn't see Joseph anymore. I guess it was all for the best.

Well, on to the next one.

*****

I decided I was going to make it even without my dad's love. I will make it. Maybe I didn't need a guy that was my age. Maybe I needed someone who was older, wiser, and with more experience. I think I found the one. He was older, and he was definitely fine. I keep running into him, on the bus of all places. Somehow we always saw each other in passing while out and about in the downtown area. One day he asked for my number so we could get to know each other. I was attracted to the thug in him; the street life of a hustler. I could tell by the clothing that he wore and the way he carried himself that he was a *bad boy* and of course, that's what I was attracted to. He took great pride in teaching me what he called the Muslim beliefs and religion. The Honorable Louis Farrakhan became a well-known name to me. The guy called Chaz for short felt the need to school me on the ins and outs of being with a Muslim. Chaz told me that Muslims believe their wife should be half their age plus 7. I was the exact age for Chaz and it seemed as though we were meant to be.

    Chaz was the age of Char, and Uncle Terry. They knew him from back in their heyday. Uncle Terry told me that Chaz was too old for me and that he was not who I should be dating. I didn't know anything about Islam; it was intriguing to listen to Minister Farrakhan and his teachings. I understood many of the points Minister Farrakhan made. Although it was not the way I had been raised to think and believe, I had to admit I agreed with some of his teachings. Maybe I was eager to agree, because I was so attracted to Chaz and I wanted to be a part of his world, even if it meant forgetting my beliefs and taking on his. Young and ignorant, I take on an identity and a religious belief I knew nothing of, just to find love in this world; a covering, a security that I should have received from my father. I wondered how many other girls my age were looking for the same thing and would gladly take on more than they could handle like I had, in search of something to fill the hurtful void of a lost father.

> Note to self: In order to survive in this environment you must forget everything you know. Forget about the Lillian who enjoys reading and loves the Lord. In order to survive you gotta become a ride-or-die chick.

No matter what goes down as long as he is in it to the end with me, I will be right there with him. Chaz showed appreciation about that with me. Not too many girls are willing to talk to a dude who is catching the bus when he should be riding in a Beamer (BMW); sitting on the bus with a big fur coat on looking like some kind of pimp when he should be driving in a car with tinted windows, and a system so loud everyone hears the car coming before they see it. I have been raised to know that Jesus is my Lord and Savior, but this Muslim thing sure is interesting. If not for any other reason it gets me away from my father, and everything he has taught me. If he himself cannot live by it, then why should I?

In my experience, dating a guy much older than you probably isn't a recipe for happily ever after. Money is what he seemed to have, and money was what I wanted. In hindsight the bus pass should have tipped me off. Fame and notoriety is what I could gain by being the girl on his arm, and I wanted every minute of it. Finally riding around town in his BMW, and having everyone watch him pick me up to and from school, I was admired by many who knew he had it going on.

    I could talk to Chaz about anything and most of the time the talks consisted of bashing my father. He refused to believe that my father wasn't my stepfather or that I was adopted. He used his Muslim religion to show me how wrong my father was for mistreating me and not being there as a father for me. He did everything in his power to make me feel like he could replace my daddy so that I could have a sense of security with him. He would hold my hand when we were out together and call me at night and stay on the phone all night long until one of us would fall asleep. Sneaking and spending time with him without my mother finding out was my only task. He was very respectful and always wanted to meet my mom, but I knew if she ever saw him she would know he was too old for me to be dating.

    Many girls wondered how I became Chaz's girlfriend. I was still in high school when we met and as I said, he was far beyond me in years. Although we had nothing in common on the outside, we bonded in a way no one would fully come to know. For some reason Chaz and Tina didn't get along. I wanted my best friend and my man to be cool with one another. I knew that her main issue with him was the age difference. She thought he should be doing federal time for even approaching me. New Year's Eve as the designated driver, Tina drove me to his house to pick him up so that he could party with us at

Missing

a relative's home. They argued the entire ride. It didn't seem as if this was going to be a good night.

We got to the house and everyone was already indulging in the festivities; Gin and Coke or Gin and orange juice, *Chronic* on the porch, wine coolers, pizza, wings, and macaroni salad, with Jell-O shots. And that was just the beginning. My very protective family members weren't fans of my very old boyfriend either. My cousin Tony kept asking him questions and trying to push his buttons. He was grilling him from every side. Chaz tried to stay cool. I was getting a bit offended and wanted to defend my man.

I sat down next to him real close as to say no matter what ya'll say or how ya'll treat him, he is still my man. As I sat down closer to him leaning my body on to his side I caressed against something hard, it felt out of place and weird. I couldn't believe what I was feeling and was praying that it was my imagination. He looked at me and I looked at him confused and in disbelief. The moment was so uncomfortable I didn't know how to react. I didn't want to make a scene because I already knew how my family felt about him.

Chaz brought a pistol to the house with him for protection. I was upset because he knew we were going to be with my family. I didn't understand why he would need protection from my family. After I thought about it, I figured he did in fact need to use caution because my cousins and uncles were not cool with him dating me because of his age and reputation as a player and a hustler. *Maybe he needed protection after all.*

Missing

My cousin Tony was adamant about grilling my boyfriends and I loved that about him. One thing's for sure, Tony took protecting his cousins very seriously, and he wouldn't leave Chaz alone. I began to get a little scared because I knew what Chaz was carrying. When there is a weapon involved as protection it always ends up being used to harm not protect, and the only people around are my blood – my family. Situations like this turn bad very quickly and once it goes on a bad track there aren't many ways to turn things back to good. I knew what I had to do and I had to do it fast. As much as Tina couldn't stand Chaz, we needed to get him away from my family before he got hurt or worse, one of my family members had gotten hurt. Leaving the party and taking Chaz back to the west side, his side of town was the best thing for us to do. Although he talked trash to Tina the entire way back, I was so glad to hear it – knowing it could have been another way if my family would have got a hold to him or knew he was carrying.

At this time in my life partying and drinking were common. I would go from one house party to the next. I was always careful of my surroundings because these parties tended to have fights break out and innocent bystanders were always the ones that got harmed. *I guess I hadn't forgotten everything I was taught.* Nevertheless, I am enjoying this life. It takes my mind off of hurtful things and that is all that matters.

Chaz and I would break up to make up. I would skip school to be with him, and he would come to the school to support me in my after school activities. Everyone always thought he was my uncle or big brother, but never my man. When his best friend became attracted to my Aunt Char, things began to go in places out of my control and I needed to get off this ride before it became a train wreck. Even though Chaz and I broke up he was still around, so that made him feel like he was entitled to have his way with me.

Uncle Terry kept telling me if he wasn't my man anymore I didn't have to give him my time or anything else. Uncle Terry said if you give up anything to a man after you tell him it's over, he knows you really don't want it to be over and you have given him the green light to walk all over you, and that is just what Chaz did – until he saw that I too had shoes to walk on him as well. When I finally decided to move on, it was hard for him to accept. I had been hypnotized into believing that he could walk on water when the reality was he was just another street hustler chasing money.

What had become of me? This Oreo cookie had turned to alcohol, men and surrounding herself with the life full of danger and crime. Something was missing and in a quest to fill the void I grabbed anything that seemed as though it could get me out of my misery. Willing to go against any and everything I have been taught and raised to know and believe, I chose to be a wild child on a mission to replace the holes in my soul that wouldn't heal.

How did I get to this place? So eager to replace the covering I had lost I was willing to change religions, risk my life and my freedom, put other's lives in danger and not even care. I found out that sex doesn't replace what's missing. I found out that not having sex could be used as ammunition to end the relationship. I felt myself lowering my expectations not only for me but also for the people I was surrounded by. I was surprised I wasn't dead yet; surprised that I hadn't been incarcerated yet. All the while wondering if there was a higher power keeping me safe, protecting me from dangers I refused to acknowledge. Everything I did was to get my father's attention. My reckless lifestyle was masterfully crafted to land me in trouble, then straight into my daddy's arms. The only problem was I never got caught. This made me wonder whether my plan was faulty or maybe someone was looking out for me. Who was strong enough to be my covering even when I didn't want to be covered? Who could rescue this Oreo cookie when the one who should have been there to save me was missing?

CHAPTER 4

LOST

I wanted to be loved. I went from one guy to the next, never taking a moment to think that one day this would all come back to haunt me. Uncle Terry gave me hardcore advice, words I really didn't want to hear because I knew they were the truth. It wasn't until I start dating another guy from school who was my age that life noticeably began changing for me. He had money, he had street clout, he had a car and he had been put out of school. He portrayed himself to be a thug. *Sounds like the perfect guy to move on to.*

Our relationship was good until I started getting phone calls from his ex, who was also his baby mama. The girl he had a child with and I happened to know each other and was cool. I didn't know he was her man. When I confronted him, he denied being in a relationship with her and told me she was just his baby mama. I began feeling uncomfortable in the relationship. For many reasons it needed to end quickly. He was controlling and seemed to have a mean streak about him. He thought that I wanted to be his baby mama too, but he was wrong. After that, I knew I didn't want to keep him around me at all. I was not interested in having sex with him, and he would have to accept the fact that he would not get anything from me. I was biding my time.

> Note to self: Just a few fun dates to the bumper car track and the arcade, let him spend a few dollars on me and I think I will be done with this one.

Before the relationship could begin it was over.

I thought breaking up with him would be easy. Another guy at school was interested in me; in time I began turning my interest towards him. I needed to build the courage to tell my boyfriend it was over between us. I told him that he may need to get back with his baby mama and take care of that business instead of trying to start something new with me. I guess he felt like the relationship was ending too quickly, and he wasn't willing to let this be a smooth breakup. *No matter what he says he is my ex and I am on to the next.* I think that if he sees me with a new guy maybe he will finally get the picture, so I start to hang out with C-Lover.

C-Lover has wanted to get close to me for a while now, and I liked him too. My friends liked C-Lover way more than my soon-to-be-ex so it is official. I have traded in my thug for C-Lover. One problem though – Thug feels cheated and was not ready for things to end. He began stalking me, waiting for me outside of my job, and coming up to the school looking for me. I would hide behind buses and ask people for rides so that I could get away from him. He would page me 911 emergency codes for me to call him back, but I would just avoid him. There was a time when I was attracted to him, when he was giving me his drug money and I was spending it on jewelry for myself, but now I wanted everything to be over. At the bus stop one morning getting ready to go to school he pulled up and told me he would drive me to school and that he needed to talk to me. I didn't want to go so I told him no and that I was going to catch the bus. He angrily demanded that I get in the car. To avoid causing a scene I got in the car with him and would regret that decision for the rest of my life.

    He took me to his house where no one was home but him and me. He took me upstairs to his room and we sat down on his bed. He began telling me how much he cared about me and he didn't like the way I had been giving him the cold shoulder. I sat next to him on the bed stone-faced, acting as if I could care less about what he was saying and was more concerned about getting to school. This made him angry. He felt that I should care more about him because he chose to be with me over his baby mama. In all actuality he was still involved with his baby's mother and was only upset because I decided to end our relationship. When he saw that I wasn't buying it he started yelling at me and forced himself on top of me and we began to wrestle. He used his heavy weight to pin me down as I began to yell back at him telling him I didn't want to be with him anymore and to get off of me. He didn't care, and he was not accepting any more rejection from me. I struggled to get him off of me and the more I fought the harder he pressed down on me. He grabbed my face covering my nose and mouth and I began having trouble breathing. I closed my eyes to find strength to keep fighting as I felt my clothes being pulled off of me. He held both of my wrists down as he began to kiss me all over my face and down my chest. I kept wiggling and moving, kicking and trying to bite him. With no way out my body became stiff as reality set in. I had no more fight in me.

As I lay there with him on top of me a single tear rolled down the side of my face. He looked down at me and told me he loved me. Does love really feel like this? Does love rip your clothes off? Does love - no matter how you position yourself, force you into physical submission as you are pinned down with no more hope? Does love make you give in and stop fighting, praying that you live through this moment and forget it ever happened?

It was my fault. I never should have gotten in the car with him. I should have kept arguing with him at the bus stop until the bus came. I should have jumped on the bus, fleeing for dear life. Weeks later I was in excruciating pain slumped over in my aunt and uncle's living room on the floor. The pain in my body was unbearable and I knew it wasn't just cramps - something was wrong. My mother came to pick me up and she took me to the doctor's office. The doctor ran tests and gave me a shot on my rear to take the pain away. The doctor asked me was I sexually active and I told her yes. She told me that I was possibly exposed to a sexually transmitted disease and that I needed to be on antibiotics. Flashes of visions came across my mind every time I would close my eyes remembering what my thug boyfriend had done and knowing he didn't use a condom. Could he have given me a disease? What if he had given me HIV? What if the HIV had progressed to AIDS? What if I had become pregnant? I couldn't believe what I was hearing. I was devastated at myself for not speaking up and saying how and what had happened to me. The look of disappointment on my mother's face I wouldn't dare make things worse for her by telling her what really happened to me.

    I couldn't tell my new boyfriend C-Lover what happened. They knew each other and that would not have been good. Thug would have flipped the story and tried to make me out to be some type of whore. I just wanted to relax and have a typical boyfriend/girlfriend high school relationship with no sex, no drugs, no guns –just peace. But would that have really been a typical high school relationship, or just my desires given the trauma I had just been through? I thought I was able to move on and things seemed to be working out fine. My new boyfriend had no clue what had taken place and I wanted to keep it that way. C-Lover would pick me up from work and drive me home. We would be together in school and things seemed real cool.

    I was on the drill team, and as captain the East High Drill Team a.k.a. the EDT was my extracurricular after school activity. I wasn't a cheerleader, nor did I play a sport, but everyone knew me from the drill team giving it all I had on the floor during the basketball game's halftime performance. The drill team didn't get uniforms paid for by the school, so we went out and got spray painted t-shirts with our individual nicknames on them as a uniform. Spray painting and tagging nicknames on your clothes was in style, and was a must for me. I had my favorite cousin Kevin spray paint me a t-shirt that had me and C-Lover's name on the back of it too. I wore it to school as a sign that C-Lover and me were in a relationship. C-Lover was excited to show it off to everyone.

It came time for our high school dance after one of the basketball games. I was sitting in the common area at the dance enjoying the evening until I heard someone banging on the window behind me. I turned around and it was my ex, the thug. He kept telling me to come outside, but I acted like I couldn't understand him. C-Lover was there, and I didn't want them to get in contact with each other so my friends and I had to put a game plan in action. Once the dance was over we rushed to C-Lover's car so that he could take us all home. C-Lover never said anything to me about my ex being at the dance. I was relieved.

My ex showed up to my house a few days later wanting to see my drill team t-shirt. I couldn't understand why and was frustrated that he kept showing up everywhere. I didn't know that he and C-Lover actually did have a conversation that night at the dance and the truth was revealed that I had moved on. Reluctantly I showed him my drill team t-shirt and he calmed down when he didn't see C-Lover's name spray painted on my shirt as he was told it would be. My uncle's brother was home with me and was ready to handle him had things got out of hand, but he left peacefully. So many times I

Lost

wondered if I would just tell someone what he did to me maybe he would leave me alone, but out of fear I kept my mouth shut and decided to erase that moment from my memory.

    Being C-Lover's girlfriend I tried to forget what my ex had done, but the thoughts wouldn't go away. When C-Lover and I were alone I would be so close to telling him what happened, but then I would hold back. C-Lover was a gun carrying hustler too, and I didn't want him to feel like he had to punish my ex for what he had done to me. No matter how much I wanted harm to come to him, I knew that it wouldn't end with him and there was way too much blood being shed in Rochester already. I knew of his violent past, and had to bow out of this battle realizing it had the potential to become deadly. I didn't want my friends or my family to find out because somehow situations like that always seem to get turned on the girl. This Oreo cookie has already disappointed her family, no need in bringing on more shame.

    Christmas was coming and I was still holding some money my ex forgot he had me stash away. I used the money to buy C-Lover the shell-toed Adidas he wanted for Christmas. I thought about what my ex had done to me and I hated him. I had no one to tell, and feeling so ashamed I vowed to keep it to myself. Spending his money on C-Lover was my twisted way of revenge. As time passed and I kept ignoring his phone calls and pop-ups he had to become clever to reach me. He knew my schedule, when and where I worked and what buses I would catch. If I saw him at one corner waiting for me, I would run the opposite direction and catch another bus. I had my co-workers on the lookout making sure he wasn't around so that I would be safe. He would time my bus routes and drive next to the bus honking his horn to get my attention. He would even get on the buses to see if I was on there, and I would calmly hide out of his sight so that he wouldn't see me and get off the bus.

If C-Lover couldn't drive me home from work at night, I thoroughly looked around making sure the coast was clear to catch the bus home. One evening I got on the bus and walked to the back when I was suddenly yanked down into a seat. I was so frightened, I couldn't believe that my ex had hidden himself as I had done to him so many times so that I would get on the bus not knowing he was on there. The entire ride on the bus he was calling me names and degrading me. I was trapped with nowhere to go and no one seemed to care enough to get me away from him. When he saw that no one was going to say anything to him, he began punching me in the face. He was so angry asking me did I think that breaking up with him was going to be easy. Pow! He asked me did I really like my new boyfriend. Pow! I looked at the bus driver looking through his rearview mirror, never saying a word. He kept punching me in my face over and over again. People on the bus just sat there but no one would speak up. Everyone on the bus seemed terrified of him and refused to get in the middle of what seemed to be a domestic dispute. I couldn't believe that out of all the people on the bus there wasn't one person bold enough to help me. No one would make eye contact with me and definitely not with him. I felt hopeless and lost knowing my return hits didn't faze him at all. With every blow to the head I became dizzy and disoriented. When we got to the stop where he lived he pushed me out of the chair and shoved me on to the floor dragging me out of the back door of the bus. I was trying my hardest to hold on and not get thrown off thinking someone was going to help me, but no one came to my rescue. No one came to my aid.

    As we walked down the street to his house he kept pushing me and hitting me letting out his anger and frustration and at the same time laughing an evil laugh as if he was enjoying every moment. I was too scared feeling defeated and just took it as we approached his house. I kept saying I have to go home I have to babysit but he wouldn't listen to me. He knew he didn't want my uncle to come looking for me, and agreed that he would just get his car keys from his house and take me home. I knew one thing, dead or alive I wasn't going to allow him to get me into his house. I couldn't survive going through him forcing himself on me ever again. I looked around for a weapon anything that I could injure him with so that I could get away. I was so angry with myself for not carrying at a time when I needed to.

    As we stood on his porch he asked me why I made him do the things he did to me. He rubbed my face and said that he used to love me and how he wanted to spend his life with me. I knew then that he was crazier than I thought he was. I *made* him do those things to me? He *loves* me and wanted to spend the rest of his life with me? How

Lost

could he possibly be in love with me when we hadn't dated long enough for feelings to be that strong? He said that he was now willing to let me go since he had humiliated me on the bus the entire way home. With tears in his eyes he says to me he was sorry for all that he had done and that I could go. I thought he was going to drive me home, instead he laughed and told me he wasn't ever going to drive me anywhere - walk. I was glad that he wasn't going to drive me because I just wanted to get away from him. As I turned to walk away he pushed me one last time down the stairs and into a large snow bank. Snow was all over my face, in my mouth, in my hair, up my nose, in my sleeves, and all over my coat, pants and boots. I wept as I got up out of the snow, stood there in shock, and then walked down the street. I was hurting, but I knew it was finally over.

    I told my aunt and uncle partially what happened to me to explain why I was late coming home. I had cried the entire way there so that I could be tough when explaining, trying not to show any sign of hurt. My uncle wondered if I was going to tell C-Lover what had taken place. I didn't want to because I didn't want there to be a beef between the two of them, not knowing that they had already been in each other's face. Needless to say that with my ex hanging around it was beginning to be too much for C-Lover and that relationship ended too. My uncle was always the one to drop a line of sense in every situation. This time all he said was, "You will learn you can only have one boyfriend at a time." Although I was with one guy at one time, I didn't need to jump from one guy to the next so quickly.

That could be why some guys were really trying to push up on me thinking that I was an easy hit, a girl that they could have their way with. I never stopped to see how it looked. People were probably wondering and believing that I was having sex with every guy I dated, took money from, or hung out with when that was far from the truth. I wish I had better judgment back then. Everyone seemed to think that because I had lots of male friends, all I was doing was ending my future and soon, willingly adding statistics to the teenage pregnancy rate. It was and still is amazing to me how adults can be judgmental of a child's actions, while refusing to sit down and make themselves available to help them see their way through. My immature mind deceived me into thinking if I had just one person I felt I could talk to, maybe my life would have been different.

> Note to self: Why hadn't anyone talked to me about college? Wasn't anyone interested in my future? You know what? I'm done waiting for someone else to miraculously appear in my life and give me what I need. From now on, I'm looking out for myself.

I couldn't wait until this part of my life was over. I wondered why no one asked if I wanted to pursue my education further. I had to come to terms with my life as it was. I was graduating from high school soon. It was time for me to move on from the chaos that was my life, and find my own way; a better way. Enough of the girl battles between schools, east and west side beefs, boyfriend grudges, and baby mama drama. It was my senior year in high school and I was all about making that paper for me and taking that paper from anyone I caught slipping. No better way to end my high school years than to have a Jamaican boyfriend.

We had just begun kicking it when he decided to break a girl's virginity because she asked him to. I couldn't understand it initially, but after thinking about it what guy wouldn't jump at the chance to do something like that with no strings attached. I am pretty sure there are many guys who would love for a girl to make that request of them. I couldn't help but look at this girl and see one of the dumbest females I had ever come in contact with. I confronted her and asked her was Jamaica her man and she said no. I really wanted to believe that Jamaica was trying to talk to me and her at the same time, but she said no –Jamaica wasn't her boyfriend. I told her if he wasn't, from that day forward he was mine and if she needed any more firsts she needed to find someone else to carry that out with. I was so busy thinking about how stupid she was, I spent less time thinking about what his respect level for a female was that he would actually go along with her request. I was hurt that Jamaica had done this, but rationalized in my head that I could move on from it. That was the very beginning, and I should have cut things off, accepting that Jamaica wasn't a guy that I needed to involve myself with. But I didn't.

Jamaica and I would talk on the phone for hours cracking jokes, laughing and making up some of the funniest sayings. He even loved to sing so we would sing church songs on the phone with a reggae twist. We had good times, amusing each other and putting a smile on each other's faces even if only temporarily. After school I would get on the yellow school bus with my friend Carolyn who lived around the corner from him. Initially I acted as if I didn't know he rode the same bus as she did. I was going to her house to hang out with her, but hardly ever really spent any time at her house. He couldn't resist getting me over to his house, and I enjoyed being there with him. There were no rules, no mom or dad in the home to monitor the activities that took place there. He was the youngest of his brothers and sisters that also stayed there. Countless hours I spent there with him and gradually my clothing began to be there too. I felt care free there sleeping, eating, and bathing as if this was my permanent place of residence. Too bad my dad is too busy to notice, I wonder if he would even have a clue where to find me if he cared enough to question where I was.

  Jamaica, although a fun and loving guy to be around, had a mean side to him as well. Jamaica wasn't like my ex who violated me so his forceful ways were more like protection rather than mistreatment – (I chose to believe). Many girls wanted to be with Jamaica, so I disregarded his overbearing ways, to maintain my reputation as his girl. Very controlling at times and as much as I have always been ready and willing to fight whether it is a boy or a girl, with him there was a fear but also a will to fight back. He enjoyed marking me, leaving passion marks on my body was his way of displaying I belonged to him – as if I were a piece of property.

Things began to be less and less fun and more aggressive when he would tell me what I could and could not do and who I could and could not talk to. My friends were even intimidated by him and would use caution when he was around. I was accustomed to speaking my mind and expressing how I felt. He took this as a challenge. No female could talk to him and say whatever was on her mind. Expect to feel pain if it sounds in any way disrespectful to him. I just took the pushing and the shoving and the hitting as part of the relationship. That is how Jamaican's are right? Very controlling and demanding, and I just have to get use to it if I am going to remain his girl.

I cried and complained to his sister about him; what he did to me and how he treated me, yet I wouldn't walk away from the relationship. I kept hanging around for more, and more was what I got: more surprises, more passion marks, and more pain. I wanted to leave but being with him had become my identity. Many of the Caribbean people I dealt with only knew me because I was his girl. I wasn't one to play with and neither was he; two stubborn people together could be a dangerous combination. We fought, we made love, and we fought again, and made more love. We fought, I got bruised, he was sorry, he made some jokes, I laughed and we made love. Over and over the cycle goes and where it will end nobody knows.

Jamaica would be my last boyfriend in high school. Soon I would be graduating. I have the well-known Jamaican boyfriend that at first glance may not have been the cutest guy, but had whip-appeal. He was younger than me and I thought that would make a difference. All the guys I dated were typically older than me so I figured if I dated someone younger things would be different. He was just as immature and grossly disrespectful as any other guy I had dated. As the relationship grew stronger – meaning the love I thought I had for him, and the love I thought he had for me, I found out he had a baby on the way. And not only one baby, but a couple of babies by different women.

    It was graduation time and I was getting out of there. I may not have known long term what I was going to do after graduation, but the one plan that was a must to be carried out was to celebrate leaving high school by going to my favorite eating spot; Country Sweet Chicken and Ribs. At the graduation rehearsals I noticed one of the teachers from the school watching me. He was a bit young, but old enough to be an employee of the school. He had a flirtatious way about himself and so did I. I was not attracted to him, but he did act like he was interested in giving me some attention. There he was at the graduation rehearsal telling me where to stand, where to lineup, and how to march to get my high school diploma. Graduation night he was there, right there, cheering for me and rooting for me. Then everything changed. I began being attracted to him. However, nothing appropriate about it. I knew that as a student I shouldn't be attracted to an employee of the school nor should the employee be attracted to me. Nothing felt right about it. At the same time it felt

Lost

innocent. I didn't know who this guy was, or what he was about, but there was something about him that I couldn't get out of my mind.

I was in a relationship. Although I wanted out I was still in it. I didn't fit in with that lifestyle I had to admit. My identity was misplaced and I was truly off course – maybe because I was confused by what my identity should be. My White side or my Black side neither was feeling the drugs, alcohol and wild life living. I was tired of the abuse, the unfaithfulness, and the lies. What was I to do? Where could I go from here? What does it mean to be lost? My definition of lost is one who was unable to find their way to a certain place and I was definitely unsure of which way to go or where I was going. There were no plans for my future, no detailed ideals for my life. I was living one day at a time. Lost could also be described as not being used properly; being wasted; and no longer in existence. I squandered my life trying so hard to carry on the tale, watching as time passed me by. The one called an Oreo cookie; hurting on the inside, firm on the outside, and lost without my covering.

Chapter 5

New World Changes

I began living with Jamaica's sister Calla. Calla and I became very close. I'd never had a sister/friend who looked out for me like she did. She didn't judge me. She was supportive of me and she knew how much I cared for her brother, no matter how dumb it was of me. In my neighborhood the Jamaicans played a major role in the drug game. They had their own turf and territory and were not to be toyed with. Along with the Jamaicans are people Calla and I called Ja'fakins –the fake Jamaicans. There were plenty of them that developed an island accent, a hustle and did all they could to garner street credit. Real or fake, one thing was for certain, if you crossed the wrong person life as you knew it would come to an abrupt end.

Calla and I spent a lot of time together. Life wasn't at all what we thought it would be after graduating high school, but we made the best of it. It seemed as though she and I were dealt a bad hand, but we decided since we couldn't do anything about the past, we might as well have a blast. Regardless of the craziness buzzing around us we refused to let the condition of our lives bring us down, especially when we realized that we were much better off than many other young girls our age.

In a one bedroom apartment on the first floor of a single family home on the west side of the city, Calla and I made the best of the life we had. I slept on the couch the days I didn't stay at home with her brother. With us living off of minimum wage, there was nothing like going to the corner meat market and getting $5 worth of chicken wings to fry for dinner. Calla had to have rice with her meals, so no matter what was for dinner there had to be a pot of rice on the stove. I am allergic to rice, so she never had to worry about me eating her favorite food. Calla had recently had little DonDon, her baby. Finding love and wanting love is something she and I both had in common; I with her brother and she with her child's father. Watching the television show *Cops*, we would sing the theme song as if we were auditioning for a talent show; "Bad boys, bad boys. Whatcha gonna do, whatcha gonna do when they come for you?" Using the nightstand radio as a boom box stereo we would jam to our music as if we were living the good life.

Yeah, we lived the good life alright, if the good life is when people are after you, you don't know who they are and you aren't sure why. I spent many days looking over my shoulder, wondering if someone was after me because of my past or my boyfriend Jamaica's

New World Changes

current lifestyle. I lived in the fear of danger constantly; the fear of us being kidnapped and held for ransom, drive-by shootings, burglaries, all of these things were a constant possibility in my world and could happen at any time to me or to someone I loved. You reap what you sew, and I had sewn a lot of evil. My life consisted of circling around the neighborhood numerous times to make sure we weren't being followed. Our good life turned out to be not so good after all.

Calla's friend was in a gun fight one night and was shot. She went up to the hospital to bring him fresh clothes because the clothes he had on were drenched in blood. Bringing him clothing turned into helping him escape from the hospital before another attempt on his life was made. She called the house and told me to be on the lookout. Watching from the side window of the house where I could see who was coming inconspicuously, I sat discretely on my post. Calla and her friend had the cab driver speeding and going through shortcuts to make sure no one was following them. I sat there waiting and shaking praying that no one saw them leaving the hospital and that no more shooting would take place. Thoughts began to run in my head of all the 'what ifs'. What if someone does follow them here and shoots this house up? What if they don't make it out of the hospital? What if someone already knows where we are and is waiting for us to be off our guard? What if, what if, what if? Suddenly the doorbell rang frantically and I looked out to make sure that it was them. I ran to the door and let them in and for the rest of the night my stomach was uneasy. He stayed with us for a couple of days and Calla took care of

New World Changes

him while he healed. That's the kind of person she was, so caring about those around her even if she wasn't getting it back in return.

Living that street life had become very dangerous. Being aggressive and protecting yourself is no longer an option. It is a must. In the life we lived, no matter who you looked out for, took care of, or whose back you had, the bottom line is that you better cover your own back too.

*****

There was an unspoken tradition that graduates go back and visit East High to check on old friends that were still there. It is part of the custom to return and see how the new seniors were doing at school. I was the Homecoming Queen my senior year so it was exciting to go back to see everyone and hang out for the games. East High was one of the most dangerous schools to attend with shootings, stabbings, and fights breaking out in and around the school randomly. It resembled a war zone at times. It wasn't uncommon to see numerous police cars and news vans with reporters at the school for good and bad stories to report on. Known for our competitiveness in sports, East High was a school that groomed many gifted and talented athletes. Of course there were scholar programs and honor students that showed East High wasn't totally viewed as a dangerous learning environment. Great men and women rose through and above the negative aspects and are a part of the outstanding East High alumni. Walking through the halls, talking to the teachers and administrators and watching my old step team caused me to have mixed feelings about my old school.

While in high school I couldn't wait to graduate. I was looking forward to not having to study for exams, not having to get to class on time or listen to adults telling me what to do. However, with high school over I started to miss my comrades, being on the year book committee, singing in the gospel choir, sitting in the commons area, running from the school police that would drive their patrol cars right up on the sidewalk to the door, with no problem handcuffing you and throwing you in the back seat until they found out you weren't who they were looking for. I missed Mr. Law and Sheriff Lobo and the other sentries that would follow you in the hallway to make sure you got to class, saying your name over the walky-talky so that every sentry on every floor began looking for you.

Skipping classes and drinking alcohol down the street from the school with the anxiety of getting caught looming over your head was worn as a badge of honor for any who had attempted it. Being proud when you got a good grade in class after believing you did terrible. Talent shows, step shows, football, volley ball and most of all basketball games. That life is done now. I reflected and wondered if I made good use of the time I spent here, or did I let the time fritter away. How would I be remembered at East High? Did everyone know about my Oreo cookie dilemma, or do they only know one side – the Black side, or the White side? Will anyone ever know who I really am? Do I know who I am?

New World Changes

I received a $500 scholarship for college while singing in the gospel choir at my high school, but no one ever talked to me about going to college. No matter how well I sang, it just wasn't in the conversations. I'd never had a legitimate thought about me actually being a success, going to college and making something of myself. As a child, I was involved in many afterschool and weekend activities at colleges, hospitals, and political offices all to gratify my White side. But my reality was the Avenue D Recreation Center, double-dutch, crime, sneakiness, neighborhood tomboy/church girl, yes my Black side. Now this Oreo cookie has a job and a boyfriend that gives me money so college isn't a place I plan to be. My parents weren't going to pay for me to go to college and I definitely wasn't going to try and pay for school myself. College was out of the question for me. It was never really a question to begin with. My parents didn't - if the truth be told, talk to me about furthering my education. My life was so full of negativity and drama, that there was no space for school to fit in. I always wondered why my family didn't encourage me to go when they had done so for my older sister. She was accepted to a college and my parents were very proud and excited. I didn't even get the offer to help fill out an application to a college or a university.

My sister never made it to college and my big brother didn't go to school either. I guess it was an unspoken expectation that I would follow suit and not receive any higher learning too. No one in my immediate family had a college degree. My father went to one of

New World Changes

those business vocational schools, and my mother went to nursing school. My mother, struggling to keep our family together kept pushing and didn't stop until she completed her courses and received her LPN (License Practical Nurse) license. We were so proud of her and how she toughed it out going to school with four children, under pressure to make ends meet all while dealing with a failing marriage. She worked at a Jewish nursing home and was a faithful employee. It seemed as though my big sister would follow in her footsteps. As for me, there was only a grim future for me at best. No hope. No promise. No way out of the life I had made for myself. I spent my time helping Jamaica complete his homework assignments since he was still in high school. He didn't seem to care that I wasn't pursuing a higher education, just as long as I was helping him get through his senior year.

There was a time when my mom didn't need to work. She stayed home and took care of us. Daddy always seemed proud to have a wife that was a good mother to her children because it made him look like a good man and caregiver. We didn't want for anything because he was the provider for us. Mom didn't have her driver's license so Daddy was our transportation; everywhere we needed to go he got us there. When things began to go horribly wrong in their marriage, Mom saw that Dad would certainly be leaving her in a bad position having to fend for her and us children. She put the plan in motion and got her LPN so that she had a way to provide for our family with or without my father's help. She didn't stop there, but at

New World Changes

the age of 40, and after years and years of catching the bus, she finally got her license to drive and purchased herself a van to fit us all in. It was hard for her, but she did it. She did it to show her girls that we have to be strong and be able to take care of ourselves in the event there is no husband to take care of us. I never wanted to put myself in a position where a man thinks that he has total control over me simply because he is my financial provider. In my experience, that is too much power for a man to have over a woman. There are too many angles where that power can be abused and misused to manipulate the relationship.

    I worked. Working was something that I was determined to do. Dating different guys that had fat pockets taught me a few things, and one was that I have to have my own money. It is fine and good to have a guy that will give you money, but if you are making your own, you can take his and spend it how you choose, and put your money up for a rainy day. Saving is my specialty and all my work paychecks began to pile up, never cashing them so that I wouldn't be tempted to spend them. Since the age of thirteen I have always worked. I was the one of my siblings that wanted to work whether it was babysitting or being a cashier. I didn't care what kind of job I had, as long as I had income. I will never forget the look of despair on my mother's face when she felt like she was all alone to provide for her children because my father was too stubborn to work their marital issues out with her. She looked as if she was a deer in headlights, frozen in time wondering how in the world she got to this place. The devastation of depending on my father and the disappointment of being let down by him over and over was why I was determined to never depend on a man and end up let down the way my mom had been.

    I worked in a kitchen at a place called The Hill. There were about five or six of us young ladies that graduated, worked and hung out together enjoying life after high school. Every concert, college party, comedy show or club that was advertised as the place to be, we were there and we were there in number. We had each other's backs and never had a fear of anything or anyone when we were together. Through the good and the bad we were always there for each other. Hiring, firing, breakups, make-ups, births and deaths we were all there and a sisterhood bond was formed.

    We all knew we needed to do more than work in a kitchen at a nursing home, and I listened to some of the girls talk about enrolling into the local community college. I didn't want to apply because I didn't want to be told I couldn't get in. I had become so consumed with my outside – my Black side that I didn't want to acknowledge my inside – what was called my White side, the side yearning to learn and grow to be fulfilled. Everyone was receiving assistance in one way or another for school, but my mom wasn't going to get a loan for me and I didn't qualify for any grants. I went down to the school to see if there was any other way that I could get into school. I didn't really want to go. I was afraid of failing. In the end I went to apply but only so I could at least look my girlfriends in the face and say that I did.

In my travels downtown catching the bus to and from work I bumped into that very same high school employee that showed interest in me during graduation time. He said I was out of high school now, and available to date. I blurted out my number real fast, and told him if he remembered the number that he could call me. He remembered the number, gave me a call, and we went out on a date. *What a gentleman he is, and he really acts like he is digging me.* I'm afraid to say it because I am fully committed to the relationship with Jamaica, but I am digging him too. I know the relationship with Jamaica was very unhealthy and it was hurting me to stay, although I wasn't sure how to leave.

Every day that I would go home to my relationship with Jamaica I would fall into a slump. I wanted out. I was tired of being the one that had to be locked up in the bedroom while he hung out; tired of being the one that is now the side-chick to his baby mama. I was tired of barely seeing my family while secretly wishing that I could have my own. Every time I tried to get away from my relationship with Jamaica I ended up getting stuck all over again. He would not let me leave and things were getting way too physical for me. Soon I became afraid that no one else would want to date me because I had been with him. I was afraid that Jamaica would make good on his threats to hurt me when we were in a heated arguments. I was tired and no longer willing to deal with a gun pointed at my face, slapping me, pushing me around and making me feel as though I was nothing.

There is far too much drama in my relationship with Jamaica; the girls he's gotten pregnant, his controlling behavior, the abuse, the lies, hurt and pain. He had an imaginary chain around my neck. I would sit on my imaginary prison bench with no thoughts or ideas to free myself because I didn't know how to lose the chain around my neck. I couldn't see it, but I could feel it. If I attempted to free myself, stand up for myself or run away, the chain tightened and I choked. Trying to explain the chain was pointless; it was invisible. No one understood why I stayed, why I took it, why I didn't defend myself, and neither did I. I could not see the chain he had around me because it was imperceptible, but it was real because I could feel it. Jamaica made it real. Everyone around me could see my way out, but I was blinded by fear of what I didn't know and depressed by what I did. I fooled myself into believing that things would get better; that his treatment of me would change for the better. I wanted this to end with us happily ever after. I stayed, waited, settled, took the hurt with hopes that change was going to come. But it didn't.

Jamaica was careless and his carelessness caused a lot of animosity between females that weren't acquainted with each other prior to their dealings with him. The more careless he was, the more reckless he became. Jamaica would let his frustration out on me both verbally and physically. *Now I know it's time for me to go.*

Michael was my way out; the first guy I was interested in that wasn't a thug. Unlike my previous boyfriends, he had intelligent things to talk about. He treated me like a lady. Here I am in jeans and

New World Changes

Hi-Tech boots, and he's treating me as though I was wearing a business suit. He took me to his place where I told him all about my current relationship and how I wanted out. Jamaica was unfaithful and I didn't want to be in the relationship anymore. I told Michael all about how Jamaica broke my heart when he admitted to me that he slept with another girl at our high school because she asked him to be her first. I told him all about the pregnancies and the verbal and physical mistreatment. Michael was such a good friend lending an ear to sit and listen to my problems. He encouraged me to get out of the relationship and promised he would be there for me all the while. He even encouraged me to go to college.

> ```
> Note to self: This is what I need. I need a man
> who is concerned about me.
> ```

Everything about Michael suddenly felt right. Countless nights we would meet up with each other and I would cry over the relationship I was in. He would hold me, caress me and make me feel like everything was going to be alright. He is the type of guy that my mom would have no problem accepting as her son-in-law. He came to my job with a statistics textbook wrapped in a red bow. He told me that I could have the book if I promised that I would go through with community college. He was the first one to care about me doing something positive with my life. It wasn't him trying to steal me from Jamaica; he wasn't in it for what he could get. Michael wanted to give something to me. Happy as I was inside because of my new friend there was still a huge void and I felt I had nowhere to go.

New World Changes

Where would I go? I had no place to go. Jamaica continued to make me feel as though I would never be able to leave him. I want to leave, but I don't. I believed that he would make good on the threats he made towards me when I mentioned leaving. I hated the way he walked around as if I wouldn't be able to survive without him. Calla is moving and I can't just assume that she will let me stay with her. I can't go back to my aunt and uncle's home because things have changed there. After I moved out, Char and uncle Terry had their own marriage and relationship issues to deal with.

My mom is going through more changes because Daddy has finally decided to leave her for good. He has been cheating on her and decided to move in with his mistress. Mommy said I could always come home, but the memories there are just as painful. I don't understand why she wants to continue living there. Soon nothing mattered but my safety. I decided I needed to leave Jamaica for good. I called mom and asked her if I could come over to wash clothes. She came to pick me up thinking I was bringing a load of laundry, but she was in for a surprise. I packed up everything I could put my hands on and left Jamaica for good. It was safer for me to return to the painful memories within my childhood home than to stay another day with Jamaica.

Surprisingly, what mentally seemed hard to do was really quite simple. The chain was loosened a little and I took the opportunity to get away. My fear of him was still there, the hurt was still there, the disappointment was still there, but I was free. I was free and I wasn't going to return to that place of intimidation again. His sister always told me that I could do it and I did. I did it. I was free. Or was I?

*****

I tried to bury my foolish choice to be in a relationship with Jamaica, but there were roots planted deeper than I knew. I could never be with two men at the same time, but Jamaica had taken a part of my heart and owned it. I couldn't stand to listen to Jamaican music or watch the music videos anymore. I tried to act as if that part of my life never took place. Michael would be my distraction; he had his own relationship problems to work through as well. His relationship with his son's mom seemed to be up and down and I wasn't sure if there was really anything to it. He would tell me how she wasn't an affectionate person and he was concerned about his son. He cried so hard over her one night, that I couldn't believe I actually sat there and listened. I told him that I had to give to him the tough love that he gave to me and told him he needed to get over her and get over her quickly. We both were hurting and thankful we could talk to each other, but it came to a point where we needed to let go of our past and make it history. We were both playing the part as the other man or other woman and needed to give that up for a serious relationship. He said he was willing and so was I.

Michael was adamant about my going to college. So much so that he enrolled in some courses as well. After all, he was a former educator and took encouraging students to go to college seriously.

New World Changes

I'm not even a student at the high school anymore, and he treats me like I am a project he is not willing to give up on. He and I were in some classes together and did our homework together as well. We couldn't get enough of each other. He made me feel right in more ways than I ever imagined. He told me that I had a beautiful body and that I shouldn't have it covered up in baggy pants, boots and sweat suits. He took me to the department store and had me try on different dresses. I tried them on feeling really uncomfortable showing my body. When I would come out of the dressing room his eyes made me feel like he was looking at an angel. If me in a dress made him light up like that I was willing to wear whatever dress he wanted me to wear. Casual clothing, as he called it, was what I needed to invest in and leave the street and thug life clothing in the past.

He introduced me to a whole new world where the sky was the only limit. Every morning I woke up, my mind was on spending the day with him, even if it was sitting in the car with him holding hands or talking for hours on end. I couldn't imagine being in any another place. He's the reason I was in college. He is the reason I was able to leave my abusive relationship. He's my hero, my knight in shining armor, my protector, and eventually he became my lover.

I had nothing to lose and everything to gain with this relationship. Every day there was something new with Michael. He was full of surprises and excitement. My friends weren't particularly fond of him because he worked at the high school, but he kept a smile on my face. I loved going up to the school as if I were going to visit friends just so I could see him in the hallways or visit his classroom. One day flowers, the next day dinner, another day a poem, and every day intimacy. He was very cautious about his son's mom knowing he had moved on. I understood that she was going to give him a hard time about it although she really didn't want to be in a relationship with him either (so he said).

The care that he had for his son was amazing and refreshing. You hear a lot about guys who refused to be a part of their child's life or are waiting on blood tests, but here he is taking his child along with us on dates and wanting to spend every moment he is not with me with his son. I would cook breakfast at my mother's house for them and do all I could to make sure his son felt comfortable around me. I didn't want any children, but I respected that he had a son. I don't want any beef with the mom so I agreed to lay low while trying to figure out where we were going to take this relationship.

Mom really loved Michael because he seemed to bring out a side of me my family hadn't seen for a long time. While my friends and I are still going to the community college, one by one they seem to drop out. We all are taking different jobs, moving on to different things, some getting pregnant, some wasting grant money, some doing too much partying, and others simply not making the grades. I didn't have that luxury and had to think things through a bit differently. My uncle Bill convinced me to take out loans to go to community college. I told him I wasn't willing to take out a loan and he told me that if I graduated I would be able to get a great job and paying the loans off would be easy. So I did. I got a loan and purchased books and supplies for school and took out enough for spending money for the semester. I knew I owed this money back, so I was determined to finish school and get that great job uncle Bill promised I would get so that I could pay off my loans. Although Michael was the driving force, if it wasn't for my uncle Bill convincing me to take out a student loan, I wouldn't have gone to college.

My major in college was Communications/Media Arts. Michael pushed me to understand that if I decided that I would pursue this life, I need to do something that I am good at doing and something I had taken an interest in. Oprah Winfrey made me want to go into television. I wanted to tell the news because I was a curious person and wanted to be the first to know it all and the first to tell it all with taste, class, and dignity. I felt that if I were on television there would be other little Black girls that were called Oreo cookies as I had been; little girls that I could encourage to pursue their dreams and love themselves inside and out minus the stereotypes. They would be free to be whomever they chose to be. I had gone through enough to realize that I should not have gone through any of it. This was my second chance at life. A chance to change my tragic beginning to a triumphant ending and have the family I never dreamed I could have; the family that had become what I yearned for and desired most of all.

New World Changes

My classes were interesting and they were bringing me out of my closed-in, secluded self. Journalism, broadcasting and verbal and non-verbal communications were a breeze for me. I was able to talk in these classes without feeling like I needed to dumb down my capabilities. Finally this Oreo cookie was getting a sense of belonging – even if I was the only Black person in some of my classes.

The professor informed us there was an opportunity to travel to London for the winter semester and anyone that has the funding to go is eligible. I wanted to go, but I had a lot of odds stacked up against me. First of all money is something that I didn't have, my parents don't have and there was no way I would be able to come up with it otherwise. I had never flown out of the country anywhere and would be the first Black in my neighborhood to have done something like this. Mom was encouraging about it and wanted me to go. I decided I would. Although my mother was struggling financially because of my father's choice to leave our family and support another woman and her family, she never stopped doing all she could for us. Mom began helping me with fundraisers and the church – yes, my childhood church, now named Redeem Bethel even held a special service and gave me a token of love to get to London. I was on my way. But what would become of this relationship I am developing with Michael? Should there even be a relationship? He wanted me to go and was so proud of me for being involved in school.

New World Changes

I really want to go. This journey would be the complete opposite of the road I was traveling just months prior. I couldn't help but sit back and wonder what in the world is happening to my life. The guy I was so in love with, Jamaica, is now facing drug charges after the house I just removed myself from was raided by the police. What if I didn't leave that environment and was caught up in the raid? Would I have the opportunity set before me right now? Somebody is covering me – what other logical explanation could there be? Mom's prayers for me are being answered and all I could do is say "Thank you Jesus!" Yes, that is the phrase of praise, the words uttered when we get something we don't deserve, and don't get something that we do deserve. I am thankful for all that is being done in my life.

As I packed my bags to prepare to go to London for school all I could think about was Michael. He was glad that I was going, but we were going to miss each other. I would be spending New Years thousands of miles away from him, and New Year's Day was his birthday. He was worried about me being far away and if anything happened to me who would come and rescue me? He bought me a fanny pack to put my money in and a big bright orange whistle with a small can of mace for safety. Michael took me to get a passport and do a little shopping for things I would need for the trip. He was there for every detail of preparation. Everyone sent me their well wishes and support, all my family and friends were so proud of me. I was actually doing something that no one in my family had ever done. As

New World Changes

my mother, Michael and I got to the airport it all became so real, and I was overwhelmed with how my life was changing right before my eyes. As we sat waiting for my time to board the plane, Michael sat close to me hugging me over and over again. My mother grinned at how lovey-dovey we were being with each other as if we had been together for years.

  I was the only Black student going to a place I had never gone before. I had never flown on a plane, over water, to another continent, by myself, no brother, no sister, no parents, no Michael – just me. It was just a few months ago I was in a relationship feeling unloved, broken, defeated, rejected, ugly, bruised, and ashamed. I wondered if my dad would be proud of this moment right now. I wondered what my friends that have dropped out of college would think right now. I wondered if there is anyone finally interested in getting to know my inside – what they call my White side that is getting on this plane with all these other White people and feeling like I am getting ready to explode with excitement. What is this moisture coming down my face and why? Pure tears of joy, tears of thankfulness, tears of appreciation, and tears of great expectation. I am on my way. To no particular final destination; just gone from where I was and steadily moving with no intentions of ever getting stuck again. My seatbelt fastened, the plane accelerating forward, we lift off the ground as I look down from my window. I am on my way.

  London is cold and rainy. I am excited to learn their communications systems, the BBC, the radio, television, the news,

New World Changes

the music. I have never been to a live television show, had never been behind the scenes or behind a camera. The British accent is very strong here and it takes me a minute to understand what people are saying. One thing I do understand is "Mind the Gap!" On the subway between every stop, with every opening of the door that is what you would hear. What is the gap? And what do they mean by minding it? Watch your step may be what we would say in America. There is a gap between the train and platform and if you are not careful you will lose your step. I love it. My classmates and I for the rest of the trip continued to say "mind the gap please" to each other with our thick made-up British accents.

    Being 5 hours ahead of EST (Eastern Standard Time) when it was time for me to be resting Michael would still be at school. He would call me every chance he got. I purchased phone cards to call back to the states as well, and as soon as I would get out of class he would be one of the first phone calls that I made. We would stay on the phone for hours talking about how much we missed each other. His birthday was coming up and I hated that I was not going to be there with him to celebrate and bring in the New Year together. Having a room to myself I wanted to play my romance music all night as I talked with him on the phone and set the mood for us. I went to plug my radio in, and it wouldn't work. The outlets in London are different from the ones we have in the states. Michael told me that he loved me and that he couldn't wait for me to get back to New York. I was so glad to hear these words from him because I knew all I felt for him at that moment was love. If it wasn't for him being so aggressive and passionate about me going to school I would not have been in London and I truly love him for wanting me to do better with my life. I have sent post cards home to everyone that supported me with a message of thanks, but I wished there was a way I could have been able to share this moment even more with them. It was astonishing, the sites, the palaces, the history, the nut cracker, the theatres, the arts, the museums, the cathedrals, the parliament, the statues, the cars, the traffic, Big Ben, the shopping, the prices. I LOVE LONDON!

As we meet in the evening after classes to discuss the day's events, all the students seem to have coined me as the spokesperson for the African American race. We were at a bar where there was an African bartender who began telling us how he doesn't appreciate Black Americans calling themselves African Americans. My White classmates wanted to know how I felt about it. The African bartender explained that in his opinion, those people who come to America from Africa are African Americans not Black Americans, and there is a big difference to him. Africans come to America with a yearning and a desire to learn. They learn the language and overcome enormous stumbling blocks that would impede most people from excelling to their fullest potential. African American's work hard and take advantage of all the freedom and opportunities in America. African Americans don't feel like they are owed anything, but work hard to own as much as they possibly can. African Americans don't kill each other over minuscule materialistic things. Instead they gain all they can to give back to their families that they left behind. To see Black Americans that refuse to work and wait for the government to feed them, clothe them, and shelter them is a disgrace. Sitting in a classroom and refusing to gain knowledge that will better your future and afford you the chance to go beyond the perimeter set before you is preposterous. To have all these opportunities and do nothing with them is not an option for the African American that the Black American takes for granted.

    I didn't come on this trip to be the spokesperson for the African American or the Black American race. We are all entitled to feel how we want. How we feel is mostly based on our upbringing and because we didn't all come from the same places, we all may have different thoughts. I was not born in Africa therefore I cannot defend or dispute the bartender's feelings. My mother used welfare and was able to feed us when she didn't have the means to provide for us any other way. She didn't stay on welfare forever, but I sure am glad it was there for her when we needed it.

    I don't feel the need to move out of the city and get a home in the suburbs once my pockets afford me to do so. I don't have to become a lawyer or a doctor because that is where the money supposedly is. I want to be me, and be the best me I can be. And if that means not being in a courtroom arguing a case because that is not my interest so be it. If that means I am not one that can stand the sight of someone else's blood as a doctor then I am fine with that.

New World Changes

If I want to live where houses are so close together that my nosey neighbor can hear what is going on in my home I have that right. I may need their help in case of an emergency one day. I want to have a sidewalk and street lights and know who the neighborhood thieves are. Where everyone in the neighborhood knows each other's routines and is able to give a detailed description of what I look like and what I had on the last time they saw me. I don't want to live gated-up and worried about who is going to break into my home and seclude myself from the world we live in. If it takes the police a long time to get to my house let it be because they were on another call, not because my house was so far out and hidden that they couldn't find it.

If I want to be where all the elderly neighborhood women had the right to beat my behind when I stepped out of line whether they knew my mother or not doesn't mean I am lazy. It doesn't mean that I am not striving to reach my full potential. It doesn't mean that I am not taking advantage of opportunities. It simply means I appreciate the culture that was developed for my survival. It means I value the ethnicity created out of hurt and pain. It means I respect those that came before me that died so that I could have what I have.

Some choose to go further and some choose to stay where they are. Does it really make one right and the other wrong? I can't speak for the entire race. I don't feel it is my place. I know that is not what I came on this trip for, and I don't plan to take on that role. Truth is I am in college finally getting to know me. I am in college trying to figure out who I want to be. I am in college an Oreo cookie with two sides of me my Black side and my White side both warring with each other to my destiny's end, and now they wanted to add my African side too. I choose to be me, to be free and to be all that I want to be, not what today's statistics say I should be. Not who White people say I can or cannot be. Not even what my own Black people say that I will be. I choose to just be me, so let me be.

New Year's Eve is a few days away and I am missing the new love of my life bad. Talking on the phone for an hour or so every day was not enough for me. I needed more and so did he. I didn't want to do anything for New Years, but stay in my room all alone wishing and missing. The other students wanted to go down to Trafalgar Square which is like New York's Time Square to bring the New Year in. Michael told me that I should go and so reluctantly I went. It was electrifying watching the people dancing and screaming and being so happy. Five, Four, Three, Two, One, Happy New Year!! Everyone is hugging and saying Happy New Year. This very dark skinned, tall guy comes up to me and quickly grabs me around my waist, pulling me into his body he closes his eyes tilts his head and puckered up his lips. I couldn't believe what was happening as it happened all of a sudden. I didn't know what to do and I definitely wasn't going to let some random stranger put his lips on me. I reached into my chest grabbed my whistle and blew as his lips hit my whistle instead of my lips. It wasn't until I looked around and saw others just grabbing one another that I realized all he was doing was trying to say Happy New Year. Talk about culture shock!

Once over those jitters it was time to party. We drank and went from club to club enjoying the night life in London celebrating our future, our success, our determination to excel in communications. Getting back to the hotel, I went to the phone booth to call Michael and say to him Happy New Year. I know it wasn't the New Year yet in the states, but I wanted to be the first to say Happy New Year and Happy Birthday. The phone rang and rang, and I couldn't reach him. This was the first time I had ever called and he was not there. I was disappointed, but I also knew that it was New Year's Eve and it was his birthday and he had every right to go out and be with his friends to celebrate especially since I was not there to celebrate with him. He deserved it. Besides, I was out having a good time and finally enjoying myself, so it's only fair that he does the same.

This was the longest time we had gone without speaking on the phone. This did nothing but make me desire him more and looked forward to going home and being with him. Before I left he told me how he felt about me and I took it all in wondering if he was for real. It's true, absence makes the heart grow fonder and now whether he was for real or not, I am. I can't wait to get back home to show him just how I really feel. He took the time to show me that I can have more than what I was settling for and I want that more to be with

New World Changes

him. With every missed call I cherished deeper and deeper our connection, yearning to hear his voice again.

At last, my baby is on the line. I get to tell him happy birthday and want to hear all about how he celebrated. I want to hear how his friends kept him company because I was away. I want to hear what happened in the ROC (Rochester, NY) and what was the best New Year festivities that took place. What did he wear? Where did he eat? What time he went to bed and leave out no details. I told him how I used the whistle, how Trafalgar Square was just like Times Square. I told him how we partied and the London night life was fun and exciting with the strong liquor I indulged in. I told him that it would have been even more fun if he was there with me to enjoy it all.

The silence on the phone made me a bit curious. We never sat on the phone with nothing to say. I think he has a surprise for me like I have for him. I want to tell him I am in love with him and maybe he wants to say the same thing to me. What is it, I can't wait any longer. I was so sleepy, but wide awake at the same time. I wanted to hear him talking to me while he plays Prince - our favorite musical artist, in the background. I wanted to hear Prince singing Adore because I knew that is how Michael feel's about me. As the music played and Michael was silent I asked him if everything was alright. He stayed quiet and I began to feel bad for him because I knew he missed me. I felt the same way about him.

Finally, he speaks. He tells me how much he misses me. He tells me how he wishes I was home. He tells me that he has been having a hard time without me. He tells me that on New Year's Eve he didn't want to be out with his friends so he decided to bring the New Year in with his son. He tells me that his son's mom allowed him to come over so that he could be with his son at the dawning of the New Year and his birthday. He tells me that while there alone with his son and his son's mom he had sex with her. He tells me he didn't mean it, and that he is so sorry. He tells me that it was a mistake, and it was in the heat of the moment as a result of missing me. He tells me that he doesn't mean to hurt me and that he hopes I can forgive him.

  I am not sure I heard him correctly. There is a five hour difference between us so maybe I was too tired to comprehend what he was saying. I am sorry, and I still want to be with you. What? How do you love someone and sleep with someone else? How do you do this while the person you say you love is thousands of miles away? How do you form the words in your mouth to tell me this over the phone in a place where I am all alone with no type of support to help me through this? How could my hero do this to me? He wasn't a thug. He wasn't a drug dealer. He wasn't my typical boyfriend. How could this happen? My heart felt as though it had been hit with a ton of bricks with a feather on top. Just heavy enough to make me break. I was open, vulnerable, ready and willing for anything for everything with him. So dangerously exposed I could never imagine anything like this happening. The hurt is far too great to explain in words and I am not sure if this is something I can get over. Not with him.

New World Changes

He had to see if there was something left between the two of them. He had to find out if there was any chance of him and his son's mom ever truly being back together. One thing led to another, but he realizes now that the relationship is truly over. Yes he slept with her, but it will never happen again because that finalized the break up. She may not be happy with it and may want to keep him from his son, but that road with her has come to an end. Could I find it in my heart to understand this? Do I really believe that it is over between them and he and I can now move on? Do I want to go forward in a relationship with a man who has crushed my expectations of him?

I don't even know how to cry over this or even if I should. This cannot be happening to me right now. Not now, when things are just starting to look good for my life. When I am in London feeling like I am living on top of the world. When I feel like there's a boatload of females who would love to be me right now. When I have finally moved on from my past and accepted this second chance at life to become something and someone special. This happened just when my inside – my White side, was preparing to take the lead over my outside – my Black side. This Oreo cookie is confused, blindsided, upset, wounded, naïve, gullible, dense and feeling really low.

I went out and had a few drinks to get my mind together, but all that did was make my mind cloudier. I don't smoke. I never did. I don't do drugs. I never did. But at that moment I was in such a state of disbelief I really wanted to do something to take me out of this world for a while; to have some time to myself by myself. I was so far gone I didn't know what to say or if there was anything to say. I felt as though I had been played like an out of tune piano. I reasoned with myself that I had to find a way out of this. I had classes to attend where people would be expecting me to have input in the conversations because I was in a Communications major. *I must learn how to communicate, to say what is on my mind and mean what I say when I say it.* The problem was I didn't know what to say.

I couldn't sleep and didn't want to eat and was up in my room all alone when the phone rang. It was Michael calling me to see if I was alright, checking on me to make sure that I was okay. How could I be after that blow? All I could say was yes I am fine knowing I wanted to curse him passionately. He told me when I came back things would be different and that he wanted to show me that I am all he wants and who he wanted to be with. I went out and did what I knew to do that day – shopping. I purchased a few pair of boots that I thought no one over in the states would have. I purchased some t-shirts and a few outfits. Normally this would have made me feel better, but this time it didn't. There had been some real new world changes in my life. Most had been for my good, to better me. But one thing about these changes that remained was that I realized all over again how much it hurts without a covering.

CHAPTER 6

FALSE SECURITY

Everyone makes mistakes right? I know I have. Since meeting Michael he had done nothing but inspire me to do better. Where I felt I had no future he encouraged me to believe differently. I knew how hard it was to leave someone that you were used to being with. I knew what it felt like to say goodbye to someone you thought you wanted. I knew what it felt like to realize that your relationship would never work. I understood the fear of starting over again and dating someone new that you would have to get to know. In my heart I really cared for Michael. I appreciated him believing in me when I didn't believe in myself. I had to forgive him. I had to help us both move on from this.

As I prepared to return to the states, I pondered whether I would be able to forgive Michael and forget what he did. It's not as though we were married and he had an affair. I packed my bags with great anticipation of going home. I enjoyed London, but I was glad to be leaving. I learned a great deal and made new acquaintances for life. It was all worth the trip if only to say I had travelled out of the ROC (Rochester, NY). No one believed that I would be in college

False Security

and there I was all the way in London for class. If I didn't do anything else in this life, I had proven many people wrong just by being in London, including myself. I wasn't pregnant, I wasn't in jail, I wasn't on the street corner, I was not on welfare, and I was not dead. This Oreo cookie had traveled abroad and far beyond her expectations.

    Landing back home my stomach was in knots. I was not sure what to expect. I knew Michael would be there to pick me up from the airport. I wondered what we would do. I couldn't help but think our seeing each other was going to be awkward. The terminal walkway seemed longer than usual, and my carryon was heavier than I remembered. With every step I took my boots seem to weigh me down. I felt as though I couldn't take another step. I came through the doorway, looked up and there he was. With a huge smile on his face he embraced me hugging me tightly. Grabbing my face looking down on me he kissed me and gently whispered welcome home.

    I wanted to see everyone, my mom, brother, sisters and nephews and let them know how much I missed them all. I had many stories to tell about the people I met, the places I travelled; the full experience of London. That would all have to wait, because Michael had something else planned. We went to his apartment to be alone. I knew where things were going to lead. Part of me wanted it to go there and the other part of me was considerably hesitant. I wanted him to see, know and feel what he could have with me so there would be no going back to his baby mama. I wanted him to understand that

False Security

everything he was looking for in a woman I could provide. I guess we both had something to prove that day and neither of us held anything back. I knew he wanted me and I wanted him. I knew from that day forward we would never miss a day of being together.

> Note to self: Never say never.

*****

I loved to drink. Drinking kept me at ease. When I drank I felt free. I was a jokester when I drank. I was guaranteed to make you laugh unless the joke was on you. I became even more truthful when I drank, saying whatever came to mind. Drinking kept me feeling my outside - my Black side, and drowned what was called my inside – the White side. Drinking was my comfort. Drinking made this Oreo cookie feel like I could do anything I wanted to do.

The hangover was my reality.

The hangover told me the truth, that my body didn't want this poison in it no matter how good it feels going down. The hangover showed me just how much liquor should not be in my blood stream.

I continued to drink because I could. Michael wasn't into drinking. As long as I'd known him I hadn't seen him take one drink. One day he sat me down to have a heart-to-heart. He expressed his care for me as usual, but then told me that he never wanted to be with a woman that drank or abused drugs. I was proud to say I was not that kind of female. I was not an alcoholic, and I had never smoked a cigarette, or weed or done any kind of drugs. He became more explicit letting me know that he didn't want to be with a woman that drank period.

The history behind his logic is quite reasonable. He saw how controlled substances govern and have the power ultimately ruin your life. He knew firsthand by his own mother. He took the time to go into detail and tell me what it was like to have a mother that acted like your sister, to have your grandmother raise you because your mother was unable to. He loved his mom and I saw in his eyes how he wished he could take her away and make everything better for her and his younger siblings. Grandma was there to raise him while his biological mother battled her addictions. I saw his hurt. I understood his pain and I am again appreciative of his concern for me. I do all I can to stop drinking – well, at least to stop drinking around him.

We wanted to do everything together, never spending any free time apart. While he was at the high school working, I was at the college campus or at my job. Once all of our responsibilities were done for the day we found ways to make sure our evenings were spent with each other. I never heard much about his son's mom anymore. I guess things there are finished and I was glad they were. Michael loved his son and didn't want to do anything that would jeopardize his time with him, and I understood that. He enlightened me on his life without his father being there full time. There were days that his father promised to do special things with him, but never made good on those promises. There were days Michael wanted to talk to his father, but his father was nowhere to be found. Michael told me he wanted to be a father to his child and wanted to do everything he could to make sure he made a different life for his son. Even if it meant his son's mother couldn't know about me. So she didn't.

I had to go to the beauty supply store and Michael, being the kind man that he is offered to take me there. We had just spent the day together and were feeling real good. For some reason we couldn't get enough of each other and were preparing to be together for the rest of the night. He mistakenly spilled pen ink on his suit and began blotting it as I got out the car to go into the store. I figured he wasn't going to come in because it wouldn't take me long to pick up the things I needed. As I went around the store picking up the products that I needed a group of ladies walked into the store. As they came into the store, I noticed that one of them was his son's mom. She was in the store with her family and her son. She put him down so he could walk around as they all looked at different products. I didn't know what to do.

I wondered how Michael was going to get out of this one. I saw his son come around the corner asking for his daddy. He began walking in my direction, so I turned to walk away. A family member came and grabbed him, but he asked again. I knew they didn't know who he was talking to or even what he was saying since he was such a little boy, but I knew exactly.

If this family figured out who I was would they want to fight me? Would she want to fight for the love of her son's father? Being

False Security

with him caused me to leave that type of life in my past, but if push came to shove I was prepared to defend myself. I was sure she would be upset to find that her son knew who I was. I walked away from the products I had gathered and went to the door to go out of the store and noticed that Michael was gone. He left. I couldn't believe that he left me there. They purchased their products and were getting ready to leave the store. I was glad they were leaving so that Michael could come back to get me. I went to the register to pay for my products and saw out the corner of my eye that they were coming back into the store. Immediately I put up my defenses, knowing that if an altercation took place outside it is definitely about to go down in here. As she walks towards me at the register she tells the clerk she can't find her keys. I was relieved and glad that our cover wasn't blown, but now I needed for them to hurry up and find the keys before Michael pulled up.

    I bowed my head down in a moment of desperation to pray to God that nothing goes down here today and as looked down, there were the keys. They were sitting in a box of candy at the cash register. I immediately said here are your keys and they were all thankful and appreciative. All I could think was that they had no clue who I was and if they did they wouldn't be so kind to me.

    They left out of the store and I finished paying for my items. I walked slowly to the door not knowing what to expect, examining items on the shelf to prolong the time. There was nothing left for me to do but go outside and face the issue at hand. I opened the door and walked outside and Michael was driving into the parking lot as his son's mother and her family drove out. I hurried to the car to discuss what happened. Michael had left the parking lot before his son's mother got there. He had no clue what I had been through on my random trip to the beauty supply store. We both wondered if they saw him as he picked me up. As we rode down the street on our way to his house his phone rang. It was raining really hard outside and the raindrops seemed to hit the windshield like rocks. He looked at his phone and then looked over at me with that look that the guys on cheaters have when the lights and camera's come on. He immediately pulled over, turned the car and the windshield wipers off to get it as quiet as we could. He answered the phone and began speaking to her. It was at that moment I began to wonder, why was I so worried about him being seen with me? Why am I worried about what his son's mother or her family would think about me? He pursued me. He expressed interest in me. He went out of his way to make me feel good from the inside out. I never asked him to be with me, but he insisted on spending any free moment available with me. Am I settling for one thing when I know I can do better? Is there a man out there that wants to be with me and there are no strings attached?

      Michael worked over time trying to make sure that I knew he only wanted to be with me. I accepted his every attempt and believed him when he said he couldn't imagine being with someone else. He had his own insecurities about me as well with the lingering connection between me and Jamaica. Working at the high school

Michael wanted to be very cautious. He was concerned that with Jamaica still at the school, there would be a conflict between the two of them because of me. I assured him that everything was over between Jamaica and I, but felt that things should be kept quiet about us, just to be safe.

We scheduled our lives around each other which meant my friendships with everyone else began to diminish. Tarchia and Meghan, my two best girlfriends totally disagreed with the relationship because of his age and place of employment. I had fallen head over heels for him for all that he had done for me, so there was nothing that they could say to me that would cause me to end this. It was known at the school that we were involved, but we didn't publicize it. Although I was no longer a student, I didn't want him to get into any kind of trouble. Every now and then when I would go up to the school I would make my visits with him short, not to draw any unwanted attention to us.

It's Valentine's Day. The day of love and romance. The day for couples all around the world to express their love for one another. I have some expressions of my own that I wanted to show to Michael. He had been the one showering me with gifts and surprises, and today I want to show him I too can be spontaneous. He was spearheading an event at school that involved hugs. I looked in the phone book to get an idea of something special to have delivered to him. Searching through the telephone book I found a delivery company that had the perfect gift to send to him. It was a coffee mug that had a bear hugging it with a bouquet of flowers inside it. The writing on the coffee cup said "Big Hug Mug". It was just right. When it was delivered to the school for him, he was pleasantly surprised that I had gone to such measures. He was even more taken aback when I showed up at the school that afternoon. That was the real surprise.

He was keeping students after school for detention and I went up to his classroom to chat briefly and see how he liked the gift I'd had delivered. I had his sentry friend radio to him that I was on my way up to see him. He met me in the doorway of his classroom with a big smile on his face and I knew I had made his day. As we stood in the doorway talking out the corner of my eye I saw someone walking towards us. I turned to see who it was, and noticed it was a familiar face. It was the young girl that had asked Jamaica to break her virginity. When she recognized me she stopped in her tracks, and then turned and went another way. In the back of my head I wondered why she changed her direction once she saw me, I didn't think of myself as being threatening to her, and my relationship with Jamaica is over so it is bygone to me.

Michael quickly dismissed it after I told him who I'd seen. He told me he knew who Virginity-girl was and that he saw her around the school. He swiftly grabbed me pulling me behind the door where his students couldn't see and began to kiss me. Telling me that this was his way of showing his appreciation for the gift for now, and later that evening he planned to continue showing his gratitude to me. I looked forward to it. I knew he would keep his word.

There was nothing left to do but make it official. In my young mind we were a power couple. He had skills with the computer and so did I. He loved music and so did I. He had that drive to be an entrepreneur and so did I. I guess it is time to take things to the next level and move in with each other. Why not? We spend most of our time together anyway. We both know that this relationship is a bit sketchy, but we were willing to make things work. We had been there for each other during life changing events and neither of us wanted to lose the attachment we had developed. Whatever it is about me that drives him to be all the man I want him to be to me, is the same thing that drives me to be the woman he wants me to be for him. Being with him caused me to open myself in new ways and I was better for it. Together we would travel on a journey exploring all that had developed between us. Everything felt right.

We began moving things out of his downtown loft to his grandmother's home. Looking all over the city for a place to stay, we finally found another downtown apartment close to where he was living before. We loved the thought of living downtown for the benefit of being in the heart of the city. While moving his things temporarily to his grandmother's, we would sneak into his unfurnished loft for old time's sake. After having our midday rendezvous I had to go back to work. I decided I would catch the bus since I was already downtown and it was convenient for the both of

False Security

us. The bus stop was right across the street from his old loft so I went to wait for the bus as he drove off to finish moving his things. I see a familiar face trying to get into the building where his loft is. It was Virginity-girl. I wondered who she knew in the building. Whoever she was looking for must have been unavailable, because she couldn't get in. Bells went off, but I couldn't imagine Michael knowing her outside of his job after I specifically told him how much it bothered me when Jamaica did what he did with Virginity-girl.

We moved in together into a comfortable loft downtown. We shopped for little things to go around the house. We both had great taste and ideas for the loft and I was overjoyed that things were moving the way they were with us. Michael had a black and white picture of a naked man and woman entangled with each other that was a sexy addition to our place. He wanted to have it mounted and framed so we could hang it in our living room. The black and white picture hung over our black leather sofa. We made love countless times under that picture, and every time was more passionate then the last. We couldn't get enough of each other. With no protection and no cares in the world we opened ourselves to each other to reach the satisfaction our bodies yearned.

My family likes Michael. For the first time everyone seems okay with my choice of partner. I was clearly fine with him and more and more in love with him as the days went by. I loved living with him, but I didn't like knowing that he had secrets. I was uncomfortable with the fact that I couldn't answer the phone. He said to me that if I answered the phone when his baby mama called she would stop him from being able to see his son. I didn't want to be the reason his child couldn't have a relationship with him. I knew what that felt like. I made sure I didn't answer the phone when I thought it was her calling. He had his son with him a lot. I would cook meals for both of them. I didn't want any children of my own, but his son was a sweet little boy and I didn't mind having him around.

Community college is a two year institution. Graduating would be historical for me and my family. Who am I kidding? Graduating from community college is more than a great accomplishment. I've actually completed this journey and the first in my family to do so. Michael didn't finish and does not have a degree, but he pushed for me to finish and to get mine. What an unselfish act. Michael planned a huge surprise graduation party for me and it was a blast. My family was overjoyed with him because he displayed how much he loved me in all he would say and do. I had no idea that he had secretly planned this for me and all of my family showed up to support me. All these people that I didn't think had a sincere care about me were there to celebrate me because they cared, they always did.

I have graduated from college. The first in my family. Sure, to some a two year degree is small potatoes but to me that moment would be, for the rest of my life, a grand thing to celebrate. To go against the odds and clear every hurdle set before me will always mean a lot to me. Graduating from college, with no children, working at Kinko's; I am doing pretty well for myself.

Tina, my best friend from church, was back in Rochester and had graduated too. She had given birth to a precious baby girl- my first niece and god-daughter Kyana. Dyna had given birth to a little girl named Jazmine prior too so I had two god-daughters with no need for having children of my own especially including my nephews; the two boys Quincy and Thomas my older sister gave birth to. My other church best friend Johnnie was at the University of Buffalo doing well as a football player. Michael didn't like Johnnie because I told him about our children's-church crush and our pretend-marriage. Michael had to know that no one would ever take the place of Johnnie - my first love. When Johnnie wanted to talk to me he would always use my sister to call me on three-way. Johnnie never wanted any beef with Michael, but he cared about me and wanted to make sure that I was being treated right.

I did all I could to prove to Michael that there was no one else I desired, but it was never enough for him. Arguments ensued and breakups swarmed without manifesting. I couldn't understand why Michael would want to ruin something that seemed so good. Living with someone was different than spending the night with each other here and there. At times it seemed to be more than we could handle. Living with him left me to wonder if there was more to the relationship with his son's mom than I realized; like he had been able to deceive me about their relationship.

False Security

We lived together and neither one of us planned on leaving the other so I felt his son's mom needed to know that I existed and I am here for the long run. I was tired of not being able to answer my home phone and began to believe that these secrets were going to hurt me more than I realized. I started thinking that it wasn't me that Michael was protecting. Maybe he was covering up his own secrets. I didn't want to feel as though I was in competition with the mother of his son, but I loved him and I was willing to fight for our relationship. We had come so far. The sky was the limit to what we could have together.

My home phone rang and I answered. Sick and tired of being in the dark, I answered. With no care about the consequences, I answered. Ready to face things head on and deal with them, I answered. There was confusion on both ends of the phone as we both tried to figure out who the other was. The voice on the other line certainly wasn't his son's mom, so who was it? I lived here, and this was my phone, so I had no reason to hide who I was. What I wanted to know was who in the world this was on the other line? I had been dating this man for years now. He had been welcomed into my family and me into his. Who could it possibly be? *How do you know me, but I have no clue who you are?* The disgust in her voice that said I should have known who she was made me very angry and my body became uptight.

It had been a long time since I had been in soldier do-or-die, ready to take out the world mode, and this didn't feel good at all. I was listening to this female on the line tell me that she was in a relationship with the same man that I was in a relationship with. I heard her tell me that I was not his lady because she was. *Who is she? She is Virginity-girl. WHAT?! How in the world does this girl go from sleeping with the guy I was in love with in high school to sleeping with the guy I am in love with now?* Virginity-girl began to tell me how she had been involved with Michael since she met him in high school. She went further to tell me how she was now in college and he came down to her campus to visit her and how she paid for them to stay in hotels when he visited. I was in too much shock to comprehend what was being said to me.

She gave me her number and I told her that I would call her back. I started to call him and curse his lying, cheating, two timing self out, but I stopped myself. I deleted her number off the caller-id and went to my mother's house. Over there I called this girl back to get details about their so-called relationship. My anger began to shift from him to her because I couldn't help but think that she was trying to be funny and somehow got a kick out of chasing after the men I was involved with. I needed to know where she was so that I could go plant my foot in her rear and school her on messing with someone like me. Her and her roommates took turns telling me about the times Michael came to the campus to see her, and how he was very controlling of her. They said that Michael was always in need of cash, and she was dumb enough to give it to him. He told her he needed money to pay the cable bill for his house and she gave him that money too.

Just when I felt like she was just a dumb broad being used for her money she stopped me in my tracks. She began to describe the inside of my house. Yes our house that we had together she described from one room to the next. She knew what kind of window curtains I had in my walk-in closet. She knew what was under my bed. She knew what my bathroom and my kitchen looked like. She had been in my home – according to her story, numerous times. This suddenly got too real for me. I thought there was nothing else that she could say to me to take my anger to another level, when she told me that the black and white photo that hung above our sofa in the living room was a gift to him from her.

Not only has this chick been in my home, she has paid some of my utility bills and has artifacts hanging as if her name was on the lease as well. I told her that I wasn't going anywhere and that was my house. I thanked her stupid self for paying my household bills, and let her know the money she gave to him he was spending it on me. I told her I deleted her number off the caller-id so Michael would have no clue that she called. I told her to call back later in the night when we are both home so that we can confront him together. In all my toughness I was hurting and again in disbelief. How could a man that showed me he loved me daily hurt me so badly? I was ready to face his son's mother, but this side swiped me worse than I could imagine.

My mother begged me not to do anything irrational – I had come too far from that type of life to resort back to a criminal mind.

I went home and began to look around at what I thought he and I had put together. Every step I took on my carpet I imagined that Virginity-girl had stepped there too at some point and I was just dismayed. I decided that I would cook him a nice meal. Being a vegetarian it wouldn't take me long to put something together that would have the house smelling good when he came home. I sat on the sofa beneath the infamous black and white picture as he walked through the door. Overjoyed with the smell of dinner he didn't recognize the pain on my face. Shortly after, the phone rang and he was in for a rude awakening. Thinking that I would do my typical ignoring of the phone, he was shockingly surprised that I answered with a sweet voice saying hello. He immediately jumped up wondering what was wrong with me. I told him it was Virginity-girl on the line and that he should pick up the other phone to hear what she has been telling me. He knew he was caught and there was nothing that he could do about it.

The yelling and the screaming began along with the denial and the lies. He said Virginity-girl and her friends were lying and that they weren't in a relationship. He was using her for the money and nothing more. He cursed her and told her to never call his house again. I stood so stunned wondering did he really believe cursing her out and hanging up on her was going to make me feel better. This wasn't just any random girl off the street, this was Virginity-girl. I have history with this girl getting in bed with the same man I was sleeping with. This hurts more than finding out he was cheating on me. I felt like Michael did this to tear my heart into irreparable pieces. I wondered why he would do this particular thing to me. Why her?

As the phone rang with her calling back I picked it up and he snatched it out of my hands. I begged him to tell the truth and not attempt to lie his way out of this. I needed for him to look me in my eyes and be honest for a change. She went into detail, describing my house again to me with him on the phone – something that cannot be disputed, and he is silenced. He told her that it was over and hung up on her again. The phone rang again and he walked out of the door. I told her that he left, but she needed to know where I stood in the situation. He wasn't some Jamaican boyfriend in high school. Michael and I had invested in this relationship and it was not going to be easy for either one of us to deal with this. I told her it was best that she made sure I never saw her again, because I would not be responsible for what I would do to her when I saw her. She replied that she loved him too and she was just as hurt to know that he and I had a life together – a life she wish she had. I told her this was our place – both of our names were on the lease and I was not moving. She needed to know that she may have been able to sleep with both of the men I loved so much, but she would never have a life with either of them. Hearing the hurt in her voice, and realizing how much younger she is than both me and Michael I again turned my anger off of her and back on to him.

I hung up the phone. I sat down on the sofa and stared at the walls. It was eerily quiet in the loft. I could hear every breath I was taking. I felt my heart beating through my shirt and suddenly I felt moisture on my face. This was not normal for me. The longer I sat there, the harder it was for me to try and control myself. Michael was gone and I was alone, and I had to let it out. I cried. I screamed and I cried. I stomped and I cried. I ran into the kitchen and grabbed a chef knife. I went back into the living room and took that black and white photo off the wall. I began breaking the frame and started stabbing the male and female in the picture. I took a red marker and wrote all over it vulgar names that I felt the both of them deserved to be called.

Michael's grandmother called and wanted to know what was going on. He had gone to her house upset in tears and she wanted to know why. In between gasping for breath as I cried my heart out I told her what had taken place and what he had done. She reassured me that he loved me and only me. Seriously?! How could she say these words to me? She asked me did I love him; did I believe he loved me; does he make me happy; do I think I make him happy? I was astonished at her line of questioning, and taken aback when she said that she was sending him back home to work things out with me. She explained to me that one thing she knew if she didn't know anything else was that her son loved me. His grandmother told me that he at times felt insecure in the relationship thinking that I had someone on the side as well. I couldn't believe what she was telling me. She told me that if I loved him I needed to try and work things out. As she was encouraging me he walked back through the door. I told her that he was there and she hung up pleading with me to work things out.

I sat on the floor in tears. I didn't think I would ever stop crying. This hurt worse than finding out about his New Year's infidelity back in London. I couldn't let him touch me. I didn't even want to sleep in my bed out of fear that those sheets had been used with Virginity-girl. Neither one of us slept that night. He went around the house cleaning up the things that I destroyed, trying to pick up every piece of glass that I shattered throughout the loft. I lay on the floor crying until there were no sounds coming out of my mouth. He pulled me off the floor and into the bed with him and I felt sick to my stomach. He kept apologizing and explaining that Virginity-girl didn't mean anything to him. She gave him oral sex that he loved, and she knew that he and I were together. She didn't care because she felt I had taken her man back in high school. Michael knew that sorry was not going to cut it this time around. He tried to do everything to make me speak to him but I couldn't.

I had opened myself up to this man. I opened my heart, my body and soul to him. My family loved him. His family seemed to love me. Everywhere we went people told us we were a cute couple. We even dressed to complement each other. I had dedicated my life to pleasing him after he had given so much to me. I chose to be with him instead of running away from him when I knew our relationship was inappropriate because of his position at my high school. Things have changed drastically and I had no clarity as to how I should deal with this. He attempted to take my clothes off; I screamed and cried. He begged me to please forgive him and to calm down. I knew what he wanted to do. He knew what would make me reconsider throwing away this relationship. He used his mouth and tongue to caress every inch of my body leaving no spot untouched.

After being deprived of sleep the entire night I couldn't move the next morning. I couldn't close my eyes to go to sleep and my body felt as though it had shut completely down. Michael got on the phone and called Virginity-girl. He told her that he could no longer go on with his relationship with her and that he was done. Michael told her he realized just how much he loved me and was going to do all he could to repair our relationship to make me happy. He admitted he took money from her to give to me. He admitted that he pawned a ring she purchased for him and gave that money to me as well. He wanted to get everything out in the open so there were no more secrets, confessing that she had been in our loft apartment. He admitted that he played her and never had real feelings for her. He told her she could never replace me. She furiously accepted his words and told him to never call her again. For some strange reason I felt I had won, and was glad that he said those things to her so she wouldn't think she had won. I was naïve. In reality we both lost and I hadn't won anything.

I honestly wanted my brother, cousins and uncles to come and do some serious damage to him, but every time I tried to make the call I couldn't. Michael had charmed himself into my life and my family would have a hard time believing what he had done. I kept hearing his grandmother's words ringing in my head. So full of wisdom and desperately seeking peace between us she did and said all she could to keep us together. I knew we had the lease and other bills together and it felt like this was going to be more costly to break things off. I stayed.

Everyday Michael dedicated his mouth to my body to reassure me over and over again that I was who he wanted. He wants all of me and promises to never hurt me again. I accepted his gesture of love because I loved him too. I wanted to be loved, and I wanted to be loved by Michael specifically. For months he was afraid to eat my food thinking I would poison him. His grandmother and my mother constantly checked in to make sure that he was alright. I knew it was going to take time to heal. What I didn't know was if I would be willing to allow the healing to take place.

I sought to hurt him the way he hurt me, but I didn't want to give my body to anyone else. I am not nor have I ever been that type of woman. No matter how many guys tried to talk to me I rejected their advances because I loved Michael. He had done so many wonderful things for me and to me and I loved him. I had to accept that I had been cheated on and I needed to move on from that. I could never understand why my mom stayed around after she knew that my father was unfaithful to her. I was not married with children, but now I think I understood.

I didn't want to tell Johnnie what Michael had done out of fear of what Johnnie would want to do. Johnnie knew that something was wrong, but I couldn't talk to him the way that I wanted to tell him what happened. I needed to move beyond all of this anyway and leave it in the past.

I sat and listened to Oprah on television as she repeated, "When someone shows you and tells you who and what they are, believe them." Profound. True. I felt as if she was speaking directly to me and it was a sign that I needed to get out of this relationship. Yet the love I had for Michael was stronger than I could imagine, so we continued on with our relationship in hopes of making things better. With every sign of progress, I felt like I had made the right decision to stay around and work things out. Oprah said to believe who and what people say they are – and a lot can be said about a person not with words, but with actions.

Michael had shown me that he could be a loving, gentle and caring person and that made me happy. He loved in the way he looked out for others. His attraction to me caused him to put in overtime turning my behaviors from street-minded to business-minded. He invested in me, turning my lack of desire for education to a hunger for education and eventually that turned into a degree. My thirst for alcohol turned into a challenge to find excitement without the inebriation. He is gentle in the way he holds me when he knows I

False Security

am hurt. Gently he caresses my skin and my face until our breathing syncs and we become one. Gentle in the way he seduces me causing me to desire him more and more, over and over again. He shows how much he cares when he bends down and kisses my tears. He cares when I don't ask for anything, but he knows my needs and helps without hesitation. Yes Michael has shown me the loving, gentle, caring side of him.

One thing I have come to know by being an Oreo cookie is that there are two sides to a person. As enticing as this side of Michael is, the other side is not very appealing. The unfaithful, lying, stealing, controlling and manipulative side that makes me hurt. So unfaithful in the women he decides to have relationships with while he is supposed to be committed to me. Such a liar, lying at times when there was no reason to lie. A thief in that has stolen not simply material things but most importantly my heart. In a very conniving way controlling my whereabouts, my friends, my finances. Manipulating me in every way to swindle me into believing I owe him for all he has done for me. He used me for his support and credit, taking full advantage of my desires he uses me for his material, financial, emotional and sexual gain.

I was living with this man as if we were married. I cooked for him, supported him and I was there for him as if I were his wife. I had no ring, there was no engagement, yet I was there as if my last name had changed. We had not gone before God and entered into a covenant. He had not made a promise before God and my family to be my lawfully wedded husband, to have and to hold from this day forward, for better or for worse, for richer or for poorer, in sickness and in health, to love, cherish, till death us do part, according to God's holy ordinance.

I felt far removed from how I had been raised. My mother wasn't pleased with the way I was living but she knew she had taught me right and it was now up to me to do right. As a leader in the church teaching young woman a holy way to live, I stayed far away from the church. I can imagine the shame she must have felt knowing that I had no desires to be anywhere near a church and was in a relationship committing more sins than I wanted to admit. I had strayed away from what I knew was right. Entangled in a web of love and lust I was painfully experiencing an uncontrolled life. I had mistaken this false security as my covering.

Chapter 7

Hope

I had to admit that I loved Michael. Even in spite of all the lies and deceit that had taken place. Truthfully I hadn't been completely honest myself. Although I'd never cheated, my heart hadn't been fully devoted to him either. Regardless, I loved him no matter what. I reasoned that it wasn't the worst thing that he was a little unfaithful and told a bunch of lies. He loved me. It is what it is, right? I told myself men couldn't be faithful to women; that his unfaithful behavior was something that I would have to get used to. The fact that a man refused to be with one woman at a time was appalling, but if that was the case and it was impossible for him to act any differently, I might as well settle down and accept it with him. Although he had done great things to encourage me, he had done just as much or more to hurt me. Our relationship should have been over, but it wasn't.

Everyone thought Michael complemented me well. We had been going to a lot of weddings and different events together, and we always received kind remarks from everyone. His friends and people I knew are getting married and that "marriage fever" could jump on you quickly. Watching the brides and the grooms with their wedding parties, it was easy to start getting ideas for yourself. Why wouldn't he want to marry me? I'm in my twenties now and at the age where I think I am ready to be a wife. I had shown and proven that I was a ride or die chick. I didn't have any children so he didn't have to deal with a crazy baby daddy. The loving is off the chain. I had put up with more than I should have. What else did he need to get him to the conclusion that I was good wife material? I wanted to be married. Getting married would be perfect for Michael and me. If we were married he would do better. He would be faithful to me. If we were married that would secure me in the number one spot, coming in second to none.

With each passing day somehow the topic of marriage came up. Initially I felt he would bring it up because there was nothing left for him to use as bait to keep me around. I had graduated from falling for high school foolishness so he needed to come with something more durable. In elementary school you could make me a card using crayons making a rainbow with hearts. In middle school you could get me a stuffed animal and some candy. In high school you could buy me some sneakers or give me your hustle money. After college – I didn't want or need anything from a man. I could make myself a card, get my own stuffed animals, buy my own sneakers, and I made my own money. What he did for me was extra – I didn't need it, but I would take it. But if he gave me a ring, that would mean something. That would be special.

Being with a man that was unfaithful gave you an uneasiness that was difficult to explain. No matter how much I loved Michael, I did not trust him. I wished there was a way that he could gain back my trust, but I didn't feel that there was. I stayed with him because I loved him and I knew him. I didn't want to meet someone new and have to go through the same hurt all over again. For the most part he satisfied me in every other way so why not make it work? When he was not home, I spent my days looking through his things trying to find traces of illicit behavior. I searched the caller-id and checked his emails for information to satisfy my suspicions. His unfaithfulness to me had him worried and wondering if I was going to retaliate and be unfaithful as well.

With all the snooping and the distrust, there was tension in our house. We argued over the smallest things. Michael thought that the squeaky clean image he had with my family had been ruined because of his mistreatment of me. What he didn't know was that my family wasn't aware of everything that happened. My mom still loved him and continued to think that we looked good together as an item; although she wished we weren't living in sin shacking together. She too hoped and wished that if we are going to stay together we do it the right way and get married.

I didn't want to cook for him anymore. I wanted to go out with my friends. But what friends did I have? When I committed to this relationship with him, those friendships that I had were completely neglected. The fun was gone and we barely looked at each other. Most days I found myself waiting for the phone to ring for someone else to say that he was cheating on me again.

*****

Out with Tina getting a break from being home, I purposely wouldn't tell Michael where I was or who I was with. I wanted him to feel what he made me feel, that sense of insecurity. So at the mall and out to eat we went. I really needed time away from all the drama going on at home. I started thinking of how Michael would let his friends use our apartment as a creeping pad, allowing them to bring the women they were cheating with to our home. I began to wonder if his friends did the same for him with their places. I wondered if someone was at my place right now. *I needed to go home.*

As Tina pulled up to the loft we saw a yellow sticky note on the door. Assuming Michael left me a note to say where he was since he couldn't contact me, Tina waited to see what the note said. We were surprised to see the note was blank. I went to put my key in the door and my key wouldn't fit. I took another look at the lock and realized Michael had changed the lock on the door. I was furious. All I could think about was that I would have been stranded outside with no phone or transportation if Tina had pulled off.

I got back into the car with Tina and we went to my mother's house. I was so upset and couldn't believe that he would do something like that. Michael had taken things to another level and if he wasn't careful things were going to start getting ugly between us. He made his point and I hope it was worth it for him. All this did was show me that he was willing to hurt me and humiliate me in any way he could. Where was the concern for me? What happened to the love?

I was beginning to feel as though he didn't want me around anymore. I didn't want to be around either. When I finally returned to our place, I couldn't stand the vibe I felt there. Many things were left unsaid. So many issues had not been addressed. Not communicating is a sure way to end a relationship. Assumptions began to fly and I couldn't stand it anymore. I chose to hang out at my mother's house instead of sitting around in the house with him. It seemed as though he was trying to make me give up on our relationship.

Every time I looked at the space where that black and white photo hung I was angered all over again. He didn't deserve a woman like me and why should I continue to hang on his arm and make him look good? He had the nerve to act as if he doesn't trust me. What had I done to earn his distrust? *Is he trying to flip the script on me as a smoke screen to cover up something else he is doing?*

I refused to sit in the house with him not talking to me and me not talking to him another minute. I needed to get out for a moment and get some fresh air. Tina was living with my mother and Mom was cooking a good meal for dinner. I decided I would eat dinner with them instead of staying home. I went into the bedroom to call my mother and as I was talking to her I saw Michael begin to get very agitated. I asked mom could she come and pick me up and she said sure and was on her way. Before I could completely hang the phone up, Michael began pulling my clothing out of the drawers and screaming at me to get out. I didn't understand what was going on and began yelling back at him. All he kept saying was that if I wanted out of the relationship I needed to get out. I couldn't understand how my mother coming to get me to eat dinner at her house meant that I was done with the relationship.

Mommy pulled up and was not expecting the both of us to be behaving the way were. He came outside throwing my things into the van as if he was putting me out. I told him not to touch another one of my belongings and that I didn't need his help. Michael stayed outside talking to my mom as I went up and down the steps removing my things from the loft. I couldn't believe what I was doing. My name was on the lease just like his. We both lived there so why was I the one getting out? I felt like he was rejecting me and that really hurt. I got in the passenger seat and look straight ahead not making any eye contact with him as I let my mother know that I was ready to go. We pulled off and I did all I could to hold back my tears.

Why would I cry? Why should I cry? This was the guy that cheated on me while I was thousands of miles away in London for school. This was the guy who knew Virginity-girl and the history behind her, yet he chose to develop a relationship with her. This was the guy who didn't want his son's mom to know who I was, and I believed it was because he still had a relationship with her. This was the guy that accused me of cheating with my best friend Johnnie just to cause a commotion so his unfaithful acts wouldn't be exposed.

This was the guy that would have me sitting in the house and not be able to answer my own phone. This was the guy who allowed Virginity-girl to come into my home giving her full access to my most private space. Now I was crying.

    I cried. I cried because I loved him. I cried because I didn't want to be without him. I cried because after all I had been through with him, I deserved to be happy with him. I cried because I remembered him sitting with me countless nights begging me to get out of an abusive relationship with someone else. I cried because he was the reason I went to college. I cried because he sat me down and encouraged me to stop drinking. I cried because he was the one that got me out of Timberlands and Hi-Tech boots and into heels and business suits. I cried because when no one else believed in me he did. I cried because I forgave him. I cried because of all that I went through with him. I cried because I knew he could be a good man, and I didn't want him to be a good man to anyone but me. Crying was not typical behavior for me, but I was crying. Yes, I cried. My body didn't know what else to do.

    I didn't want to face another day or accept our breakup. We had invested years into our relationship for it to have ended like this. There were plenty of guys that wanted to date me, begging for a chance to take me out or get my number. I could've been with any one of the guys that had an interest in me. But I didn't, and I wouldn't. I loved Michael. I could not believe that even after all I had endured; that was what came to my mind. I loved him. I was hurting without him and I didn't know what I was going to do. I couldn't imagine this being for the best. I couldn't imagine our break up was meant to happen. I couldn't imagine that the man I love is going to be with someone else.

My mind was all over the place and my emotions were too. I loved him, but my Black side, my outside wouldn't allow him to make me look like a fool. He wanted me out? Well out I would be. *Who am I kidding?* I was not going to make it through one day without my inside, what was called the White side thinking about him. This was not going to be good. Looking around my childhood bedroom I wondered what I was going to do. I didn't want our relationship to end, but I was not going to show any sign of weakness. I heard the doorbell ring and there he was standing before me. He hovered over me looking down telling me to get my things together and come home. All I could do was stand there. He told me he didn't want to live without me and he was sorry. He wanted me to come home. It hadn't been 24 hours and he wanted me to come home. *Should I be tough and say no? Should I be real and go?* I grabbed my things and I went home. He loved me and I knew he did. I loved him and there was no need to say it, we would go home and show each other the only way we knew how.

*****

I wanted to be married and have my last name changed. No need in me keeping the one I had because I didn't want any lingering connections with my father. Michael and I looked so good together;

he couldn't have been a better soul mate. Someone was always asking us when we were going to get married. We both acted as if we didn't understand the questions when asked. All the while Michael would string me along looking at diamonds and pricing out rings as if the day would really come. After I landed my job at the Urban League of Rochester, our relationship had become more public. Many women would question why a man of his age would date someone as young as me. I asked that question myself, but it felt too good to let go. I loved the fact that other women desired or inquired about what was mine.

Michael and I had been working on our relationship and I saw that things were getting better between us. I couldn't believe we had been together this long and we were finally growing strong. I cherished him and I wondered if he knew just how much I truly loved him. Michael believed that the reason my father and I didn't get along was because I did not know how to communicate. He expressed concern over my need to communicate. Oddly enough I had earned an Associate's Degree in Communications but had yet to master the skill of performing it.

Working at the Urban League and helping youth prepare to take their GED was a rewarding job. I loved the fact that I literally lived right down the street and could walk to work. I was enrolled at SUNY Brockport (State University of New York College at Brockport) and I was working on my Bachelor's Degree. Michael and I had been praying together and every now and then we would drive by a church. My confidence level had risen drastically and I was surer of myself and my success in life than I had ever been. The exposure at the Urban League introduced me to new acquaintances and opportunities.

Everyone seemed to be a Christian talking about the Lord and inviting me to church. I went when mom was being honored and any special programs that she was in charge of. Church was generally not a place I wanted to be especially with all the hypocrisy that I saw as a child. One of the directors of a youth program at the Urban League was a minister in his church, but he was a liar on the job. Every other question I asked I could bet his answer will be a lie. One day I asked him a question, and for some strange reason he couldn't answer me. Every time he would open his mouth, his words would get jumbled like he couldn't speak English. When I asked him what was wrong with him, he told me that he had anointed his tongue with holy oil, so every time he got ready to say something wrong or tell a lie God wouldn't allow him to. It was funny and shameful the entire day hearing him babble when all he had to do was tell the truth.

Mr. Harris was the teacher for another GED class and he attended a Church of God In Christ church like my mother. He was nothing like the hypocritical babbling minister. He even knew my mom and took the time out to tell me about the Lord. My heart was getting softer and I could see that I needed to make some changes in my life. Soon it would be five years that Michael and I had been in a relationship, and it really was time to start thinking about where our

Hope

relationship was going. I was a young lady with a good job, no children, looking good and feeling good about myself. I was too young to hang around waiting to see what would happen. I had to make things happen for myself.

I took a look at the young women that I helped find jobs and prepared to take the GED and I was thankful. I could have been any one of them. I could be at the Urban League on the other side of my desk asking for help instead of offering help. I could be the one with the criminal record looking for a second chance at life. These women with their children were having such a hard time; angry at the world because they felt like failures in life with no hope. Where was the hope? I took my job personally. I would go a little further, invest a little more time, advise a little harder, because I wanted to see each one of the young men and women succeed in life. I remembered when I needed someone to show me that they were concerned for my future and now I wanted to return the favor to these young people.

Michael always made appearances at my job. Some of the women there would whisper amongst each other when he would come around. He was more their age and I guess some really thought they could pull him from me. With lunch in hand he would show everyone that he was taking care of me. I imagined so many wished they were me and I was glad I was finally getting the good man out of Michael again. I loved it when he made me smile, when he made me happy, those days he made me feel so good that all I did was think of him all day long. While sitting at my desk in the office

Michael called me and was asking random questions. It sounded as though he was talking for his own sake, using his charm to distract me. I thought it was sweet that he didn't have anything else to do but joke around with me; that he wanted to hear my voice. He said he was coming up to my job because he had something to tell me. He told me to come to the front desk because he was on his way.

When I hung up with him before I could leave my desk my phone rang again. It was a coworker asking me was I looking out the window. I told him no and asked what was going on. I hung up with him and I went over to the window to see what he was talking about. As I looked out the window down to the sidewalk, I saw a familiar car with a black and white sign with two big red bows on each end that had my name on it. The sign said: LILLIAN, WILL YOU MARRY ME? I put my hands over my mouth as I saw Tina waving up at me then I started screaming. I turned around and there he was in a black suit with a dozen red roses. He got down on one knee and proposed to me in front of all my coworkers and students. All I could do was cry and say yes. I loved this man with all my heart and all my being. He completed me.

Engaged to be married and boy was I excited about it. Tina and I went to the mall that night and all I could do was look at my ring. I couldn't believe it was finally happening for me. I couldn't believe I was proposed to that way. So much excitement, so much love, so much to look forward to. After all we had been through he wanted to make it legal. He wanted to spend the rest of his life with me – not just as his lady, but as his wife.

On our engagement night, after celebrating with my family we went home to our apartment. It made things seem so real, and so right, more right than it had ever been before. With this engagement ring he promised to never leave me, to always be by my side, to love and to cherish me, to spoil me, to be faithful to me, and do right by me. As I lay next to him in our bed looking at the ring he gave me, going over the promises he made I was overjoyed and ready to spend the rest of my life with him. Passionately we held each other, caressed each other and made intimate love all night long. We tried to make it last forever, because that was how we wanted our marriage to be – forever.

I had it all. The one everyone expected to be imprisoned, dead, or pregnant was the one now getting ready to have a Bachelor's degree, engaged to be married, and had a wonderful job. I beat the statistics that said I should have contracted HIV by now, or have babies, or a prison record. Instead my dreams were coming true. I had wedding appointments. I had material to pick out, and a honeymoon to schedule. Planning our wedding was my top priority. I wanted us to hurry and be married. I didn't want to wait and neither did he. Getting married was the best thing to do. Getting married would help him to be faithful to me and draw my heart closer to him. Marriage would be the daily reminder to the both of us that we were to be faithful to one another and love one another with all of our heart.

Hopefully he would stay faithful to me. That would certainly be enough to cause my heart to have love for only him.

We had already purchased the honeymoon package, and I needed to get the material for the dresses. Since everyone looked to us as this high class power couple, our wedding could be nothing less. I was so focused about our wedding, and getting situated for what was to come. I was running here and there, and anxiety would take over causing me to stress sometimes. I was beginning to feel sick. *Maybe I caught the flu. I'm probably stressed out from all the wedding planning.* Of course that was it; just stress. *Once the wedding is taking care of I will be fine.* I was concerned because the stress was causing my cycle to be off schedule. I needed to calm down and relax so that I wouldn't break down. No matter how much I tried to relax, I still felt sick. Michael being the man that he was didn't help me get our wedding prepared. He kept telling me to calm down and to slow down, but I was way too excited. He should have known that trying to slow an engaged woman down was pointless.

No matter what I did, I was not able to shake my sickness. Michael told me to take a pregnancy test. He thought that I was pregnant. I couldn't understand why he would think that unless that was what he wanted. After many tests, reading many results and sitting in disbelief it was true. I was pregnant. How did he know? Why didn't I know? What am I going to do now? All these years we've been together and I never got pregnant. Now that we were engaged this comes up. Why? What am I going to tell my mom?

Hope

I was amazed how quickly things changed. In the blink of an eye life could go from high to low, from peace to chaos. It was just a few months ago I was proposed to, engaged, living with my fiancé, planning a wedding, enjoying my youth and freedom, while attending college to receive my Bachelor's degree. Then I got sick. In and out of the hospital, big as a house and planning a baby shower instead of a bridal shower. I couldn't stand the smell of my fiancé or the smell of our apartment. Just being in our apartment made me want to vomit, so I moved home with my mom to prepare to deliver a baby that I could not believe I was having. No more drinking, no more going out, no more fun for me. I never wanted to be the type of mother still in the club while my child had to stay with grandparents. I refused to let my child think that his grandmother was his guardian and parent. I was the one who got pregnant and I would be the one to raise this child – along with his father.

There was no more discussion of the wedding. Michael did all he could to divert from facing the issue that the wedding date was approaching and we were not ready to be married. All the money we spent on the reception, the material purchased, and the honeymoon paid in full now feels like a waste of time and money. Instead of Michael and me getting closer to one another we seemed to be drifting apart again. I hadn't been staying at our apartment and I knew he was feeling neglected. I dropped my mom off at one of her church services across town and decided to stop by the apartment to be with Michael for a while. I wanted to show him that although my belly was huge and I got sick every time I walked into our apartment, I was willing to endure it because I loved him. He needed to know I was still his woman; his nauseous, pregnant, slightly irritable woman.

I got to the apartment and saw his car parked. I was glad he was home, because he didn't know I was coming so this would be a wonderful spontaneous surprise. I heard people say all the time, doing things sporadically and unplanned kept excitement and fire in the relationship. I took out my keys, unlocked the door and walked up the stairs to get into the apartment. I heard music playing and I got excited about what was getting ready to take place. I got to the second entry doorway but I was taking my time because the baby caused me to lose my breath while going up the flight of stairs. I turned the knob to open the door and the door wouldn't open. *This is strange, this door never locks, and as a matter of fact, I don't even have the key to unlock it.*

I looked through the window on the door calling out Michael's name. I noticed that he didn't have the radio playing. It was the television. I saw the lights from the television glaring off the back wall, and I was wondering why the television was so loud. I begin banging on the door and screaming Michael's name assuming that he was in the bathroom and could not hear me. I paused for a moment when I heard another man's voice that wasn't Michael. I heard moaning and groaning and became curious as to what was going on. Next I heard a woman's voice as she screamed with pleasure. It sounded as though he was watching a sex tape on the television.

I began screaming Michael's name again for him to come and open the door. I couldn't understand why he wouldn't answer knowing that I was standing there. I looked through the glass window again and I saw a shadow – not one but two. On the wall a light was shining through the bedroom window perfectly where I couldn't see who was in the apartment, but I knew it was a male and a female. Their shadows projected on the bedroom wall as they were in our walk-in closet. I saw Michael's shadow holding the female's face, he rubbed her face and he kissed her.

My heart dropped and I could feel my child moving a mile a minute inside my belly. I picked up a garbage can and begin banging it against the glass to break the door window to get in. Furiously I was piecing together that Michael was not in there alone, and he was not just watching a random show on cable. He was in our apartment with another woman and they were in the middle of their rendezvous when I decided to pop up and surprise him – at OUR home.

I watched the closet door close and couldn't stop screaming. Moments later I saw the closet door reopen, but only one shadow appeared. Now I was wondering was I seeing things. Could I have mistaken the curtains or clothes as another person? What happened to the other shadow that looked like a short female that I thought I just saw Michael kiss? As my baby continues to move fiercely in my stomach I looked up and saw Michael angrily coming towards the door naked. He opened the door yelling and screaming at me and grabed me by my clothing. He cursed me out asking me if I was crazy. I yelled back demanding to know who was in my house.

He grabbed me by my hair and began to pull me into the kitchen and asked if I saw anyone in there. He then pulled me into the bathroom and yanked back the shower curtain and asked me did I see anyone in there. He grabbed me by my throat and violently tried to pull me out the bathroom and I fell to the floor. Grabbing my stomach I yelled for him to stop and to let me go. I looked into his eyes and he stared down at me as if he could care less that I was carrying his unborn child. When I wouldn't get up, he grabbed me by my hair and dragged me across the floor from the bathroom, through the living room to the bedroom and asked again do you see anyone in here. I lay on the floor and cried no. He stood over me and called me stupid and other terrible names.

Angrily he said to me that since I became pregnant, I wasn't giving him enough sexual attention. He said that he put in a video to gratify himself and that he wasn't in there with anyone. I knew there was only one way in and out of the apartment. I also knew my mind could not be playing tricks on me and I saw someone else in this apartment, but where did they go?

There was no sign of anyone being there, and at this point I no longer cared. I could not understand how in the world a man would drag a pregnant woman across a floor as he did and be angry all because I interrupted him from masturbating. Why not welcome me in so that I could please you – unless someone was there and they hid themselves very well. What kind of father would put his unborn child and mother in danger like this? I laid in disbelief trying to catch my breath and calm down as I felt tightness in my stomach.

The same man that claimed to love me and care for me just put me and his child's life at risk out of frustration. I was sick and distraught, but I couldn't move as my stomach became tighter and tighter with pain. He towered over me in a stance of intimidation, but this Oreo cookie refused to let him think that what he had done was okay. I didn't know where the strength came from, but I picked myself up, cursed him out and with every pang of tightness in my belly I kept moving, grabbing my things to leave. At the stoplight I put my head down on the steering wheel and began to pray asking God to let nothing happen to me or this baby. *I need you God to help me get through this and make these pains go away. I am only seven months pregnant; it is too early to have my baby.*

Because of Michael's abusive tirade, for the rest of the pregnancy I was considered high risk, and put on bed rest limiting my activities. I didn't want the doctor to insert a cup in me to keep the baby inside until the due date, so I promised to do my best to relax. Of course, Michael attempted to show he was sorry sexually and as usual I accepted. I didn't tell anyone what he did to me, keeping it to myself would be best. I didn't want to tarnish the good guy reputation he had. It was my fault anyway because I shouldn't have come to my own home unannounced. I should not have accused him of having someone in my home after he already promised me that he would never do that again. What was I thinking? I know. I wasn't thinking. I wasn't thinking that my fiancé would harm me. I wasn't thinking that he would drag me across the floor from room to room in our apartment. I wasn't thinking that surprising him was going to surprise me. I wasn't thinking that I would see male and female shadows that suddenly disappeared. I wasn't thinking that I would see a side of the man I loved that would forever change the way I thought of him.

I am not a victim, I am a survivor. I had dealt with more pain in my life than I was willing to recall, and I felt that enough was enough. I could no longer return to that apartment and call it my home. I was violated there and my child and I would never live there and call that place home. Whatever I had to do to get my own place I would do, but I would never allow a man to believe that he could treat me the way Michael had and think that I was going to look to him for safety and protection. I could make it on my own.

My best friend Tina had gone through a rough time after her boyfriend was murdered and she had recently been shot. I could hardly believe what happened to her. There seemed to be trouble everywhere I looked. Tina relocated to Baltimore and left her daughter with me. Michael used me taking in my goddaughter as the reason for us not to reconcile. He barely wanted to take responsibility or make mention of the child he made with me, and now here I was trying to take care of my goddaughter as well. He was not pleased with my decision.

Hope

My best friend Johnnie was home for the summer and we spent a lot of time with each other while I was on bed rest from work. He treated me kind and lovingly, so much so that sometimes I wished he was the father of my child. He showed me that I didn't have to tolerate the fluctuating treatment from Michael. I was glad they never met each other. I wouldn't tell Johnnie what was happening, but he could tell that I wasn't happy. He had his own girlfriend to deal with and I didn't want to add to that. Even being fat and pregnant Johnnie still made me feel special. Johnnie took the time out to show concern for me. It meant a lot and showed that no matter how old we got or how much we had moved on with our lives, we would always be friends. We would always love one another.

*****

Three months later my mother and her sisters were going to the gravesite of my grandmother Lillie Mae Brumfield as they did every year on the anniversary of her death. I wanted to go take time and reflect on my grandmother and reminisce on the relationship we had. If there was anyone on this earth that knew how to make me feel like I was somebody with a purpose, it was my grandmother. I missed her and I wished she was here to talk me through some of these issues that I didn't want to share with anyone else. I wondered what she would think of Michael and the way our relationship had turned out.

Getting back into the van I felt those pains in my belly again and they were strong. I keep it to myself because the last thing that I want to do is deliver my baby on the day that my grandmother passed away. I went back to my mom's house and the pain wouldn't stop. I called Michael, and he wouldn't answer. Over and over again I dialed his number leaving him messages and he would not answer nor would he return the calls. Mommy ended up taking me to the hospital where they gave me some medication to get some rest, and sent me back home because I wasn't in labor, just needed to sleep.

The next morning my mother stayed home from church – which was a first. She must have known that my baby was really getting ready to come. No more false labor, this was the real deal. I made it to the hospital where I cursed every nurse out that wasn't willing to help me get this baby out of me immediately. Finally Michael made it to the hospital before the birth. He looked so nervous and excited at the same time. In no time, after two pushes, naturally with no pain medication or epidural Zion Noble emerged; Zion a name in the Bible which represents strength and Noble meaning man of high honor. From birth, my son was named to represent strength and honor. He was named on purpose.

The pain was finally over and I only had two stitches. Michael kissed me on my forehead as tears developed in his eyes. He told me how much he loved me and for a moment it felt like things were going to be okay. He was so happy to see his newborn son and I was so happy to see him happy again.

My son. My first born. My child. My baby. Oh my God. I was a mother now and there was no taking that back. My life as I knew it was over, and I was embarking on a new journey in life as a provider and protector of my offspring. Anointing him every morning with the blessed oil I had the pastor pray over at the church, I believed that God would protect my son better than I or his father ever could. The time had come for us to leave the hospital, but we must first complete the birth certificate information. I let the nurse know that Zion's dad stepped out but would be back to take me home. I told her he would sign the paperwork when he returned.

Michael came after I completed my portion of the paperwork. I handed the paperwork to him to complete his part and he placed them down. The nurse came in to get the papers and Michael acted as if he was so engulfed in his son he didn't see or hear her. I told him he needed to sign the paperwork so that the nurse could get it processed, and he looked at me and then looked at her and then looked at me again. He cleared his throat and looking me straight in my eyes said he was not comfortable signing the birth certificate and therefore was not going to do it.

Numb and stunned I was once again in a state of shock and pure disbelief. I was embarrassed and speechless as the White nurse walked out of the room as if she already knew that was going to happen. How could Michael say he wasn't sure that this was his son when he knew he was the only man I had been with? There was never a question of fidelity, not with me. I was faithful and had sworn to this over and over again, yet he didn't want to claim his son. Why hold him, and be at the hospital with me looking into this child's face, and not accept him as your blood? My beautiful baby. What a

Hope

handsome son he is, and the documentation showed and confirms that he is mine, all mine. How many times and in how many different ways would this man continue to break my heart and my spirit?

I hated men and despised the ground they walked on. Almost every man I had come in contact with treated women as second-class citizens and we stood by and watched. So desperate to make things work we tolerated things we wouldn't dare allow our daughters to accept. My mind raced with hatred, bitterness, disappointment and pain. I began to understand why some women run away from men, never to return. I feel lost. I refuse to go against what my body was made for, the natural companionship between a man and a woman, but I've been hurt so badly by men who were supposed to love me. How could I ever trust a man again? How would I ever find comfort again? I realized that my comfort had to come from God.

Shaking, shattered, tattered and bruised it is to Him I go, broken with the humble and sincere request for Him to put my damaged pieces back together again. I know I have done a lot of wrong in my life. All I can do now is ask God to have mercy on me, if not for my sake, for my child's sake. He doesn't know what he has been born into, and didn't ask to come into this world. *God, no matter how hurt I am, please allow me to show my son love, peace and happiness. He needs to know that if no one is there for him, to claim him, to love him, to raise and take care of him, I will always be there no matter what comes and what goes – mommy will be there.*

Hope

> Note to self: It's funny how when bad things happen in our life we suddenly feel the need to pray. We get right down on our knees as if we had been praying all along and have a serious good standing relationship with God. We know right from wrong and decided to do wrong, but then we look to God to help us when we are in trouble, and heal us when our heart has been broken.

I wanted to love Zion unconditionally like I wanted my father to love me, like I wanted to love his father, and like I wanted his father to love me. All the love I had stored away in the deepest part of me I will invest and pour into him so that he will be a whole man when gets older. I could only hope that this is a phase that his father is going through. I hope that we both remember when and how I got pregnant in the first place. I never want my son to treat a woman the way his father had treated me, and I can only hope that his father's ways change so that he becomes a good example of a real man for his son. Until then no longer am I assessing my covering, I am in a phase of hope accepting the role as the covering for my son.

Chapter 8

Soul Ties

Finding childcare wasn't easy, but after four weeks of being home, I needed to get back to work. I had gone through three different babysitters before finding the perfect family that I could entrust to take care of my child while I worked. I was back at the Urban League and going to school at night. I had to complete my degree so that I could get a better job to provide for Zion and me. No longer was I looking to his father to provide anything for us. If he did anything it would be extra. I could not depend on him. He said he would help pay the babysitter, but then I would have to come up with all of the money. I found my own apartment and baby boy and I were doing just fine.

I co-signed for a car with Michael so he took me to and from work every now and then, or I had the car to take myself. I was going to church more often with my mom. My 'big sister' Michelle would come to pick me up and take me to church too. I went because I wanted to, not because I was looking for anything. The last thing I was going to do was be a hypocrite pretending to live holy knowing that I was not committed to living a Christian life.

Michael and I argued more and more, and made up more and more. With each make up and each break up I got confused as to where our relationship was going. Now I was getting sick all over again – feeling the flu like symptoms. My child was just a newborn, and I thought that I was pregnant again. As if this were all a dream, the doctor confirmed that I was pregnant. However because of the poor condition my body was in, this baby would not make it. I was confused. I thought I heard my doctor tell me that in order for me to live and to eliminate all health risks my only recourse was to abort my baby? Was I actually scheduling a session for this fetus to be taken out of my womb?

My doctor explained that I may never have children again. I may become pregnant, but won't be able to bring forth a child unless I put my life in danger to do so. I could go to counseling to discuss how this made me feel if I wanted, she advises me. What she didn't know, was that I never imagined I would have any children, so if I didn't have another I would not be sad. I already had Zion and he was just a baby. If something happened to me who would take care of him? I couldn't risk my life for another child and leave them both on this earth motherless – I rationalized in my head. It was best that I looked after myself so that I could continue to raise and protect my son.

Pressure from Michael didn't help. He tried his best to act as if he cared about my health and was pushing me to end the pregnancy immediately. The doctor seemed to believe that the pregnancy was going to end on its own anyway, but Michael wanted me to get out of this situation as soon as possible. Who knew that internally my body was damaged? On the outside I look like a healthy young woman, but on the inside I am far from it. Who knew getting pregnant again would send me into a dangerous health risk that I wasn't ready or mature enough to deal with. My Black side knew there was more to this than I was willing to acknowledge, and my White side was paralyzed with fear. This was no condition for an Oreo cookie to be in.

All I could think about was my son. If something were to happen to me who would raise him? Michael hadn't cared enough to claim Zion so I knew him caring for our unborn child, risk or no risk, was out of the equation. This same man who was eager for me to get well did so not out of concern for me and my health, but because he didn't want the responsibility of taking care of his son, let alone an additional child.

It was not that he couldn't raise Zion, but he had shown me that he wouldn't and I refused to leave the responsibility of raising two children to my mother. I couldn't and wouldn't ever have any more children with Michael unless he was my husband. Right then he was not, so another child was not an option. It seemed easy but it wasn't. The choice I made was done with great deliberation. In the end, I made my choice and told myself that was that. But it wasn't.

A part of my soul left me on that day. Ignorant to the depth of pain I would feel, I with limited information and few options chose to do what I thought was best. Everything was done covertly from the appointment to the location at the hospital. As I walked down the long hallway at the hospital going through security checkpoints, making sure no one saw me or knew my name I wondered how long I could carry this baby in my belly in the condition I was in? Are things really as bad as my mind perceived them to be? What if I don't make any choices right now? What if I waited to see what would happen? If I miscarried, I miscarried. Wondering which I would be more accepting of, losing a full term baby that died at birth, or a fetus I would never see. *God forgive me because I don't see any way out of this.* I was waiting for a sign from God that there was another way, waiting for some divine intervention, a miraculous healing of my body. No sign ever came.

 I was in and out of the hospital within hours as if nothing ever happened. I could act as though nothing happened, but I knew it had. I went to sleep that night and relived the day over and over again in my dreams. Every time I looked into my son's eyes I wondered about the what-if, the could've, should've, would've. With this uneasiness, I guarded my body and my son's as if our lives depended on it all the while wondering – where was my covering, where was my sign to show me a better way?

 Michael moved on with no problem. As a matter of fact I had solved his problems for him. I was no longer living with him, he only has one child with me and he knew that whether he provided for my son or not, Zion would be taken care of. I couldn't help but think all of the persuasive conversations were just to make sure he manipulated me into handling the situation the way he wanted me to. My mother was my reminder to never depend on a man. My mother showed me the danger in allowing a man to think that you need him for your survival. When a man thinks this way, he can and will have total control over your life. I made sure I stayed employed because I wanted Michael to know that while I don't need him, I want him. I want my son to be raised with his father. I want my son to experience the love of a father, the love I felt that I had lost. The only way to show a man that he wants you more than you want him is to move on without him. I knew I couldn't do this on my own, and I needed divine intervention.

I couldn't keep saying that I was tired of breaking up to make up. I felt we needed to make more definitive decisions. I decided not to wear my engagement ring on my finger, nor would I wear it hanging from a chain around my neck. To show Michael that I was serious I handed him the ring. I needed him to understand that the ball was in his court. Fuming with anger he smashed the ring until it was flat and the diamond almost popped out. His fury had become too much for me, and I wasn't going to put myself in the same abusive situations I had in the past. I had a child to care for, a responsibility and an obligation to provide and protect this child, and if that meant distancing myself from Michael I would.

I had been attending church every now and then and it seems to calm the resentment and the hurt that I feel inside. Michael and I always believed and agreed that we didn't need to be in an actual church to have a relationship with God. I had gone through enough church drama to get caught up in attending a building, but now I feel different. I wondered if not attending church in that building was what had me in the terrible place I was in.

Growing up in the church I saw a lot of things that were both good and bad. Now as an adult, I made the choice not to do the "church thing" until I knew I was 100% into it. I didn't want to be a fake, pretending that I was living a holy life but knowing truthfully that I was not. I watched that type of behavior too many times growing up, and I didn't want to have that reputation. It proved too difficult to keep up with the facades – worldly here, saintly there; it was a real turn-off for me. Many gifted people sang and lead choirs, musicians, preachers and missionaries, married and single taking advantage of their knowledge of church and the gifts God has given them for personal gratification. It was sad to see ones that I considered mother figures or father figures, big brothers and sisters in the church behaving worse than my friends that have never stepped foot in a sanctuary. No. I don't want that reputation, it was best that I be me.

*****

My mother asked me to go on the Women's Retreat with the church, and I was reluctant to go. I felt I was moving at my own pace getting closer to God on my own, and didn't need to move faster than the pace I was going. I knew other ladies that planned to go so I figured - why not? I honestly wanted to get away, but I hadn't left my son before except for work or school. The only person that cared for him was our babysitter who we paid, and she did an awesome job. At no time had I ever asked Zion's sitter to care for him over the weekend. I did not intend to start that now. Making it seem as if I was unable to find a babysitter was my way of stalling, holding out on making a decision – not sure if I wanted to go while simultaneously understanding that I needed to go.

    I let Michael know that I was going to the Women's Retreat and it seemed as if he could care less. That left me thinking and believing that he was glad I was going away so this would be one weekend he didn't have to worry about where I was, and with less chances of me popping up on him. I dropped my baby boy to my cousin's girlfriend and was off to the retreat. This was my first time in a year being by myself with no child. I felt lost. My baby boy had become my person, my reason, my home. I felt incomplete without having him around. No diaper to change, no bottle to make, no feedings, no bubble baths. This felt nice, but I missed him. *Is this what bittersweet feels like?*

    I missed his dad too, and began to pray things would get better between us. We were together, but we aren't on the same page. I didn't want to lose him, but it was hurting me to keep him. I endured the hurt because I wanted my son to be around his father. When Michael showed me he loved me, he showed me hard, but those moments that he didn't show me love hurt worse than I could describe.

Listening all weekend to the women carrying on spiritually tore down a wall that I had placed up. From Friday night to Saturday my heart was getting softer and softer. I realized that I was fooling myself into believing my life was all good. I knew that the life I had itemized out was not all I pumped it up to be. I was unmarried, and I had a child. I had an Associate's degree but I needed a Bachelor's. I had a nice job, but my finances were still not where I wanted them to be – where I was fully independent of Michael and soaring on my own. No matter how together I displayed myself to be, I was a teardrop away from falling apart.

I feel loved at this retreat and I was glad everyone received me just as I was. I could see God using those women to show me that it was alright to admit my wrong and to be vulnerable before God. For so long I had exposed my vulnerabilities to the wrong people, and I was in a place where God showed me He was all I needed. God had more to give to me and it included the joy and happiness that I had wanted for years. I vacillated from one relationship to the next never finding that exclusive love that I was seeking. Saturday night after joking around and getting a good laugh in here and there it was time to go to bed, and I went with tears forming in the corners of my eyes. I felt different. I *wanted* to be around the church women. I *wanted* something more in my life. I *wanted* to be a part of this lovely, liberating "church thing".

Waking up early Sunday morning I felt refreshed. We picked up Zion in my mom's minivan. I was actually excited about going to church as I listened to the radio with the song saying "I Got Just What I Wanted". *I'm really feeling this song.* It wasn't the old school version, but a new one with a nice groove to it putting a smile on my face. I felt the spirit of the Lord coming into the service, and I heard myself saying "Yes Lord". No longer was I on my life schedule, but I was surrendering my life to Christ saying "Yes".

November 14, 1999 I became a new creature in Christ Jesus. I felt so free and renewed; not a care in the world. With tears in my eyes I went before the entire church and asked them to forgive me for my past behavior and professed on that day that I had been redeemed. Everyone seemed so happy for me and I felt so loved I didn't want the moment to pass. I wanted to feel this feeling for the rest of my life.

Reality was it's time for me to go home and when I go home there will be a man there that I loved. He would need to be informed of this weekend's events. I was professing salvation now so I could no longer be Michael's bed partner unless we are married. I didn't want him to marry me just so we could continue with life as we knew it. I wanted things to be better, and if not, it was time to move on. Now that I know God is with me, I am no longer afraid of the world being against me. As soon as I got relaxed in my apartment, Michael came over.

We sat down on the futon in my living room and I told him I had some important news. Nonchalantly he said, "What," as if he didn't want to hear what I had to say. I continued with my story despite his dismissive reply, explaining that this past weekend at the Women's Retreat God softened my heart. I told Michael that this softening caused me to surrender my life to God during the Sunday morning service. The happy feeling I felt all day began to turn into uncertainty as Michael's face displayed his displeasure in my news. We both agreed that we wouldn't do the "church thing" and now he is making it seem as if I had gone back on my word. I didn't go back on my word. This was bigger than any agreement with a man. This was my covenant with God.

I felt boldness as I never had before as I told him that we couldn't continue on in this relationship the way we were and there will need to be some changes made. Something new in me was coming out – not back, but out. Times before my tough exterior manifested from fear, out of frustration, out of disappointment. Now there was boldness that came from God, and love. A boldness that gave me peace, that made me feel protected, no longer inferior, but on the winning side. Michael noticed this new confidence, he saw that it was not going to be easy to dissuade me. Belittling the transformation that had taken place in my life, he considered it a phase that I was going through and was willing to stick around until I gave it up. That night I showed him how serious I was, and as he attempted to spend the night and have sex with me I rejected the advances. Michael needed to know that this was real for me and not just a stage I was going through.

*****

Michael had been spending more time at my house and there had been no arguments or disagreements between us. I was going to school and he was working and things seemed to be peaceful. However, not having sexual relations with Michael was not as easy as I thought and it was breaking my heart to let God down. Numerous nights as Michael would lay on top of me making love to me it would feel so good because my body yearned for it. But afterward I would cry because I knew I had let God down knowing what I was doing is fornication. I knew for myself that it was a sin. Not only did I know in my mind, but I knew in my spirit and I grieved. It was as though I was in mourning. I didn't want to sin. I wanted to be real for God, but I didn't know how to do it while in this relationship.

For several years this had been our life, our routine with one another, and it was not easy to break things off and do what was right. Michael and I went to counseling with my pastor to discuss what we were going through. Michael expressed his unhappiness with me being in church all of the time. Not wanting to sleep with him anymore, crying afterwards and turning into a different person after invested so many years into our relationship was unfair to him, he explained. Michael felt that I needed to spend less time at church and devote more time with him and our son. My pastor so eloquently responded to Michael's displeasure by telling him that although he and I have been together for so long, we were not married, and I was not obligated to do anything with him.

Michael agreed to attend services every now and then, but now and then hardly ever came, and I was on my own with this decision to live for God. I did all I could to make this relationship work because I wanted my son to have his father. Since Michael doesn't want to respect my new body in Christ I decided to pray. I don't know what else to do so I pray. I wanted to know if God believes me when I say I cannot live a phony life in Him. I wanted to know if God sees that I am for real about living a holy life and I needed His help. I asked God to take the desire away from me so that when Michael came around I wouldn't feel tempted. I didn't even want an attraction there if he was not going to be my husband. I went on a fast, turning down my plate as a sign of sacrifice and through faith I believed God was going to do something to this relationship and make things better.

The car that I co-signed for with Michael is up for repossession. It is sitting in the back yard of my apartment, but I can't drive it. I am getting rides from friends and borrowing my mom's vehicle to get around, but there is a car in my name that I cannot use. Never knowing how I am going to pick my child up from daycare or how I am going to get back and forth from school is getting played out. One would think that a man who cared for me, who said he loved me would be there to support me when I needed him, especially since I was still a constant support to him.

I wanted to move to a better place. My son is getting bigger and he needs space to play around the house. The apartment that I lived in at the time was a one bedroom with just a kitchen, bathroom and living room area. There was no space for him at all, and he had been sleeping on the futon or with me when his dad wasn't there instead of having his own bed to sleep in. My lease was coming to an end, and I really didn't know if I could afford to move. This has been the cheapest place to live in because it was small, and now I want to move but I am not sure if I can pay for something bigger. I fast and pray and look to God for a sign on which way I should go. I believed He would direct me and everything would be just fine.

I got a raise on my job, and I am now able to afford a bigger place. I looked into an apartment that happened to be owned by my old East high school gym teacher, and without hesitation, she rented the house to me. There was a newly married couple at my church that was looking for a starter place to live, and I told them that I was moving out and my landlord was willing to rent to them. Just like that God showed me that He was with me and not only ready to bless me, but to bless those around me as well. This was the right thing to do and I was ready to move into my new place.

My son had his own room and we both have more closet space than before. This place has an outdoor grill and we can have cookouts. My kitchen and bathroom are spacious and updated. Randolph Street, I loved that place. There was plenty of grass in the front and backyard for my son to play in. I even lived closer to

Michelle so she can pick me up and take me back and forth to church. My son now had his own little toddler bed. I had a dining room and a kitchen table for us to sit at and enjoy meals. My stove is a regular family size stove instead of a small studio apartment sized old fashioned one. I have an indoor porch, and my son is able to use that as his play area. He has so many toys, books and gadgets it looks like a day care. I found this place without Michael's help, and there was no need for him to have keys. His name is not on this lease, and I am proud that this place belongs to me and me alone.

All that keeps ringing in my head is don't let this man do you like your father treated your mother. Do not allow a man to have control over you because you can't do for yourself. God is with me now so I cannot be afraid. I have to go back to what I know so I called my Uncle Terry. Uncle Terry knew a guy who was trying to sell a little car. He came and picked me up so that I could take a look at it. My student loan was enough to pay for the semester, my books and there was a couple hundred dollars left over. I didn't stay on the college campus, but working full time I was able to pay my rent. With the left over money, I finally purchased my own car. Michael didn't have anything to do with it and I was so happy. He had no attachment to this accomplishment so he couldn't hold it over my head. I was so proud of my 1988 4-door white and rust hatch back Mercury Tracer. I treasured that car and treated it like it was brand new, fresh off the lot.

God was so good to me and showed His love towards me. I had a new car, a new home, school was going well and I was finding happiness in Jesus and no longer in man. I did all I could to avoid nights with Michael and just as I asked, God began removing the attraction. I no longer stressed myself about being with him. Our season had passed and I was thankful.

Michael decided to go hard on me to make me feel what it would be like if he was not around. He stopped paying his share of the daycare, and stopped helping with the care of our son. I was close to finishing school, and I needed someone to help me keep the baby occupied while I did my homework. Instead of helping, Michael made it difficult for me as a form of punishment. Instead of giving in like I normally would, God gave me a new outlook on this situation and I pressed on. No matter how much water splashed on my text books and notes because I am bathing my son as I studied and completed my homework, I kept moving forward. For so long Michael held over my head and took partial ownership of my Associate's degree because he was the one pushing, he was the one encouraging, and he was the one at the finish line with a celebration. This time, it was God on my side – He would get all the glory, and I didn't need anyone else. Slowly but surely God was releasing me from my soul tie for my soul to be connected to Him and Him alone.

Tired from late night studying I still wake up early every morning to get Zion off to the babysitter and head to work. Many nights I picked my child up from the Church of Jesus Christ because

Soul Ties

that was where his babysitter could always be found. I was stressed about many things, but childcare was not one of them. Mrs. Mable Taylor was the best child care provider ever to walk the earth. She took care of my son as if he was her own. I didn't worry about him being with her or her husband and children. There were plenty of times when I had to stay at school late and she never got upset about watching the baby after hours. She took him to church with her and he fit right in with the rest of her children. What a lasting impression she made on me and my son. I loved her like family because she was a wonderful help to me by keeping my mind at peace regarding the safety and wellbeing of my child.

*****

My baby had a cold and was not feeling the best; I needed to take him to his doctor. He'd had a fever over 102 for two weeks and Tylenol and other child medications were not breaking the fever. Initially I assumed he was teething and the fever and cold symptoms would go away. Once his body began to turn red I knew it was something more. Dr. Lisa Harris, the wife of teacher Torey Harris that I work with at the Urban League was my son's pediatrician. She was all that I could ever want in a doctor. She was an educated Black woman who believed in God. We had a lot in common. Zion's hands, feet and mouth were swelling and turning red with fever. She not only treated him but she was a great comfort to me.

When Dr. Harris came into the room she pulled out a small bottle of blessed oil – yes blessed oil; oil that had been prayed over, similar to the oil that my baby boy came into this world being anointed with. Before she did any medical probing, she laid hands on him and prayed. She then looked at him and said he needed to go to the hospital for further examining. Things had been going well in my life. I was not expecting something bad to happen, and it caught me off guard when the emergency doctor told me that my baby had to be admitted into the hospital.

    Sitting in Strong Memorial Hospital, I wondered why God was allowing this to happen. I knew I was not perfect, but if anything else bad were to happen in my life I wanted it to happen to me, not my son. I sacrificed everything for him and couldn't imagine life without him now. I didn't understand anything the doctors were telling me. At one point I didn't even have the words to pray. I wanted my son to be well again. His fever wouldn't break and his body began swelling up like a balloon. After hours of waiting, the ER doctor tells me he has Kawasaki disease. They explained to me that it was imperative that he begin treatment immediately so that they could attempt to stop any permanent damage from occurring to his heart or his blood. I want to be the best mom in the world, I want to love him and spoil him forever. I want to be the mom that gives him whatever he wants, but I can't heal him, only God can.

    For the next week coming into Easter Sunday I spent my days and nights in the hospital. Everyone – even Michael's family, was very supportive coming up to the hospital to visit. Even my pastor came and prayed with us and left a few dollars. I really appreciated him doing that and it meant so much to me as a babe in Christ that he showed me love as my spiritual father. I always remembered him for making me feel like more than just a number or a member of the church, but as family. This couldn't have happened at a crazier time for me. We were in the middle of the semester having midterms before the spring break and testing was taking place. Missing these tests would cause me to have to withdraw from my classes and repeat them next semester. I called my teachers to tell them my situation and surprisingly they were all very understanding and willing to work with me. I was able to make up every test that I missed, but that would be considered a small thing compared to what God was getting ready to do.

Each day a group of different doctors were coming into my son's room. I finally asked one doctor why there were so many doctors checking on my son. With a smile on his face he explained to me that my son was a rare case and the doctors coming in are in medical school. There were very few if any cases of Black children having Kawasaki disease as it was typically seen in White children or children in Japan. He further explained to me that after the fifteenth day of having this disease and not having it treated, my son would have irreversible heart failure and an untreatable inflamed blood condition. As I counted back the days that he had not been feeling well with the fever, I held my hand over my mouth when I realized he was one day away from his blood condition being irreversible. Apparently the look on my face caused the doctor to be concerned for me. He asked me was it too much for me allowing the students to come in and I told him absolutely not. I wanted them all to see what God had done. This was no medical miracle, this was a miracle performed by God and God alone and each doctor needed to witness this to know that no matter how much they had learned in school there was a Master Doctor that could perform miracles like none other.

On Easter Sunday the hospital staff came around with a cart full of stuffed animals. My son was able to pick one out as an Easter gift since we were unable to celebrate outside of the hospital at church and with the family. I sat in the bed holding Zion, watching his skin peel as he healed, and a thought came across my mind. Here we are during one of the most religious times of the year for a Christian. This was the time that we celebrated Christ dying on the cross for our sins, and rising in three days. We make great emphasis on Jesus' blood and the power that is in the blood. How His blood formed a pool around the cross when he was pierced in his side. How sinners are washed in the blood and come out white as snow.

I thought about Mary, the mother of Jesus. How she had to stand by helplessly as her son was beaten, tortured and hung upon the cross. I thought about how, if she could, she would have saved him. Many from far and near came to witness this crucifixion, not fully understanding what was taking place right before their very eyes. Mary watched her own flesh and blood suffer powerlessly because she could do nothing. She knew this was something He had to do, and there was no changing or exchanging in it. My son laid on my chest, a little infant baby boy. Within his blood there was a disorder that had developed. As Mary, I could only stand by feeble and afraid of what the outcome of my child's life would be.

Doctors from all around came to see my son firsthand, not realizing or fully understanding that God was in the midst of the situation and was healing my son right before their eyes. Mary, the proud mother of Jesus may have cried when He died on the cross, but in three days He rose again with all power in His hands. As the proud mother of my son, I may have cried when he was diagnosed, but I now rejoiced knowing that because of Mary's Son, my son can live.

Knowing that God was with me meant more to me than anything. He showed me He was with me and all I had to do was trust Him. I couldn't wait to get to church once my son was released from the hospital. I gave God a shout of praise and before I could finish my testimony my son jumped out of his seat next to my mother and began to praise God too. I believed Zion knew what God had just taken him through.

Easter now has an even deeper, heightened and extraordinary meaning to me. God sacrificed His only begotten Son so that my son could have a chance at life. With His stripes my baby boy was healed. I am now more determined to live for Christ. It seems as though no matter how much I give to Him, God ends up doing so much more for me. I will never be able to repay God for all the things He has done for me. I owe Him my life for saving my son's life.

I passed all my classes for the semester and I was so close to graduating I couldn't help but be excited. This Bachelor degree was something I desired without being pushed or persuaded by anyone. I worked hard, not to make anyone happy or proud of me, but for myself. My inside – what was called my White side, was hungry and looking for an opportunity to shine. I loved my classes, teachers, and the information I was getting from this communication field. I was looking forward to getting that degree and putting it on my resume so that I could request more money for my salary. I struggled with early mornings and late nights for a better life for me and my son. Life is really good right now and I can't believe how God continues to open one door after another. I have left the Urban League and I am now working for a banking institution making more money than I have ever made in my life. I wanted to live in this moment at peace with God for as long as I could.

But of course I couldn't. As long as my soul tie is gradually unraveling and my soul and heart are getting closer and closer to God, Michael becomes more and more aggressive in his behavior. This time instead of me trying to make him happy and do whatever it takes for us to stay together, I chose not to fight anymore. Whatever will be will be. I was in the new converts' class at church and I was excited about what I was learning in the Word of God. Michael was the last thing on my mind. Yes. God is doing just what I asked and I know it, and I think Michael knows it too. I initially had a list of reasons why I loved Michael and why I wanted to spend the rest of my life with him. Here we were years later in our relationship and the list hadn't grown longer, it has actually become smaller. My number one reason for being with Michael is his son – our son. The son that he never wanted to claim needed to be around him. His son needed to grow up knowing who his father is. He needed to know where he gets his looks from, his mannerisms, his feet, eating habits and talents. I never wanted to separate my son from his father, so I stood by and sacrifice true happiness all for my son.

    I would love to start dating someone new, but I was afraid. I didn't want another man around my son. I didn't want Michael questioning my behavior and bad mouthing me as he did his older son's mom. I didn't want to fall for another guy's games and lies and get hurt all over again. I wished Michael would just do right so that we could be happy together – it would be so much easier and better for us all. I wanted a saved man, someone in the church that loved the Lord; someone like my dad before he decided to be unfaithful to my mother. I wished Dad was around for me to talk to. I could have used his support through this relationship drama. I would have loved for Daddy to sit Michael down and let him know that he had to be a better man to me. Tell him he had to step his game up and be faithful because I was a good catch. Where was my daddy to let this man know that I was worth loving and being committed to wholeheartedly?

    I was in pain. I needed my daddy. I needed my daddy to have a man-to-man talk with Michael to tell him he had to take care of responsibilities with his son at all times, not just when he felt like it. Daddy saw our names in the newspaper where they announced all the couples that had recently received a marriage license. He called to inquire if it was true or not, but he never took time out to deal with Michael as any father would when he found out a man was attempting to marry his daughter. I needed my daddy, but he was living his new life that he created with a new family, new daughters, and a new wife. There was no place or space for me in his life, so I turned to God for guidance, and trusted that He would see me through.

Why was it, that even after God had proven himself over and over to me there was still a part of me that desired to please Michael over God? After God delivered my son, continued to take me through school, blessed me with a new place and my own car, I yet had a connection to Michael that I couldn't let go of. It was gradually ending but I wanted to be done completely. I didn't want to be a hypocrite nor did I want to stop going to church. Why was it so hard to let go?

Sexual relations according to the Bible are to be conducted between married couples only. By continuously engaging in sexual acts with Michael we developed a soul tie. That kind of emotional bond or connection was what spiritually united us, causing us to be obsessively preoccupied with each other to the point that no one else mattered. Acknowledging that I had an ungodly soul tie with Michael was hard to accept but the reality was it existed. We discussed it and that's when we decided to get a marriage license, but after we got the license there were no plans for a wedding.

As tough as I was; I was always ready to fight, and could curse you out using the right choice of words making it feel like I had physically put my hands on you. As much of a weapon carrying, confrontational, argumentative, loud mouth that I had been known to be, I could not get away from my ungodly soul tie. I couldn't curse or fight my way out of it. Not naturally. His domineering ways controlled our relationship and he refused to come under the subjection of God and develop a healthy, Godly and God approved soul tie. I heard his voice over and over again in my head demeaning me, and out of fear of what he thought of me, I conform into what he wanted me to be. I did what I knew he wanted me to do. Common sense told me to run, get as far away from him as I could, but because we had connected spirits together into one united soul it was nearly impossible to physically break apart.

I mistook a soul tie for a soul mate. Sex may make you feel good for moments in time, but it doesn't cover a lifetime. Committing the act of fornication and going further and shacking only made my life more difficult. A soul mate would never take you through the things I had suffered. A soul mate makes you feel you have found your romantic destiny not feel repetitious turmoil. How could I have been so naïve and stupid to mix up a soul tie with a soul mate? A soul mate would do everything in their power to keep you happy, because seeing you happy makes them happy. And because you want to see them happy in return, it becomes an ongoing cycle of two beings doing all they can for their soul mate and basking in the joy of the Creator.

    I never truly forgave Michael for the wrong he had done to me and bitterness was building in my heart. God had given me freedom from all of this yet, the cloud lingered over my head. The more I sought God and His will, Michael had less and less manipulation and control over my thoughts and my life. God allowed my eyes to be opened to see the condition I was truly in with Michael in order to understand there was nothing healthy about this relationship. I am in desperate need of breaking this soul tie. What do you do when you have mistaken your ungodly, unfaithful soul tie as your covering?

CHAPTER 9

INDEPENDENT WOMAN

Michael was beginning to embrace my church life. He would rather me be in church crying to God instead of in the club crying to some other guy. He didn't have to wonder where I was because he knew the only place I wanted to be was in church. He knew there was no male competition at church so it doesn't worry him at all that I was there all the time. We talked to my pastor in counseling and Michael felt that my church was a little bias. He and I begin praying together, and he was even interested in visiting other churches to see if we could find a church that the both of us were comfortable with.

Moving me away from my support system was a classic scheme for a manipulator like Michael. Leaving the church where I grew up and trying to find someplace new wasn't something I wanted to do. I was willing to visit other churches, but my heart was with those who prayed me into my breakthrough. How could I now act as if I no longer needed them in my life? How could I walk away as if I no longer needed their prayers?

I couldn't help but think that this was nothing but another stalling tactic that he had to fool me into believing that things are going to change for the better with us. I prayed to God alone and asked Him to reveal Michael's true intentions towards me and to protect my heart from any further damage.

*****

I began second-guessing everything I said and did and I was feeling as though no decision I made was right or smart. I adhered to Michael's requests in hopes that we were doing the right thing for our son. He thought our relationship and situation was under his control, but what he didn't know was that God was in control.

With Michael and I living in two different homes, that gave the both of us freedom to do what we wanted without the other knowing. I no longer had keys to his place, and he didn't have keys to mine. It was better that way because I needed him to know that I could make it on my own. Although we didn't live together we were constantly at each other's place (he was at my home more than I was at his). I began to feel like he was hiding something again and this didn't feel good at all. This was his opportunity to show me that he could be faithful with or without me around.

Moonlighting as a photographer at a local club, Michael worked late at night and invited me to come along with him.

Hesitantly I went because I wanted to show him that I still had hope that we could make things work. He knew the last place that I would want to be was in a club. God had made a change in me and Michael was testing to see how real the change was. I didn't enjoy the club at all, but Michael showed respect towards me for going and taking a crack at looking at things from his perspective.

Knowing that being in the club for business or for pleasure was not something I would do Michael goes on his own and no longer asked me to accompany him. I was happy to see he was beginning to accept my new life and was praying that he would change his life as well. Michael would come to the house and say good night to the baby and me before he would go to work in the club. Every night as he departed, I would pray that God would protect him and turn his mind and heart toward Christ just as my heart had changed.

It was not unusual for Michael to call me while at the club working. When things were slow and no one was taking pictures I would lay in the bed holding the phone to my ear and enjoy peaceful dialog with him. Instead of him being in the club grinding and flirting with other women, he was on the phone with me. Sometimes the music would be too loud and I could hardly hear him, but the thought of him calling me made me feel good. I would hang up the phone with a smile on my face optimistic about our future.

Michael typically called once a night to chat. Sometimes he would call later if he planned to stop by after work, so it was no surprise to me when my phone rang late one night and it was his number on the caller-id. I answered the phone and said hello, but there was no response. I said hello again and again there is no response. I called out his name but he didn't answer. Concerned I sat up in the bed to try and hear what was happening on the other end of the line.

Listening closely, I heard an alarm beep, it was a familiar sound. It was the alarm that beeps when we enter his apartment – the loft we use to share together. I figured he called to tell me he'd made it home so I waited for him to get on the phone. I heard a female voice faintly but I couldn't make out what she was saying. I heard him ask her a question, and she replied. He offered her something to drink, telling her to get as comfortable as she wanted. I heard fumbling and muffling in the phone and could imagine what was going on. He turned the music on, and fury sets in. I can't believe my ears as he begins to play the music he and I would be romantic with – Prince. I heard *Adore* playing, and by now I was out of my bed pacing back and forth once again in disbelief. I heard this female reaching her pleasure climax and I heard him enjoying every moment of it.

I dropped the phone to the ground and threw on a pair of jeans and a t-shirt. I grabbed my son out of his bed and put him in the car seat in the back of my car. I sped over to Michael's house ready to confront him and whoever else was there. Parking my car at his front door I pushed the buzzer. I didn't have keys to get in so I was standing outside banging on the door and pressing his intercom. I yelled through the intercom that I knew he was there and for him to open the door. I kept yelling in the intercom, and then I noticed that the intercom was no longer making the response noise – he had turned the intercom off. Michael thought he was so slick and didn't park his car in the parking lot where he normally parks. Instead he parked it on the side street adjacent to his house.

    I stood out there knowing there was only one way in and one way out so I was waiting and would wait until they came out. It was chilly and through all this excitement I stopped and realized my son should not have been in the midst of this. I kept banging on the door telling Michael that his son was out there and for him to open the door to let us in. I drove across the street to the payphone and called him, but of course he wouldn't answer the phone. I wouldn't take my eye off of that front door waiting for it to open. I called my mom and told her what was happening. I asked if someone would come and get my son because I didn't want him to be out here while I was going through this. My sister came and took my baby home with her, as I parked down the street waiting for someone to come out of the apartment.

    A police officer drove by and circled back around to me. My anger heightened thinking that Michael had called the police on me. *Why call the police instead of being a man and facing the situations you have created? Why risk your son's mom getting arrested because you're a lying, cheating, selfish sorry excuse for a man?* The police officer slowly pulled up next to me and I rolled down my window and said hello. He asked was I having trouble with my car, and I told him I was fine. He asked me was I sure and I said yes, and thank you so much for checking. He said alright and told me to be careful and he pulled off. In that moment I thought about what I was doing and how badly this could end. It was not a wise thing for me to do and I needed to leave before something happened that I would not be able to take back.

Before giving my life to Christ you would never find me out late at night without some type of weapon – no matter what. Carrying, as we called it, was a must especially when you lived a dangerous life and didn't know who your enemies were or where they would show up. However, I was a changed woman, and God had to remind me of that change. I looked up to the sky and smiled as I pulled up to the back of his car. Had this been any other time I would have had an object sharp enough to flatten all of his tires. But I was a Christian and a saved lady didn't behave that way. I knew his car driver's side door was broken and couldn't lock, so I went into his car to find something. Not sure what I was looking for, I was searching angrily. Michael had one of those notepads with the pen on a string stuck to his windshield and I decided to leave him a note. The message to him was simple.

> LOOK NO MORE FOR ME BECAUSE I AM GONE – WE ARE THROUGH.

I got back into my car thanking God that I had enough strength to leave. I picked my son up from my mom's house and thanked them for coming to get him. I apologized because I knew bringing my son to confront his father was a lapse in judgment in the first place. Even though I knew and realized this was wrong, I decided to take the long way to my place and drive by Michael's apartment one last time. When I got to his apartment I noticed that his car was gone. He waited long enough for me to leave and when I went to get our son like a coward, he left. I shook my head as I passed by and drove on to my place. While driving down the road I saw in my rearview mirror a car speeding towards me as if it was going to hit me in the back. The high beams of the car started flickering on and off. I realized it was Michael and I kept driving. The further I drove the more erratic he became with his driving, so I pulled over.

    My son was awake in the back seat and asked me was I okay. When he saw his father jump in the passenger side front seat his eyes lit up and he screamed, "Daddy!" Michael said, "Hello son," and then asked me what was wrong with me. He had never used vulgar language in front of our son. I was shocked. I couldn't respond to him, and just looked at him as if he was crazy. Grabbing my arm and squeezing so tightly he then asked me why I would leave a note in his car saying that I was going to kill myself. This idiot was so high-minded and arrogant that he would believe because I said my life with him is now over that meant that I was going to commit suicide. How much more stuck on himself could he be? I had no intentions of ending my life because of him, but he continued to talk to me as if he was talking me off a ledge.

All I could say to him was get out of my car. He kept trying to grab my arm, yelling and cursing at me and again all I could say was get out of my car. Finally my son becoming afraid yelled out, "Daddy, just get out of our car!" He looked back at his son – his year old son, and got out of my car. I pulled off and hurried to my apartment. My son so innocently came into my bedroom after I had tucked him away in his bed, and asked me could he sleep in my bed instead. I picked him up onto the bed and rolled over with tears in my eyes. He started moving around and I felt him pull the cover back from over my head, he moved my hair off my face and kissed me and then said, "Good night mommy. I love you." It was his words, those priceless words that allowed me to fall asleep.

That event was enough for me to see that Michael was full of himself and there was no space for me or my son in his life. Grabbing me the way that he did in my car really startled me, because the last thing I planned on doing was to allow another man to attempt to physically abuse me. Instead of Michael being sorrowful for being with another woman he chose to instead turn the conflict around on me as if I was the problem. Talking to me in such a demeaning way as if for some reason this was my fault that he was once again caught being unfaithful. This has gone further than I had expected. Michael actually tried to drive the thought into my head that I want to do harm to myself. Maybe that was what he wanted me to do. Would that be for the better? Why would he want me gone? Who in the world would take care of our son? There is nothing left for Michael to do but tear down my mental state, but with God on my side, this attack will be defeated.

Emotional and mental abuse is real. At that time in my life it was yet another subject that wasn't discussed. Afraid that my accusations would be dismissed as me looking too deeply into things or overstating a situation, I kept my mouth closed as I had done in the past. Once again excuses are made to explain Michael's behavior, but to put it plain and simple this is abuse. Back and forth in my mind I question my existence. A seed had been planted. As my mind filled with doubt, there was little space for self-esteem. Maybe he was too good for me. Maybe I didn't deserve someone like him. Could that be why things continued to go wrong in our relationship? I wondered if I was ever good enough for any of the men in my life. Why is it that I couldn't have a man want to be with me and only me and never want to leave me? My dad, my ex-boyfriends, and now the father of my son – not one found me worthy of being loved.

For a long time I had been feeling that way and it crushed me to the very core. Who would have thought that emotional and mental abuse really did exist? Who would have thought that it would have such a long-lasting, devastating impact on me and those around me? All I wanted was for Michael to listen to what I had to say. All I wanted was for him to understand that he was hurting me. I needed him to be sincere with his apologies and never do and say another harmful thing to me again. I wanted to express how he had made me feel, but I didn't want him to be upset with me for being honest.

Maybe what he was trying to put in my head about dying wasn't such a bad idea after all. His up and down treatment of me, the unfaithfulness, the cruel and critical words, and undermining of me has killed me already. He never had to pull a trigger; he was the weapon. His words and actions were causing me to consider the course of my life. I had such doubt and distrust with everything and everyone around me. Is this considered living? Who ever made the saying "sticks and stones may break my bones, but words will never hurt me", had me fooled. Words did hurt and they left scars that were more devastating and lasted longer than a stick or a stone ever could.

I didn't feel as though I was an equal in our relationship. I didn't know if this was a relationship anymore or if it ever was. Maybe I was just a pet project for Michael, a pet that he is no longer interested in being attached to. I do everything in my power to make him happy, and no matter what, it is never enough. Like a cat or a dog that tries to please its owner so it can get a treat, there I was with Michael jumping through the same hoops with bells and whistles with no hope of things getting any better. All the times he told me he loved me and attempted to do special things for me, to me and with me, yet he would turn right around and show me just how evil and nasty he can be. I often wondered if it was me that he hated, or did he hate himself taking it out on me because I was his loyal puppy.

Ours was a mentally and emotionally abusive relationship. Neither my mom nor my dad ever prepared me for anything like it, and I had no clue how to get out of it. No one would ever believe that the relationship I was in was abusive. I was a black woman, tough with a low tolerance for foolishness. I knew how to make little become much. Surviving off of nothing and turning it into something was first nature for me. Physical abuse was common in my life and surroundings, but all that mental abuse talk was for weak women or women of another color.

Many women are in relationships that can be described as abusive. We tend to have a hard time accepting that reality. Most often when we bring up abuse we are talking about broken limbs, black eyes, bruises on the body, cracked ribs, and other physical visual signs of abuse. Mental abuse is just as brutal and painful and is a form of violence that affects the mind. That feeling of worthlessness with no sense of believing in one's self causes for a very unhealthy lifestyle.

Mental and verbal abuse is a form of aggression used to control or manipulate another person. When someone makes you feel unloved or unworthy of respect or as if you are nothing and would be nothing without them, they are abusing you. Many Black women refuse to accept it for what it is. Mental abuse along with an ungodly soul tie is a deadly mix. You are no longer thinking for yourself or about your wellbeing. You will accept things you never thought you would accept and go through many things you never imagined all in

Independent Woman

the name of love. You look around at your life as you know it and realize that none of the things you have done were your goals and dreams but are all attached to your abuser. Even if you didn't have any goals and dreams before you met him, you look in the mirror and don't recognize who you have become.

Jealousy and controlling behavior are used as his way of showing you how much he loves you, and as a sign of affection and protection. The cursing, yelling, mishandling and threatening we explain as his way of showing his manhood, a strong man taking no foolishness from anyone. We deceive ourselves into believing that we are in control of how much mistreatment we are going to accept. We have convinced ourselves into believing that we can walk away at any time when things get severe. We can't tell anyone that we are in this condition because we portray ourselves as the woman that has everything under control. We even go to the extent of trying to mentor and encourage other women that are going through the same or even worse situations.

We buy into the idea that if we weren't so strong minded we wouldn't have all these arguments. We're tricked into believing that the arguments and the aggressive behavior directed towards us is our fault. We're made to bear the shame for putting the indictment on our abusers. This good man is doing nothing but trying to make a horrible me, an Oreo cookie, better. Michael always used the saying 'you can take the girl out the ghetto, but you can't take the ghetto out of the girl,' and referenced it to me. I was Avenue C East-side hood and he was West-side, Corn Hill bread and buttered. One would think that I should embrace his treatment to bring myself up to a higher class, but was there ever anything really wrong with this ghetto woman or the side of town where I grew up? Was I ever really an Oreo cookie to begin with? Was I still carrying the pain of that label given to me by my father?

Mental abuse brings on humiliation, shame, low self-esteem and no sense of self worth at all. Bringing up my past mistakes, reminding me of who I was before I met him and what I was involved with prior to meeting him is just another part of the abuse to keep me humbled and feeling like I owe him. If I don't accept this for what it is, I will continue from one relationship to another with the same outcomes. I will be looking for this treatment from men because this is all I know about how a man should treat a woman.

Haven't I done things for myself? Haven't I made goals and accomplished things that have nothing to do with Michael? I made the choice to surrender my life to Christ without him, and I realize now that it wasn't just for me to say that I am saved and live a church life, but it was to empower me to become a woman dependent not on man, but on God. God showed me that it was time to empower myself. I had never thought of myself as a victim, and I was not ready to start. From this point on I am a survivor, a saved survivor who is no longer under the subjection of Michael but hidden in the bosom of God. The Word of God says those that keep their mind stayed on Him, will be kept in perfect peace. My mind will be focused on the

Lord, keeping Michael's voice of negativity out of my head. I am in control of what I think of myself. I am in charge of how I look and how I will dress. Slowly I will gain back my self-worth, thinking for myself and feeling what I want, being in total control of me.

I could no longer allow Michael to cause me to be frustrated or disappointed in myself. No more would I feel guilty about wanting to better myself without him. No more would I worry about what he thought of me or who he thought I should be. Keeping a diary and reflecting on my past would help me to never go back down this road again. I had to be honest about my situation and down in prayer I told God how I truly felt about the condition I was in. I released all concealed emotions of abuse and let it go. I couldn't keep it inside to eat away at my inner being killing me slowly with no chance to subsist.

What I endured was not my fault. I was not to blame for someone else's actions. I would not take that charge and accept that I had done it to myself. No matter how long it took, I knew I had to cleanse myself of any stains of abuse. I would not allow myself to live in misery, and I would not accept that I deserved to be mistreated. It was time for me to heal. God was my healer and no man could ever heal me, only God. Doctor's, counselors and specialists were there for the pulling out of deep rooted hurts and venting, but God was there for my healing, comfort and restoration.

I had strong women around me that showed me I could do and be better. My mother and her sisters, the prayer warriors that they were showed me that a closer relationship with God was what I really needed. They were powerful women who had gone through much themselves, but yet were able to be role models for me. My mom and her sisters, the Brumfield Nine, oh how I appreciated each Aunty. My Aunt Marilyn was my father's sister and she completed the best pack of Aunties any young girl could ever wish for. I was able to pull out strengths from each and every one of them for my survival. Not only were there blood relatives for me to look up to, but my spiritual sister Michelle was there for me as well. Never did Michelle turn a deaf ear when I needed someone to talk to. She didn't judge me and always made me feel like she was proud of me and my life no matter what stage I was in. I didn't look to her to rescue me, but she listened.

Sometimes that was all I needed, someone to listen. I guess it runs in her family because Michelle's sister Linda was there for me too. Her stance and approach at life I watched closely. A beautiful black woman, independent, strong and vibrant letting me know without ever saying a word that I would get there, I would be alright. It wouldn't happen overnight, but I would get there. I couldn't give up.

*****

Every time I gave Michael an opportunity to regain my trust he screwed it up. I exposed my heart and true emotions to him and he defecated on them each time. This man that started off as my knight in shining armor turned out to be the headless horseman instead. I was so glad I had accepted Christ in my life. In retrospect, that horrible and devastating night could have gone differently, but once again God saved my life, Michael's life and whoever he was with in that apartment. I was glad no one came out while I was there because I would not have represented Christ with my actions. I prayed and asked God to forgive me for the things that I was thinking and feeling about Michael. I asked Him to give me peace over this situation. I thanked Him for revealing to me just what I asked Him to reveal. I ask God to continue to lead and guide me as I surrendered my life to Him. I realized I was nothing without God and I needed Him to teach me how to live Holy and be the best mother I could be. I was finally free in my mind from Michael, and this, no matter how small it sounded, was a huge step. An independent woman was on the horizon and there was no stopping me.

Living saved was not something I had to do on Sunday only, but I must represent Christ every day. God showed me that I am just a babe in him and I have so much more growth to receive. The only way I would grow into the woman God wanted me to be was if I kept my focus and mind on Him. I was no longer putting my trust in Michael or in myself; all my trust was in God. He was the only one that hadn't failed me yet – even with my sketchy past, God treated me like royalty and for that I owe Him my life. I am no longer in debt to Michael for pushing me to get a degree, and I am no longer blaming my father for lost love. I am independent – yes an independent woman totally dependent on God. I'd rather spend my time trusting and thanking God for all He had done, and all He is going to do instead of creating blame and mustering up anger.

"Life now is sweet and my joy is complete for I'm saved, saved, saved." Yes this song rings in my heart as God continues to bless me more than I could ever imagine. Every church service I go to I try to dance the carpet off the floor. I know I am not perfect, but I can feel God perfecting me and it feels great. I can't act like my heart isn't broken, that things couldn't have been a different way with the father of my son, but I have learned that you cannot force a circle into a square hole. If it wasn't meant to be, I have to accept that it wasn't meant to be. I still love Michael and I am trying to forgive him but allowing myself to be in a relationship with him was something I could not do. I was independent now, and independence looked good on me.

I wanted to be cordial with him for our son's sake. I would tolerate his presence and communicate with him as much as possible because it is important to me that he be a part of his son's life. I know a lot of mothers who make this same sacrifice and it destroys their life as they become miserable, but with Christ in my life I found a type of peace that even I don't understand. The attraction I had for Michael that was so strong and overbearing was gone. I no longer dreamed of being with him. I didn't sit and imagine a wedding with him and living that happily ever after dream life.

The mental abuse was fading away. I stopped wondering what he was going to think about what I am doing, wearing, or saying. I was not worried whether or not he was pleased with the decisions I made. His talking down to me no longer intimidated me and his manipulating schemes were all played out.

Yes. The soul tie had been broken, but I wondered if he knew it. I was all about pleasing and serving God. I wanted to be the best mother I could be to my son and live my life without drama. Michael liked to take Zion so he can spend time with his older brother. Before I would become very insecure and jealous, but after a while I didn't mind at all. Michael thought that the reason I was not giving him grief anymore was because there was someone else in my life that I was dating. He tried to figure it out snooping around but came up with nothing. He didn't realize that I had fallen in love with Jesus.

I used to hear so many people say that and think they were phony and crazy. How in the world could you go from being in a relationship with someone for years, being intimate with this person countless times day and night, having a baby with him, loving everything about him, and now say you are in love with someone or something that you cannot see. Now that I had experienced it for myself I realized it was not what I saw, it was what I felt. Jesus was the first man in my life that made me feel this kind of happiness. So many people call Him so many different things, but I like to just call him Jesus –the lover of my soul. He is my new soul tie.

One of the church sacraments done outwardly to express what has taken place inwardly is water baptism. Growing up at Redeem Church of God in Christ, baptism took place at Sodus Point. Down at the beach the group of church members would be singing *Take me to the water, take me to the water, take me to the water to be baptized.* Before Elder Jones died he renovated the church and now there was a baptismal pool under the pulpit. Thankful for Elder Jones' labor of love, I was ready to be baptized. Michael had been lingering around, but I chose not to give him the time of day. Now that I have truly moved on, he wanted to express his readiness to be married. I would love to have married Michael if I knew that was what God wanted me to do. God had not shown this to me, so I embraced and celebrated my independence.

It was the day of my baptism and Michael wanted to come along to church as well. Why now, I asked myself, when he never wanted to come before? On the way to church he said he needed to stop at the mall. All I could think was that he was intentionally making me late for service. I was very quiet and calm not allowing him to stir up any frustration and we finally made it to the church. He was being kind and gentle with his words and demeanor. I wondered why but let it go. The church service was exhilarating and uplifting. As a baptismal candidate I was sitting on the front row while Michael had our son sitting on the other side of the church. I looked over and saw him standing to address the congregation.

With tears in his eyes I heard him say he wanted to apologize to me and the church for the way he had treated me. He admitted that he was wrong, and he wanted God to save him. I sat on the front row crying with tears in my eyes. Could this be it? Could this be the breaking point I had been waiting for? It seemed like there wasn't a dry eye in the church as he began to breakdown. I watched him, shaking and crying and taking off his glasses. I kept asking God if this was really happening. Was he really ready? Is this why he wanted to come to church today? Is this why he was being such a gentleman and so peaceful? *God please show me a sign that this is your will. Oh how I pray this is what it looks like.* No matter what happened, if God had changed this man's heart for the better I wanted to be the woman with him to enjoy the good man he would become.

My focus had been all on pleasing God and this was distracting me. I was no longer thinking about being baptized, I was thinking about if my lost dream of becoming this man's wife was really going to happen. It had been so long since I had the dreams that I can't remember how they played out. As the church praised God and the music played I sat with my face in my hands, just sitting and praying. With my eyes closed, snapshots of my life flashed before me. There flew by a glimpse of me with my dad; me dating all the wrong guys and then graduating from high school; now a glimpse of me graduating from community college; Michael's oldest son and his son's mother; London; Virginity-girl; the birth of my son; the lies; the cheating; the redialed phone call mistake. The glimpses were so vivid of all the hurt throughout my life and especially what Michael had just recently caused.

I rushed to open my eyes. As I looked up I saw a missionary rejoicing in front of the church. She was looking over at Michael and began to run towards him. As she started to run it seemed like time started moving in slow motion. Before she could take a second step, she tripped over a wire that was taped down to the carpet because of the baptism. When she tripped, her glasses flew off of her face and up into the air. As they twirled up in the air over and over again it seemed like they were never going to come back down. Finally they did, and so did she – right down to the ground. People came to get her up off the ground and she hurriedly continued over to Michael as if nothing ever happened. At that moment everything was clear to me. God couldn't have given me a better sign.

    I had been baptized and felt I had made one more giant step closer to God and being an independent woman. Drying off and getting my clothes changed I breathed a sigh of relief. I received so many hugs and kisses from everyone that were Godly proud of me and happy for what had taken place in my life. At last I got to Michael and he hugged me tightly and kissed me telling me he loved me. I looked at him and told him I loved him too. Pastor reached out to me, shook my hand, and said that we needed to come into his office. I went into the office and hugged and kissed his wife sitting there, and Michael followed. As I sat down I saw the door open again, and the Pastor said he called my mother in as well. Mom looked at me, and I looked at her, both of us wondering what was going on.

    Pastor began telling me that Michael came to him and said that he wanted to marry me…today. Yes, today. As in right now. He had the marriage license that we went down and got together, and he had a ring that he purchased at the mall that morning. I didn't see this coming, and couldn't believe it was happening. Pastor wanted to know what my mom thought about this and if we should get married. My mother immediately said without hesitation this was not a decision for her to make. She explained that she had never told me what to do regarding my relationships and this, like everything else would have to be a choice that I made, not her. She said that whatever we decided she would be thankful and supportive because she loved the both of us and wanted the best for us and our son.

I was so appreciative of mommy giving her blessing and leaving the decision making to me. Michael looked over at me and asked me to marry him. I froze. The pastor's wife asked me was there something wrong and I told her no. She then began to tell me how much of a blessing it was and that I should marry him. She said obviously he loved me to go to this extent and reminded me unnecessarily that he was the father of my son. The pastor expressed that he would be happy to marry us and he felt that it was the right thing to do. *Wow. When the pastor says that something is the right thing to do, hands down, no questions asked, it is the right thing to do.*

Everyone waited for my response sitting quietly with anticipation and expectations of an office impromptu wedding to immediately take place. I looked at them and told them all, "No". There would be no wedding. Not today. I was calm about it with no anxiety, and I felt free as the independent me saying, "No". Way too many things had taken place for me to have made a decision based off today's present emotions. Pastor nor his wife could understand why I would say no after all this time of wanting to be married to him. They see couple after couple come in and out of their office with the woman so eager to be married.

Out of love and concern for me they pushed for me to rethink saying no for my sake and my son's sake. They didn't want me to say no and regret it later. Pastor was willing to marry us and offered counseling. That didn't sound like a bad idea at all.

Without a doubt it was my dream to be married to my son's father. I never wanted to be called baby mama. I realized I had no business having a child before I got married and the least I could have done was make things line back up by marrying Michael now, but I couldn't. When I gave my life to Christ I fully believed I owed Him my life. I said yes to Him, and He promised me that He would be there for me always. He never broke that promise so my trust was totally in Him. He was the head of my life leading me and guiding me and directing my path. Making decisions without Him was no longer an option for me. When I was trying to be in charge of my life my heart continued to be broken, but when I placed my heart in His hands, He had yet to hurt me. With my loyalty and commitment to Christ I waited on Him for guidance. Every time I asked, He was right there to answer.

In church I had asked God for a sign while the service was very high and anointed. When I opened my eyes after watching some of my life play out in my mind, I saw the missionary trip right in front of me and I accepted it as a sign that was truly from God. Time after time I have been caught up in the smoke screen of things. Playing off of emotions and getting tricked into believing what I saw before my very eyes were real, when everything was trick mirrors of deception. The soul tie and mental abuse were mistaken as a soul mate and tough love. Just as that missionary tripped and fell, numerous times I came running to what I thought was real, and ended up getting tripped and falling. Her glasses twirling in the air symbolizing how blind I had been; around and around going in circles; only to fall and hit the floor face first over and over again. God said no more with Michael, and when God speaks we must listen.

My pastor, his wife, my mother and especially Michael could not believe that I refused to marry him. I chose to listen to what God was saying and not what man thought I should do. Michael was so hurt and upset and that is why I expressed my desire to have counseling. Not to give Michael false hope of us getting married, but I believed that if God saw something different in him, there might be a wedding after all. In that moment Michael was able to see he was no longer controlling me. No longer in control of my mind, manipulating my decisions and this was no longer his world. This girl from the ghetto had found independence through her dependence on

Independent Woman

God and there was nothing anyone could do about it. It was a long ride home, but we made it. I did all I could to make sure Michael understood that I didn't say no out of malice or to humiliate him. In order for me to have peace, I had to forgive him and we must be able to get along and love one another even if we aren't getting married. The marriage license was good for a year, so who knows what would take place before it expired.

After that I felt like I was as free and independent as Alice Walker's character *Celie* when she was leaving her abusive husband *Mister* in the movie *The Color Purple*.

I'm poor, black, I might even be ugly, but dear God I'm here. I'm here!

Yes this so called Oreo cookie was still here. No more would I entangle myself with the mistakes of my past. Goodbye old world – the independent me, my Black and my White side were intact. The first major decision this Oreo cookie had ever made was simply adhering to the voice of God as He spoke. I was independent, living in liberty, and all the strength I displayed had come from my Heavenly Father who was my covering.

Chapter 10

THE MOVE

It was almost summer time; time for me to begin making future plans. I would be graduating that summer and I needed to decide if I was going to stay at the new banking job I had gotten after leaving the Urban League or attempt to get better employment elsewhere. I needed to figure out what I was going to do with my new degree. I had a project due and had to prepare for the presentation. This was a group project and my team and I were determined to get a perfect grade to culminate our time at SUNY Brockport. Being a mother and an employee meant I was a non-traditional college student. I didn't stay on campus, so every time my group needed to meet, they wanted to come into the city to my apartment off campus.

As an Oreo cookie I loved being with my group because they were more acquainted with my inside – what was called my White side. Vanilla, my group partner liked to be the last to leave my house and loved playing with my son. He would give me long hugs and a kisses on my cheek. I knew he was interested in being more than classmates, but told him I couldn't. I tried my best to let him down easy and he was understanding, but made sure I knew he was waiting

The Move

by if I ever changed my mind. Dating Vanilla would have been nice because he was thoughtful and kind, but I wanted time to date myself before I moved into another relationship.

Even the security guard on campus began flirting with me, and I thought it was quite flattering. We exchanged numbers and talked daily when I travelled to and from work and school. An attractive dark-skinned gentleman, he tells me how much he loved the Lord and he is in the church too. We talked about the Bible and what we are looking for in a long-term relationship. Talking to the security guard helped me realize I wanted God to send me the man He has prepared for me. I soon discovered the security guard was not the one. I didn't want to fall for someone who has practiced the right words to say and was smooth with lies knowing how to be deceitful to get what he wanted.

I passed all my classes and this time, the graduation party was not a surprise. It was fully planned by me. My big sister Pamela was proud of me. She purchased the meat for the party and my brother Patrick was on the grill. Graduating and getting my Bachelor's degree was electrifying. I was overjoyed with all the support I received from my friends, family and church. Michael was there as well taking pictures and he made me a large poster that said: CONGRATS LILLIAN ON YOUR GRADUATION! I could tell he had some reservations, and I knew I was going to hear about it sooner or later.

I did it. Finally, I did it. One more thing I accomplished in my adult life that I didn't have to give Michael credit for. The more I saw

The Move

that independent woman showing up, the more insecure Michael seemed to become.

Family and friends came from all over and we had a wonderful time celebrating at my house. As day became night the celebration continued on. Someone called me outside and said there was guest who wanted to see me. I went out and was excited when I saw my high school friend "big brother" T-Jay and his cousin. It had been a long time since we had all seen each other, and had a lot of catching up to do. I asked how my old boyfriend Joseph was doing and his brother said I should call him. I gave him my number so we could get in contact with each other. I had given my heart to God and I knew that if Joseph was still up to the same old things he was up to back when we were dating there was no reason for him to try and talk to me. I wasn't looking to start a relationship with him, but thought it would be nice for us to see how the other was doing.

Sure enough Joseph called me later on that week. We talked for hours on the phone laughing about how we broke up and why. He informed me that he had children, and I told him about my son. He asked if I was dating anyone and I told him no. Joseph began telling me how he always thought I was a good girl, and that was what he loved about me. I told him I always thought he had the highest respect for me and that's what I loved about him. I told him I was living for God and invited him to come to church with me. He laughed, but agreed that one day, maybe, he would come.

The Move

One phone call turned into many calls, and then he asked me if he could come over. I hadn't dated anyone and the only male my son had been around was his father. I was careful because I didn't want to confuse Zion. I knew that if Joseph came over my son would wonder who he was, and I didn't want to have to explain. It was getting late and my son was falling asleep so I told Joseph it was okay for him to come over, and he did. We sat and watched television and talked the entire evening. I brought him up to speed on my college degrees and what I planned for my future. He was proud of me and behaved as he had always, like a gentleman. He was getting sleepy and so was I as we watched television on the sofa. He never tried to make any advance towards me, and we both enjoyed the other's company. After a while he drifted off to sleep and I found myself dozing off as well. I didn't want to wake him so I let him sleep on my sofa and I went into my bedroom with my son and shut the door.

The next morning I woke up to banging on the door. When I heard the pounding I knew exactly who it was. I didn't want to open the door because I knew Michael would be upset to see that Joseph had stayed the night over my house. Joseph awoke and grabbed his pocket knife as if he were preparing for battle. I asked Joseph to please stay quiet and after a while Michael would leave. Michael went around to every window in the house, banging on it for me to open the door, but I wouldn't. I couldn't. I prayed Lord please let this end peacefully with no one getting hurt. I knew that if Joseph felt his

The Move

life or my life was in danger he was going to do whatever it took to protect us. I also knew that although we weren't together anymore Michael was going to make this about him and would want to fight just to save face.

    Finally Michael gave up and left. I was worried about Joseph, and thanked him for not getting upset. Joseph was worried about me and wondered whether he should leave. Michael had gone down the street to the payphone to call and see why I wouldn't open the door. I ignored his call. I told Joseph I would be fine, and felt it was best that he left while Michael was gone. I asked Joseph to call me when he made it home so that I knew he was okay. He made the promise that he would call and make sure that I was alright as well. To the very end he remained a gentleman. I gave him a hug and a kiss and he left.

    After Joseph left I got in the shower to bathe and when I got out, I heard more banging at the door. Michael was back. I reluctantly let him in and he ferociously busted in the door walking through the house demanding to know who was with me. I told him no one was with me but he called me a liar and began looking through my bedroom, the closet and the rest of the house. He said he saw a car outside in my driveway with a Florida license plate, and he knew someone was in my house. I looked at him quizzically and told him that car belonged to guests that were visiting the people that lived upstairs from me. He was still having a hard time believing me and then questioned why I was just getting out of the shower. I told him I was getting ready to go to my mother's to do some laundry, but he refused to believe that as well. I wasn't going to tell him about Joseph because I could see that he wasn't thinking rationally.

What comes around goes around is what I was thinking in that moment. It was just months ago when I was pregnant that I came to our apartment and caught Michael there with another woman, that somehow mysteriously disappeared when he finally opened the door. Now he knew what I felt, although I hadn't slept with anyone – just the thought going through his head put him in the place that I was when he was being unfaithful to me. No, it doesn't feel good, and I was glad he finally got a taste of what he had been putting me through. This wasn't planned, but I was glad it was happening. I couldn't have planned it better if I tried.

I told him that he should leave and there was no reason for him to be in my house yelling and screaming at me. As I continued gathering my dirty clothes to take over to my mom's Michael paced back and forth through my house as if he were waiting for the owner of the vehicle in my driveway to appear in my apartment. I finished getting my son dressed, and my phone rang. I paused because I knew Joseph said that he was going to call me when he made it home, but I didn't think it would be that fast. I didn't want to answer the phone because I didn't want Michael to know who was on the other end and take the phone and start talking trash. I didn't want Joseph to come back over to my house to try and fight Michael for talking trash, so I just wouldn't answer the phone. I forgot in the moment of things that I didn't have voicemail, I had an answering machine. Before I could

The Move

run to the machine to turn it off, I heard Joseph's voice and knew that it was too late. Joseph said in his message, "Lillian you told me to call you when I made it home, and now I am calling you and you are not answering the phone. Are you alright over there?"

Michael being the intelligent man that he is quickly pieced together that Joseph was in the house when he came earlier and that was why I didn't let him in. He began grabbing me and shaking me asking me was I having sex in front of his son. I told him no, and it was none of his business what I was doing or who I was doing it with. As he called me out of my name, he lifted up his hand. I looked at the palm of his hand as it came crashing down on to my face, I could not believe that Michael had taken things to yet another unacceptable level. I fell into my Snoopy stuffed animal display case that sat in the corner of my living room. Holding my face I refused to believe what had happened. My first mind was to fight back, and make sure I disable a limb in the process, but then something said no – just go.

Michael became angrier at my reserved demeanor and punched a hole in my wall. I became thoroughly upset at that point because he knew that I was contemplating moving to another apartment, and I would not be able to get my entire security deposit back if that wall didn't get fixed. The whole scene was incredible, and eye-opening. I was completely taken aback.

I wanted to get as far away from Michael as possible so that he wouldn't hit me again. I have been in this position before, and this

The Move

time I know I will not allow myself to become a punching bag. Everything he did seemed to be more revealing than the last. Michael has just shown me how much of a man he is not and I will not tolerate it.

When I got to my mother's house, there he was. Michael was yelling at my mother telling her what he thought I had done. Telling my mother that she doesn't know how I *really* am. He tried to tell her that I was not the girl she thought I was and that I had a man in my house overnight. He said I had abortions for him, and then he told her that I had been sleeping around. He was so wound up saying that he knew my mother wasn't going to do anything about it because she never wanted us to be together and get married anyway. My mom was taken by surprise not knowing that any of this was going to happen she was compelled to tell him that was far from the truth. My mom actually loved Michael and treated him as her son. She wanted us to be married, but she wanted us to be happy. Lately, happy was the opposite of what we have been. All she could do was attempt to get us away from each other and give us time to calm down. Michael left angry and I was now there with my son looking up at me confused and my mom looking at me with concern.

Michael fixed the hole that he created in the wall and was apologetic about what he had done. *Sorry isn't enough when you put your hands on me.* He said all he did was hit me in the face, and I said all you did was way too much for me to accept. I couldn't believe that he would try to minimize the seriousness of what he had

The Move

done. It wasn't too long before when he dragged me across the floor while pregnant with our son and now he has stepped it up to hitting me in the face. For the safety of me and Zion, goodbye is in order.

*****

Michael and I met at Old Country Buffet to try and communicate with each other. I was sitting at the table with him and he pulled out forms that he said I needed to sign immediately. Looking over the forms, I understood them to be custody paperwork. He said to me that he was willing to take me to court for custody of our son because I seemed unstable. *This sounded awfully familiar. Sounds like the same claims he made against his first son's mom when he and I started dating.* I sat and listen to him go through his rant of threats and accusations. I kindly informed him that I was not signing anything and would never sign anything for him. *The audacity of him to even bring custody papers to me when he had the chance to claim his custody rights by signing Zion's birth certificate the day he was born. He refused.* Right then I knew it wasn't about him getting any parental rights. He didn't want any claim or custody; this was pure manipulation and intimidation at its best.

When I called him on it, he was no longer interested in having his name put on the birth certificate. Michael didn't want to get together and talk to me or make amends; he wanted me to be afraid of him. He wanted me to feel inferior. He wanted to put in my mind that I was not good enough, that I was damaged, and that no one wanted me, especially not with my son. He wanted to plant negative seeds in my mind that I was a failure and that I was nothing without him.

I'd had enough of the verbal abuse. As Michael watched his invisible chains being loosed and broken he tried all he could to keep them in place. I wasn't falling for the jargon any longer. The words that would come out of his mouth no longer pierced me to my inner being. For so long he treated me like he owned me because he was the one to help me get off of the dangerous path that I was traveling. I had always felt less than, as though I was his personal charity project.

I began to reflect and noticed that Michael's helping me do better over the years we had been together was not the only thing that had taken place. He had dreams and goals and I was there supporting him too. I was there in the studio as he indulged in his music career with his best friend. I was there to help him launch his *Keep It Real* greeting cards business; assisting him in gaining permission to sell them in Midtown Plaza at the All Day Sunday store. I purchased and insured his first expensive camera. I mailed out introduction letters to churches to gather clientele for his photography business. I was behind the scenes preparing things when the Chip N Dale Male Strippers show came to town. I co-signed for the black Dodge Neon he drove around, and then the old BMW he purchased with my help. I could go on and on and on.

Useless would be the last thing that came to mind when I thought of myself in this relationship. I didn't do the things I did because I was indebted to him. I did these things for him because I

The Move

had the skills and capability to do so. I was worth something. I have more value than he would ever let on or show me. He doesn't have to anymore, because my stock and value has gone up even further now that I am a child of the King.

I landed a job at a big medical insurance company which was new in the area. They were doing a mass hiring and this would be my first job utilizing my new degree. Excited about the change I saw that in the midst of turmoil God was yet blessing me. I don't like going to my apartment anymore because Michael tended to show up more and more unannounced. My son and I have been going back and forth between my mom's house and my apartment so that I would feel safe.

It wasn't until I saw his car hidden down the street from my apartment that I knew things were getting out of hand. It was the weirdest feeling because I had just passed a police patrol car, and for some reason I had an urge to ask him to follow me to my place, but I didn't. Instead I decided to just drive by my house and not pull into the driveway. By passing my house I was able to see Michael's car parked down the street in front of someone else's home, and I sped off to my mother's house. Zion and I stayed the night there, and she let me wear some of her clothing the next day so that I could go to work.

In training at my new job I could not focus wondering what Michael had planned for me if I hadn't seen his car. Once before he snuck up on me at night when I was getting out of my car and it was

The Move

an unpleasant surprise. My son was sleep and I was getting him out of his car seat, when I shut the door and looked up, Michael was standing in front of me. He aggressively snatched Zion out of my arms demanding I tell him where I had been with his son. His irregular behavior caused me to be more on guard expecting the unexpected with him.

In the middle of training at my new job, my trainer received a phone call. He called my name and told me I needed leave training class to take a call. Apparently there was someone downstairs that needed to see me right away and security wanted to speak with me on the phone. I got on the phone outside of the training class and heard someone calling my name saying it is an emergency I needed to come down to the lobby right away. It was Michael's mother, and I couldn't believe my ears. She said all she could to get me to come down to the lobby, but I refused. I had no idea what lay waiting for me down there, but I wasn't going to find out.

I went back into the classroom teary eyed because I knew this wasn't going to be the end of all the random spectacles. Things had gone so far out of the norm that there was no turning back. I was afraid to leave my job when it was time to go, because I didn't know if Michael was going to be hiding somewhere with his mother waiting to confront me. I drove my mother's car to work that day to hide from him. I rushed to my mother's car and sped to the baby sitter to pick up my son. I explained to Mrs. Taylor, my sitter, that things were rocky between Michael and me, so she knew to contact

The Move

me if he came around and was acting unseemly. She was surprised to hear of the events that had taken place and was sympathetic with me. I safely made it to my mother's house, but I was so bothered by the day's events that I couldn't eat or sleep.

I pretended with everyone that I just wanted to spend more time over my mom's house so that my son could be around his cousins. In reality I was afraid to go to my own home. Sitting at my mother's dining room table contemplating my next move the phone rang. It was Michael calling to say that he had been pulled over by the police and he needed my help because he didn't have his license. I told him that I couldn't leave my mother's and that he may need to call his mom or grandmother to help him. He begged and pleaded for me to come, and I told him I couldn't quite understand what help I would be by coming to the location he was giving me. Once again I felt that I was being set up, for what I don't know – but once again I wasn't going to find out. My mother overheard the conversation and told me that I needed to be careful. She didn't fully understand what was going on, but God gave her enough wisdom to tell me to be careful and to stay away from Michael for a while.

Here I am a college graduate, the Oreo cookie that won against all odds. I was supposed to be imprisoned or dead by now, but here I am. I was starting to feel like my luck was coming to an end. That feeling of death kept coming over me and I was scared. I had my women's devotional Bible that I read to keep me calm, but the reality was I was terrified of the what-if's. What if I had gone to

The Move

my apartment the night Michael hid his car down the street? What if I had gone down to the lobby when Michael and his mother came to my brand new job? What if I had gone to the location where he said he was pulled over by the police? What if he actually does try to harm me and take my son? Too many events were running through my mind and none of them had a happy ending.

This should have been a happy time of my life, yet I was in despair. God hadn't failed me this far and my faith in Him made me believe He would continue to carry me. Praying was all I knew to do and when I prayed, I believed things happened. I asked God to protect my son and me from dangers seen and unseen. I didn't want to tell my family what was going on out of fear that they would attempt to handle Michael for me. I knew his family could be the same way, and I didn't want a family feud to erupt. Praying does what it always does. I was transported into certain peace where I was able to think clearer.

I couldn't allow Michael to intimidate me with his usual tactics. He was subtly trying to take back control of my life. I refused to give him that type of power to manipulate me and hold me hostage from living. I refused to live in fear and decided I was going to go home to my apartment and not worry about Michael at all.

There will come a time in life when you think praying and trusting God is not enough. I didn't know that time for me was right around the corner. I drove around my apartment before pulling into the driveway to make sure Michael wasn't hiding out in any place. I didn't see his car anywhere, so I pulled into my yard thankful I had a safe ride home from my mother's house. My upstairs neighbors were coming home at the same time and I felt better because I knew I wasn't all alone. Secure in my apartment I began getting ready for bed. I heard a knock at my inside door and assumed it was my neighbors since we all had just come in at the same time. To my surprise, it wasn't my neighbors but it was Michael standing in my doorway.

Michael had a crazed look on his face and when our son saw him he ran to him calling out "Daddy". One thing I always promised myself is that I would never let our son have a bad image of his father because of something I said about him or allowed him to see. For Zion's sake I played along as if everything was alright. I walked from one room to the other praying and trusting God that He would protect us, but I felt as though I needed to do something more – I just wasn't sure what. Michael got our son ready for bed and sat holding him and playing with him. Once he fell asleep Michael said he wanted to talk to me. He told me he was tired of all the fighting and arguing and he was so sorry for all the things he had done. I had heard it so many times, I could almost say the words right along with him as he spoke.

I let Michael know that we needed to concentrate on being the best parents we could be for our son. He kept making references that he couldn't live without me and he didn't want me to be with anyone else. I stood firm, not falling into anything that he was saying. I went about my apartment straightening things up and ignoring Michael to show him it was time for him to leave and he was wasting his time talking to me. He walked in the kitchen as if he was going to the bathroom and he came back with a large knife. All I could do was stare at him as he told me he was serious, and that he wasn't going to live without me. I asked him what he wanted from me, what did he want me to do? He told me to love him and make love to him like we always had. He stood in my bedroom doorway blocking me from getting out, and I begged him to please put the knife down.

God where are you? I need you to intervene right now. As I sat on my bed I begged him not to do this because our son was in the next room. He repeated that he didn't care because if he couldn't have me he didn't want to live. A part of me wanted to tell him to go ahead and kill himself and leave me and Zion out of it, but I knew that message would not go over well. He said he didn't want me to live without him either.

I didn't want to give off any sign of weakness, but I felt the tears swelling up in my eyes. He came towards me. I guess he thought they were tears of acceptance. They weren't – they were tears of disgust and the closer he got to me the more the tears began to flow. He kept kissing me on my forehead and trying to kiss my lips as he pushed me back onto the bed. My feet went numb as if I were unable to lift them as he got on top of me telling me he wanted to love me. I didn't want to die. I didn't want him to kill himself. I felt the only way out of this was to give him what he wanted.

The Move

I lay lifeless on my bed with him on top of me. With every thrust I cried. I wanted him to know this was not what I wanted. I would not consent to it. Nothing about it felt good. There was no passion like before. No stamina or excitement. Hurt, disappointment and sadness was all I felt. I kept telling myself it was alright, I could take it. It would be over soon and I could go on and live. But then I thought what if he doesn't leave, what if he wants more, what if he decides he wants to kill me anyway. I felt him climax and could no longer hold it in. I cried so loud and hard holding nothing back.

After seven years being together how did we get to this place? *God why would you allow this to happen to me? Please don't allow me to be pregnant from this.* Michael held me as if he was consoling me. I couldn't believe he didn't realize he couldn't be the attacker and the consoler at the same time. I asked him to please release me and let me go. I told him I needed my space and that he needed to leave. The thought of my son waking up and seeing me in this condition made me clear my face and demand that he leave immediately. He had an air about him as he left like he thought he had broken me once again, and it sickened me.

I locked the doors to my apartment and slid to the floor in despair. I asked God to forgive me and help me because I didn't know which way to turn. I crawled across the kitchen floor to my bathroom and stood in the shower letting the water wash me in my face. The longer I stood in the shower the stronger I became. I told myself I was not a victim. I was an over comer. I would get through

The Move

this. God is my help. Even though it felt like He wasn't there with me, He was. He knew I could make it through this and here I am, still alive. Yes, I am alive and able to see my son. I am alive and able to raise him to be a respectable, gentle, and loving man. I am alive and will never let my son ever know what his father has taken me through. My son sees his father as a hero and if I can help it he will always remain a hero in his eyes.

God doesn't make mistakes. People do. By no means should any of the turmoil that was in my life be blamed on God. Every choice I made was mine and the outcome brought me to where I was. I thanked God I was still alive. I should not have had to go through numerous things I endured, but I did and I was still alive. I was stronger. I had more confidence, and most importantly, through my struggles I learned to trust in God. There are many women that have been placed in the same predicament as me, and they are no longer here to talk about it. Women who have gone through worse than me and are still in it feeling there is no way out.

I saw my way out, and I took it. With God's help you can get out too.

I decided that I wasn't going to keep my apartment, and began packing things to store at my mother's until I found a new place to stay. I loved my apartment and I didn't want to let it go, but I couldn't live there anymore. It was time to leave. To hurry the moving process, I decided to sell and give away all of my belongings. Some of my sisters from church came to help me and I was willing to

The Move

give them all of the clothes and shoes that Michael had purchased for me and even some things I had bought for myself. I gave away everything from the shower curtains to the food in my cabinets – everything had to go. I wanted to rid myself of anything connected to Michael save our most important attachment – our son.

I wanted to move into a new place with all new furniture to rid me of everything that took place in my last apartment. I gladly sold my bedroom furniture since I'd only had it for a few years. It was still like new, but I never wanted to lie on that mattress or in that bed ever again. The living room and the dining room sets, plates, glasses, microwave, and all the other stuff were gone. I was happy to be able to give most of my things away to those who were in need. It made me feel good that there were positives coming out of all the negativity.

I had to resign from my job at the medical insurance company. There had been too many distractions during my training, and it was leaving a bad impression with my trainer. I told him that I really wanted to work there, but I needed to step back and take a break before going any further. It was an awesome job and I hated to let it go, but God gave me that job and for Him to allow me to let it go meant He had something greater for me. I had my Bachelor's degree and I could apply to a larger array of job openings and ask for a higher salary. It was risky but I knew deep down that I would be alright.

No one needed to know how far Michael took things. I didn't want anyone feeling sorry for me, or feeling the need to retaliate against him. I didn't categorize the act as rape. I allowed what happened to take place. No, it is not what I wanted, and I didn't consent to it, but I let it happen. I felt I was saving my life and my son's life by allowing Michael to handle me the way that he did.

From that time on when Michael came around he had an arrogant persona about him. I couldn't stand it, but I tolerated it. He thought he still had control over me. He gave me demands about what he wanted for his son. He gave me orders and was egotistical. He behaved as if the world revolved around him. I knew he was doing it on purpose, but I didn't say a word to him about it.

This was the same man that was recently at my apartment holding a knife to his throat saying he didn't want to live in this world. Now he was walking around as though the world belonged to him. I knew he thought I fell for his antics and gave in because he gave a clever performance, but what he didn't know was that his one-man-show liberated me. Only a weak man would allow a woman to believe that he was going to kill himself if she didn't sleep with him. Only a weak man would threaten to kill himself or someone else because he wasn't getting his way. Only a weak man would put the mother of his child in danger and care less about the outcome. Yes, he was weak. And in Christ I was strong.

I continued attending church trying to stay in communication with everyone like normal never letting on the real pain that I had

The Move

been feeling. I didn't tell my pastor what happened because all I could think of was that he and his wife wanted me to marry Michael. If I had married him that day he would have really thought he was in control of me. The marriage plan had nothing to do with him finally wanting to settle down with me and be a good husband and father. The plan always was to manipulate and misuse his authority as a husband. The plan was to be able to legally have rights to tell me what to do and no one in the family or in the church would be able to have any say. The plan was to isolate me from those who supported me and to leave me feeling alone and desolate. The plan was to bring me to a deep depression so that he could then feel again like I needed him to rescue me.

It was family reunion time, and I really didn't want to be around family. I didn't want everyone asking me where my fiancé was. I didn't want to tell anyone that I wanted nothing to do with my son's father and that we were no longer engaged. I wanted to keep it quiet and not deal with the questions. There was no way in the world I wanted Michael to be at the reunion, but everyone was accustomed to us being together. With all of my uncles, cousins and my brother coming together the last thing I wanted to do was alert them of any wrong doing to me. No good would come of it, and I couldn't live my life knowing that harm had come on others because of me.

Father's Day was approaching and Michael had once again set directives on how he expected the day to go. My best friend Tina that had been living in Baltimore was coming home for the weekend to

The Move

visit her dad. Tina and I had been talking on the phone. She knew that I was unhappy with my life and the way things had turned out. Her and her boyfriend Chon suggested that I travel back to Baltimore with them. It was a kind gesture of them to offer their assistance but I didn't think they were sincere. I heard Tina and her boyfriend on the line as they again offered me a place to live, but I thought that it was a kind hearted suggestion, and nothing more than that.

It wasn't until they actually made it to Rochester and asked me one last time that I knew they were serious. I asked when they were leaving, and they told me they were leaving on Sunday after Tina spent time with her father for Father's Day.

> Note to self: Father's Day is tomorrow. How in the world are you going to prepare to move to an entirely new city in less than 24 hours?

With me being unemployed, I only had the money that Michael and I had together. I had a few dollars in hand and I didn't know what I should do. Sunday morning arrived and Michael came as planned to pick up our son for the day. I asked him what time he would be back, and with a smart and cynical tone, he replied later this afternoon. As soon as he pulled off with our son I began putting my plan in action.

I told my mother that I was leaving, and moving down to Baltimore with Tina. She was surprised when I told her that this was all taking place in the same day. She went on to church accepting my decision with no hesitation. I took my car to the auto store and bought

The Move

new spark plugs. I wanted to be sure it would make the trip to Baltimore. That purchase cost me less than $25 and I was able to fill my tank with gas leaving me with $20 in my pocket.

I didn't want Michael to see Tina because I knew he would become suspicious, so I told him that I would pick our son up instead of him dropping him off. I had all the belongings that I could pack in the trunk of my car. Because my car was a hatchback, I became a little worried that Michael would notice the things packed back there. I used a big green blanket to cover my things up, and it looked like I was just carrying around a trunk full of laundry.

I pulled up to Michael's place and he came downstairs with Zion. Hugging him he held him in his arms, kissed him, and told him that he loved him. There was silence between us and it felt like he was being so affectionate with our son because he knew that we were getting ready to leave him. He stood outside on the side walk waving and watching as we drove away in route to meet Tina and her boyfriend. We didn't waste any time and got on the road to Baltimore. I never got the chance to say goodbye to my sisters or my brother. None of my cousins, friends or church family could say farewell since no one knew, and I felt it was best that we kept it that way for a while. With Chon in the driver seat I pulled out after them and didn't look back.

Fred Hammond Pages of Life I & II tape was playing on the car stereo, and my son and I were on our way to a new life,

Jesus is all, the world to me,
My life, my joy, my all;

The Move

> *He is my strength from day to day,*
> *Without him I would fall.*
> *When I am sad, to him I go,*
> *No other one can cheer me so;*
> *When I am sad, he makes me glad,*
> *He's my friend.*

With tears in my eyes I accepted this hymn literally. Jesus was everything in the world to me. He had taken me from the lowest point in my life to the highest places, higher than I could imagine. In my darkest hours He had been there for me and had never failed me. He had made me glad, and He was and is my friend. Not worried about the backlash for leaving the way I had to go, I began praising God and thanking Him for His comfort in song. Fred Hammond sang and told me God will do what He said He would do. That's right, No weapon, formed against me shall prosper. God is going to come through, standing on His word and no matter what the devil tries… *It won't work.*

No longer was I second-guessing anything, because I put my total trust in God. I surrendered fully to Him and I have asked Him to lead and guide me to where he desires for me to be. It seemed as if Fred Hammond was speaking directly to me as I listened to him say, *"when you have been called to have a relationship with God and called to do something great for him sometimes it's not going to be easy"*. No matter how difficult it was going to be the Bible lets us know that every step of a righteous man (in my case, a righteous woman) is ordered by God. Although we don't understand everything, in time He would reveal His will.

I sang along with the tape as it played agreeing with every word. Yes my mountain is too high and I am tired of the climb. Oh how many times my faith has been challenged and my vision obscured. That's me hanging on by a thread waiting for that word to help me endure.

My God is my refuge and I will hide in Him. I was on the move, and in spite of what it looked like there is a smile on the bloom. I was free: soul-tie free, mentally free, physically free, sexually free and bad-relationship free. My steps were being ordered by God. I did not understand what He was doing or what He had planned for me, but my faith was in Him. My singing and praises continued with every track on the tape. I looked up as we were crossing a small bridge, and read the sign that said *"Welcome to Pennsylvania"*. I was gone – out of the State of New York and relocating to where ever God told me to go. My covering had set me free.

Chapter 11

A New Life

I could hardly believe it. Baltimore, Maryland. I never thought in a million years that I would live in a place like this. There I was in an unfamiliar city, lying on a pillow in the room of a row home with tears in my eyes as I stared at the ceiling. *Lord why did it have to get to this point?* I believed this was the right move but I was scared. I didn't think it was going to work. I didn't have a job and I didn't have any money. I was not accustomed to living off of friends or family. I needed to get on my feet quick. Tina got me a newspaper and all day long I was on the computer updating my resume sending it out to companies.

Why was I always crying? I was not accustomed to shedding tears, but it seemed like crying was all I'd been doing. I needed to get to my place of refuge. The place I know He resides. I needed to have a moment of spiritual healing and feel God's presence to know that He was with me and would continue to order my steps. More than I needed a job, more than I needed money, more than I needed my own home, I needed to go to church.

I wanted to hear the songs of adoration and lift my hands in praise. I wanted to get my shout on and thank God for His mighty hand of protection. I wanted to let Him know I would continue to trust Him no matter what my life looked like. I wanted to let Him know that I was scared, but I still believed.

The phone rang. I was home alone. I answered.

"Hello?"

"Lillian, if you do not bring my son home immediately I will come down there and kill you myself!" a familiar voice said.

"I am never coming back and I have every right to be wherever I want to be. Please don't threaten me," I replied as calmly as I could.

"This is not a threat. Bring my son home now!" Michael screamed.

"There is no turning back, you should have thought about the consequences of your actions. Now, there is no turning back," I say.

"Lillian I hate you and you are dead to me," He says all in one breath.

"Hello?" Michael's grandmother says, taking the phone from him.

A New Life

"Listen Lillian," she continued calmly, "Michael is upset right now and he really just wants his son," she said. I could always count on her to make peace amidst confusion.

"He is my son too and I am the one who takes care of him. It was not safe there for either of us and the best thing for me to do was to leave," I tell her.

"Well, are you two alright?"

"Yes Ma'am."

"Do you have a place to stay?"

"We are staying with a friend and we will be fine."

"Do you have any money?"

"No ma'am I don't. I no longer have access to my bank accounts. All the money I had is gone, but don't worry, your grandson and I will be just fine."

"Lillian, call me if you need me. You two need to take some time to cool off. You are not wrong for leaving. I understand why you did what you did. Let's make plans and try to come up with an agreement so that we can still be a part of the child's life and get to see him," she explained.

"Yes Ma'am. Thank you for being supportive and understanding." I replied.

It wasn't fair that I was the one that had to move. Why couldn't he leave so that I could stay with my family? None of my siblings have ever moved away. We all stuck together and lived nearby. With great hurt and dismay I had to leave my family and support system and travelling to a place where I had no family and no friends. I left so I could survive. Baltimore was my best option to start afresh so I could give me and my son a fair opportunity at life, but it wasn't home.

Leaving Rochester was tough for me. Rochester was all I knew. As I reflected on the fact that all of my family and friends were there I felt more alone. I uprooted myself from the life I knew because of foolishness. I felt as though my dreams and plans had been destroyed. Thankfully my spirit received rest because it was then that I remembered that I believed God. I believed He had other plans for me and whatever those plans were, I was convinced His were better than mine. I chose to hold onto what I'd said when I accepted Christ into my life... "Yes Lord".

*****

I couldn't wait until Sunday morning. I was anxious to get to the church – Mount Hebron Memorial COGIC. The pastor and his wife were good friends of my parents, and I needed to be around folks that loved the Lord. The church gave me a good feeling. *Feels a little like home, but not quite.* I knew one thing, God was there. And for that I was glad. "Mommy look, Granddad!" Zion blurted out as the Pastor greeted the congregation. "That's not Granddad Zion. Shhh. I guess they do favor each other somewhat," I replied. "Praise God for Sister Lillie Nowlin," the Pastor said. *What? How does the pastor know my name? I know he knows my parents, but he doesn't*

A New Life

know me. Oh my goodness, that mother of mine called this man and let him know I was coming.

The church turned out to be very nice and the people genuinely friendly. Looked like a nice group of young people congregated there as well. *I think I will fit in here just fine.* Whether I fit in or not one thing is for sure, I need God to lead and guide me. I had gone out on the water in the deep trusting that He wouldn't let me drown. *This church has an evening service? Getting back into that mode will be tough. Tina isn't trying to hear coming to church with me so I am on my own with this. Taking the kids with me made it easier and I planned to make it to every single service there is because I needed God.*

The preacher quoted Psalm 30:5 saying, "Weeping may endure for a night but joy, (oh joy) cometh in the morning!" He spoke powerfully, as the same excitement filled my heart that he must have been feeling. I embraced the message as if it were encrypted for me and only me to understand and hear. The Lord used the man of God to send me a message and let me know that He is here with me. I could sense His presence and my heart felt warm with His love. I got the message; I may be crying right now, but soon and very soon good change will come my way. I chose to thank God in advance. I shouted all over the church to let God know I got the message and I was patiently waiting on Him to do what He said He would do.

The pastor pulled me to the side. Do you have money? Are you looking for a job? Where are you staying? Do you have food to

A New Life

eat? *Slow down partner.* My mother neglected to tell him that I was one of those women that got uncomfortable when a man felt like he had to take care of me. I don't take money from men and surely didn't need a man's help. If I don't have it I don't need it. If I need it God will provide it.

This pastor refused to let me be the tough girl I had always been and forced me to take the gift of love he was offering. I was so upset I had to call my mom and tell her how uncomfortable it made me feel. I didn't get close to preachers and didn't need one offering me money. I wondered what his motive was. *My own daddy isn't concerned about me so why are you, Pastor?* I told my mother that his money would be repaid as soon as I got a job and that was that.

*****

It didn't take any time for my mother and my sister to come down and check on me. I was glad when they came. Familiar faces in strange places always give you the encouragement you need to continue on. I started a new life and I was determined not to be defeated. My mother let me know that I had lost a lot of weight. She was kind enough not to let on that she could tell it was from stress and not dieting. My mother also neglected to comment on the hair I'd lost from stress, and again, I was thankful for kindness. Their trip was short, just the weekend, but they spent the entire time encouraging me. They told me I had done the right thing. They even did a roll call of all the people from home that were praying for me and wishing me well. I was strengthened by their words more than I could express.

A New Life

I hated for them to go, but I knew they couldn't stay. I had been under such stress. This was all new to me. I prayed to God that he would relieve me of the anxiety and stress I was dealing with so that I would be well enough to raise my son.

The news spread that I had left Rochester. Some were happy and others sad. I heard rumors that I had kidnapped my son, or that I left to get even with Michael and hurt him for no reason at all. I could only imagine what other lies were spreading about me. For the first time in a long time, I could honestly say that I didn't care. What Michael said or thought or felt was no longer a concern of mine. I decided that I was going to keep my peace and even with the lies being told about me I refrained from bringing out the abusive, manipulating truth that was his treatment of me.

It was still my desire and goal to never have my son look at his father in a negative light. If I didn't do anything else, I would do all I could to uphold the superhero-image that Zion had of his father. I had to call my son's babysitter and explain to her what had taken place and let her know that Zion would not be coming back. Her and her husband both were sad that I had to leave the way I did, but were glad I was safe. When I hung up with her I began wondering if I would find someone as good as her in Baltimore; someone that I could trust with my son.

Uncle Big Bill visited Washington, D.C. and wanted me to drive over to see him while he was in town. I knew it gave a measure of peace when people could see for themselves that Zion and I were

A New Life

safe and in good spirits. I was excited to see Uncle Bill and I loved him so much for being concerned about me. Uncle Bill was my dad's older brother and one of my favorite uncles. He didn't have to do much to be one of my favorites; he just knew how to be the most awesome uncle ever.

I arrived at Penn Station in Baltimore to purchase my ticket and catch the MARC train to the District of Columbia. Riding the train to D.C. was a brand new experience – something I had never done before. I'm sure Zion and I looked like fish out of water. Nevertheless, I was focused. All I wanted was to get to my uncle. As we boarded the train I found a comfortable seat. Zion began asking questions and wanted to be held. I held him on my lap and rubbed his head until he fell asleep.

Looking out the window I thought about my life. *God, I just want to be loved. I want a man to love me because I deserve to be loved. Love me as if I am the only woman who matters. Love me as if his life depended on it. Love me because he wants to, not because he has to or because has a negative ulterior motive.* I didn't want to be a single mom raising a son. My child needed a male figure in his life to relate to. *Lord I want my companion to be a saved man; a man that is going to be faithful to me and fear you. I want to feel like I have never felt before when I am with him. Dear God, please don't make me wait too long, I desire this man now.* Before I knew it we were in D.C. I had fallen asleep on the train.

A New Life

Joy was obvious between Uncle Bill and me as we embraced. His genuine concern and love for me have been a constant in my life. He and Aunt Gloria gave good advice that kept me thinking about my future, while their tough love kept me in line so I could make good choices. As we caught a taxi to Uncle Bill's hotel in downtown D.C., I was amazed at what little scenery I was able to take in; the architecture and historic wrought-iron fences, the maze of streets winding to no end. Unfortunately I spent much of my sightseeing time in the corners of my mind trying to make sense of things. When I should have been enjoying myself, I was swimming in unanswered questions.

Uncle Bill was such a protector. Being with him reminded me of the safety only family could provide. I wanted to tell him how hurt I was. I wanted to tell him how scared I was. I wanted to tell him that I was not sure if I could live far away from my family. I wanted to tell him what Michael had taken me through. I wanted to open up to someone and tell them that I had been abused and I was hurting inside. Uncle Bill looked me in my eyes and told me that I would be alright. "Lillian, you have made a decision. You can do this," he said. "I will support you and send you $50 a week until you find a job and get on your feet. Just don't give up and don't look back. You can do this." he continued. I was thankful that my uncle believed in me. Knowing I had his support and encouragement meant more to me than any amount of money he could ever give.

A New Life

Our trip to D.C. was over and it was time to go. The commuter traffic was unlike anything I had ever witnessed. We had to hurry back to the station so as not to miss the train back to Baltimore. I wanted to stay with Uncle Bill and hide in his basement. But no, that's not my style. *I am a fighter, and I trust in God. I will be alright no matter what it looks like right now. I believe God is going to provide everything I ask for.*

We ran towards the train as the last passengers were boarding. Uncle Bill was out of breath running ahead of me to make sure the train didn't pull off. He gave me a great big hug and kissed Zion goodbye.

I felt the visit was too short and I was not ready to face my new reality. I grabbed hold to my uncle's love for me and his faith in me and took it as my covering. Uncle Bill had at times been like a father to me. Taking time to check up on me while on a business trip to D.C. showed me that no matter where I was he would always be there for me.

All of the hustle and bustle to get to the train made me and Zion very tired. Zion laid his head in my lap and wanted to stretch his feet out. The gentleman sitting in the third seat next to us gave up his seat so that Zion could stretch out and sleep during the ride. I was a bit nervous to fall asleep again on the train because it didn't feel safe.

I felt a tap on the shoulder. A man excuses himself and asks me if I knew what street ran parallel to the train we were on. My response was no, and that I wasn't from the area. Why did I say that?

That only led him to ask me where I was from. I told him upstate New York, and he told me that he was not from the area either. He was trying to find out if there was another route between Baltimore and D.C. and I told him I didn't know. He didn't seem dangerous so I continued conversing with him as he asked one question after another. I kindly gave him short answers and explained again that I had recently moved to the area. He apologized for asking so many questions, and then realized he hadn't asked my name. I told him I understood he was just making conversation, and politely gave him my name. He was stunned enlightening me that his grandmother and I shared the same moniker. I smiled as he gazed into my eyes.

Why does this guy want to talk to me all the way back to Baltimore? Who is he anyway? Even if I did want to take a nap I wasn't able to. I looked down at his hands, and he didn't have on a wedding band. He asked me what side of town I lived in and I told him I didn't know. He asked how I was getting home. I told him hopefully my sister would be free to pick me up but if not I would catch a taxi. He asked if I knew where to tell the taxi to take me. I told him no, but assured him I would be fine. As he asked question after question, I began to wonder what I had been thinking. I didn't have a clue as to where I was going or how I was going to get there. All I knew was what Tina told me. She said Penn Station is near North Avenue, and I could catch a taxi to the church once I got back into Baltimore if I couldn't reach her.

My new friend with his newfound concern for me and my son offered to take us wherever we wanted to go. I told him I would be fine. He insisted and I continued to say no. He compromised and offered his phone number in case anything happened. He told me if I needed his help to give him a call and he would come back for me.

I was shocked. As we got off the train and walked into the station I looked at this handsome, tall man with a muscular, athletic build. His milk chocolate skin with the nicely shaped brush-cut complimented his charming, spellbinding smile. He was neatly dressed and had a kind demeanor to match. I felt as though I knew him since we had such a long conversation on the train. Getting to know each other I find out he attended church, and he loved the Lord. He was on his way home from work so I knew he had a job. Could he be the one? I did just pray and ask God to send him to me. *Would God really answer this quickly?* He made me promise that I would call him to let him know that I had made it home safely. I put his number in my Bible and smiled as he walked out of the station looking back to make sure that I was going to be alright.

Why was he so concerned about a stranger – someone he hadn't seen before? There was something about this man. Finding words to explain our immediate connection was difficult. It was transparent, spiritual, vulnerable and easy. I couldn't wait to tell Tina all about him. My unoccupied time was now spent thinking about him; wondering where he lived, and if I would ever see him again. I called him, but he didn't answer. I left a message, but he never called

A New Life

back. Months had gone by, and I had yet to hear from him. For some reason he stayed on my mind, as a dream, a thought, a fantasy that might never be.

I realized that it was not for me to seek out the man that God had for me but to patiently wait. I withdrew from the notion of dating or 'helping God out' in sending the right man my way. God didn't need my help and showed me that I needed to trust in Him and He would take care of me. Feeling happy with God alone, I let go of the options of dating any available man at the church. I no longer wanted to entertain the attention of any man that didn't share my Christian values. I accepted the fact that just because a man goes to church doesn't mean that he is the one God has for me. I was finally at peace with not having a man in my life. Or so I thought.

*****

I was glad Zion was comfortable around the young ladies at our church who babysat for me from time to time. One of them worked at a Head Start program so I applied for him to attend. When I arrived to enroll Zion the family services coordinator was a New York native and wanted to do more than usual to help a fellow New Yorker out. She introduced me to the director of the program and told him that I had a degree and I was from New York looking for a job. The director did an impromptu interview and hired me. I couldn't believe that this girl I had never met was willing to do more than what her job required and forced her boss to talk to me and give me a job. She treated me like we knew each other, but it wasn't until I

A New Life

started working that I could recall her name, Laverne. God said He was going to take care of me, and He wasted no time doing so. I had a job. Now I am saving money and repaying my uncle so that I could find a place of my own.

Just when I thought I was the big bad Oreo cookie moving on with life and loving the changes God was making in me and for me, August comes. August 2001 was our last and final chance to use the marriage license that Michael and I went down to the courthouse to get. I was all the way in Baltimore fearing that at any moment he was going to show up and try to kill me for moving away with his son. He was in Rochester hating my very existence for the way I moved away with Zion on (of all days) Father's Day.

Our unused marriage license was reaching its expiration date. I knew that time was running out and I couldn't believe that there was still a part of me that cared. I wanted to isolate myself and not be around anyone; just let the days and hours go by. I was glad the youth from my church encouraged me to get out and have a good time. The Youth Department of my church was going on a trip to Virginia Beach, and I wanted to go. I knew Zion would enjoy it. No one knew what I was going through or what I was feeling. All I could think about was that I should've been getting married, but God had a different plan for me. I had learned not to question God and accept what He allowed.

*****

A New Life

September 11, 2001. The World Trade Center's twin towers were hit. In fear not knowing where the next attack was going to take place we were instructed to begin an evacuation of the Head Start center. Watching the towers on the news I frantically called parents to pick up their children. In between calls, I would call my family back home, but couldn't reach anyone. The phone system in New York State was bombarded with calls and none of mine could go through. The horror in everyone's eyes and the uncertainty and lack of information available had the entire states of Maryland, Virginia and the D.C. area paralyzed with fright. It was probably the most frightening, and saddest time in recent American history, and an obvious time to pray.

I made it back home to Tina's house and was down in the basement watching the news coverage of the planes crashing when the telephone rang. I looked at the number and it looked familiar. Was this who I thought it was? Yes! My handsome, talkative, concerned friend from the train finally called me. He remembered me telling him that I was from upstate New York and wanted to make sure that none of my family had been affected by the events that had taken place. I told him that we didn't live in New York City, we lived upstate, but I had not been able to reach my family. In the midst of all that was going on, I leaned back on the sofa and smiled. I could feel that he was just as happy to hear my voice as I was to hear his.

We talked about the movie *Left Behind* and I read him scriptures I had been meditating on. The more we talked the more I could imagine the connection becoming stronger between us. From that day on he promised never again would he take that long to get in contact with me. He wanted to take me out on a date. I couldn't resist and said yes. I wanted to see him again. It was something about him that made me feel comfortable and safe. We met at a shopping center parking lot for our date. I realized in my haste and excitement of our date that I'd left my purse at work. We were both nervous and laughed at our cautiousness. I ended up having to trust him allowing him to drive the both of us instead of driving separate cars. He followed me to drop my car back off at home, and then took me to get my purse. Just like that, he immediately knew where I lived and where I worked.

We went out to eat at *Jillian's* a place where I knew there would be a crowd. As we sat at the table waiting for our food, we both pulled out our licenses to prove we were who we said we were. It was funny to look at each other's ID's and call each other by our middle names. I enjoyed the evening as did he. We got to know interesting things about each other and the night was as a breath of fresh air.

As we rode down interstate 295 to go back home he asked me to sing something since I told him I knew how to sing. Reluctantly I opened up my mouth and said "I've had some good days…I've had some hills to climb," I looked over at him as he drove and saw his eyes fill up with tears. We began to talk about his grandmother and what she meant to him. He explained that he felt it was more than a coincidence us meeting on the MARC train that day and me having the same name as the woman he held so dear to his heart. I felt the same as if there was more to this connection than either of us knew in that moment.

We talked to each other every day after that. He would send me instant messages at work and talk to me on the phone all night long. We couldn't get enough of each other. He took Zion and I out, and they were attached as if we were meant to be a family. I never had another man around my son, but his presence felt natural and right. Months passed and the smile on my face remained. He and I went bowling and the entire way to the alley he kept looking over staring at me. When we pulled into the parking lot he turned off the car and told me there was something he needed to tell me. He began to say how he never felt this type of excitement with anyone. I felt the warmness of his hand grabbing mine and he leaned into me and we kissed. The dangers in kissing and what it leads to all flashed through my mind. I reasoned that I yearned to feel this passion for a long time and I didn't care about the dangers. He told me he loved me, and I knew right then I found him irresistible too.

We never made it into the bowling alley. We stayed in the car and talked. We talked about whatever came to mind. We discussed everything from the son he had to my baby daddy. We didn't want to keep anything a secret. Clean non-fornicating adoration. I was so excited because this man didn't try to have sex with me. In no way was he inappropriate and was always a gentleman. I nicknamed him

A New Life

Mr. Marc-Train to symbolize where and how we met. I couldn't wait for him to come to church with me so that everyone could meet him.

Any chance Mr. Marc-Train got he would take me out and just spoil me. We always ended the night with a passionate kiss. The kiss at the end of each night became more and more passionate as we talked about marriage and spending the rest of our lives together. Things were moving very fast, and I didn't know if I wanted to hit the brakes. I figured I would allow things to go on and see where this new relationship would lead.

We both began to share our past hurts in relationships and where we were emotionally. Finally, without pressure, without being judged or criticized I was able to tell someone what the past few years of my life entailed. He didn't try to be a hero or bad mouth my son's father. Instead he listened and comforted me. I silently wished I had met him before.

As he held me in his arms and wiped the tears from my eyes he assured me that everything I had gone through with my son's father would stay in the past and I would not have to hurt anymore. I couldn't believe he was willing to accept my baggage as his own without blinking an eye. Michael's harsh words, when he told me that no man would ever take a relationship with me seriously came to mind, and I smiled. God proved Michael wrong.

This man, without trying to tell me how I should think, look or act was standing by me and supporting my every decision. He didn't want me to be who he felt I should be; he wanted to get to know me. We were both surprised that we had become very serious so quickly, but agreed to pray and allow God to lead us. It was getting harder and harder to only kiss goodnight, but we both knew that was as far as we could go.

At times it seemed as though there were things left unsaid. He wanted to tell me something, but he didn't know how. Late nights we sat with each other holding each other but he wouldn't let it out. He finally tells me that he is having trouble with his child's mother. I jumped at the chance to encourage him the same way he had supported me. Just as he gave me confidence, I in return assured him the care and interest I had for him wasn't going anywhere.

Depending on the individuals involved, things can be peaceful or chaotic when dealing with separated parents. Engulfed in this new life as a Christian but not forgetting what I had been through, I was calmer and more understanding towards women who have strenuous relationships with the father of their child. Mr. Marc-Train had to know that no matter how crazy his child's mom behaved, it would not run me away. As long as he was honest and real with me we could work through anything. Mr. Marc-Train was there for me so why not be there for him in return? I loved this man, and I loved what he represented in a tumultuous season of my life.

He commended me for the way I handled my son's father. He told me how strong I was and how much respect he had for a woman that would stand up for herself and her child and not spend the rest of her life trying to make her child's father miserable.

A New Life

I was glad that God allowed this relationship because it was what I needed. It felt good to be loved. It felt good to have a man's attention. It felt good to have someone who made you feel like no one else in the universe existed or mattered. Mr. Marc-Train cared about my opinion and counted it a blessing to have come in contact with someone as special as me. Yes me. The same Oreo cookie that had been broken into pieces is now a delicacy someone is eager to swallow whole.

Knowing that he supported me because he wanted to and not because I was giving up anything was the greatest feeling on earth. I had no pressure from him, nothing but compliments and kind words. He was more like a best friend than a boyfriend. God is allowing this, and Mr. Marc-Train is everything I want and need in my life so I am open to take this relationship where ever it may lead.

I'm open? What does that mean? I want this bad and it feels so right that I am willing to do whatever it takes to make sure it works. He complimented each side of me, my outside – the Black side, and my inside – the White side. Both felt a connection with him as if he is the only one in the world that holds the key to my entire being. He remains a gentleman to me, but I can feel he wants to take this relationship a step further and so do I. I let him know that I was saved and I meant to live my life in a way that represents Christ. The last thing I intended to do was become a fornicator and have God be displeased with me.

A New Life

He showed me so much respect for holding to my position and it made us more attracted to each other. There was nothing stopping me from taking this relationship into territories that it should not go. I saw him fighting the urges and he saw that I was serious about living upright as a single Christian woman.

I kept telling Mr. Marc-Train it had been a long time since I had been this happy, but the truth was, I had never been that happy before. I couldn't get him off my mind. I invited him to church, but he hadn't had the time to come. He expressed his willingness to be at my church, but told me how God was calling him to be a minister elsewhere.

He worked a job in Washington D.C. that required him to be away a lot. When he was home, church was not on his mind. When I was at church I was thinking about getting home to him even if it was just to hear his voice on the telephone. Constantly I was looking at my cell phone to see if he had called me. In the choir stand I daydreamed about the time we'd spent together. I had no interest in anyone but Mr. Marc-Train.

I was so in love with him and there was nothing anyone could say to change that. Completely head over heels love, the kind of love that makes you leave everything you know to travel to the unknown, not caring or having any caution towards potential harm. The love I had for him I had never felt for anyone. I thought I had experienced every emotion there was with my son's father, but this had reached new heights. Mr. Marc-Train was his own person looking for me to

A New Life

be my own person as we both expanded into the best versions of ourselves together. Neither one of us was dominant over the other; neither one of us inferior. Together we desired to be happy in life and in love.

Who is this man that was willing to understand my every tear as he wiped them away with his lips gently off my face? Where do you find a man that knows from day one that you are someone he wants to spend the rest of his life with, and believed this without hesitation? He showed me his vulnerabilities and trusted that I would not take advantage of him. I opened myself to him, he knew me thoroughly in and out, and yet he stayed around and seemed to love me even more. Knowing my flaws and seeing me for who I am, through his eyes he looks at me as if he were laying eyes on a real life princess for the very first time; someone he would never want to take his eyes off of.

Mr. Marc-Train is a man of few words. Every time he speaks his words are sweet and lovely to me. I am waiting to see the other side of him, but there is none. I wondered if he (like every other guy I have come in contact with) has to have some evil twin that will pop up sooner or later. The more I anticipate and wait on him to run me away by doing something crazy, the more he does to draw me near doing just the opposite of the bad I expect.

We were getting closer and closer. We had reached a point where we hardly wanted to be apart. My emotions reminded me of my past, and caused me to be cautious. I never wanted to get so engulfed into a man again that I lose sight of my life.

Just when I felt as though I was protecting myself from getting engulfed in him, he made everything be about me. Whatever I wanted, whatever I thought, wherever I wanted to go. He was certainly not trying to be the controller in this relationship. Before he made any move, he considered how it was going to affect me. He was concerned about how I felt, interested in what I thought. He respected my opinion and he listened to every word that I said.

I loved the wa y Mr. Marc-Train made a daily routine of connecting with me over the phone or internet. Even when his job took him out of town he stayed in touch with me. I smiled with every email, blushed with every instant message, and when I picked up the phone and heard his voice, immediately I melted. The words, "I Love You" rolled off his tongue so naturally as if we had been together for years. He now calls me, "Baby," and his shyness was cute. He's turning out to be a big teddy bear, one that I would love to cuddle with.

Mr. Marc-Train always made sure I wasn't late for church even though he wasn't interested coming with me. He checked on me to make sure I had offering money together so that I was giving what I desired and even more to the ministry. Whenever I went to church at night or when he was out of town for work, he called me in the evenings to make sure that I had made it home and Zion and I were safe. Sometimes I wondered why he was so cautious, why was he so protective? It wasn't a controlling type of cautiousness; not a manipulating way of protecting us. Mr. Marc-Train didn't try to pull me away from what I knew or who I was, but rather expanded what I knew and evolved who I was.

I felt a strong sense of independence with him. I was in no way pressuring him nor did I feel any pressure with him. I was taking as much advice as I was giving and it all worked out for my good. I was able to hold my head up with him, never feeling less than, never feeling unworthy. This sense of independence made me grateful to God while unclear of the full picture, but loving this segment with Mr. Marc-Train.

When the nightmares of feeling ugly, unwanted and unlovable arose, without hesitation he knew just what to say to make me feel beautiful, desired, and loved beyond measure. He took the time out to be a friend to me, not my man, my Romeo, or my lover, but a real true friend. That meant everything to me.

Mr. Marc-Train never questioned me about the clothes I wore. He never asked me why I didn't wear makeup or why I didn't have pierced ears. He liked that I wore my natural hair. He joked a lot about my height since I am short and he towered over me. I loved that he wasn't a flashy guy. He didn't drive a big fancy car with a loud sound system. He was low key and muscular but not a macho man with a chip on his shoulder with something to prove.

I enjoyed when we talked about the Lord and expounded on a scriptures that had special meaning to us. After hearing him say he believed God called him to be a preacher, I didn't say it to him, but I don't think he will be. I believed he could be inspirational; he was an encourager and highly motivational. He was charismatic and it was obvious I loved to be around him. I did not, however, believe him to be a preacher.

    I looked forward to us going to church and worshiping God together. I couldn't wait to go to Sunday school where maybe he could be a teacher of the class. Whatever he did in the church, my mind hadn't changed; I didn't want my future husband to be a preacher. He could be an usher, deacon, or even in the choir, but preacher –absolutely not. I was glad he had a mind to be in church and not simply talking to me *about* church. I was fine with that. I figured if he hadn't visited church with me yet, he at least goes to his own.

    I could imagine spending the rest of my life with him. Talking about having babies with him and the names we would choose; how many children we wanted to have; how many boys and how many girls to make our home a happy clan. *I must really feel something for him to want to even try to have children. I know my condition, but it doesn't hurt to imagine.* We loved talking about what they would look like with his dimples and smile, my complexion, his height, my eyes. I didn't want to go so fast, nor did I want God to think that I was trying to help Him again. I know God didn't need my help – I needed His.

A New Life

Instead of trying to see how much money I had in my bank account with a hidden agenda to take it from me, he educated me about saving and investing money. He never asked me for a dime, but was always willing to spend for me and my son. He was amazed to hear how much money I gave to the church in offerings, especially with me wanting to make big moves. I didn't want his money and took the time to let him know this. The last thing I would ever want another man to be able to say is that he takes care of me. No man has to take care of me because God has that job and He does it well. Even in the midst of struggles, He is still opening doors and making ways for me that I could not have done on my own.

Up to this point I had done all I could to be obedient to God's word and walk circumspectly representing Christ in my daily life. For a long time after breaking up with my son's father I refused relationships seeking only a relationship with God. There were men that I hurt and disappointed because I accepted my assignment as doing what God told me to do and not what I wanted. Nevertheless I allowed the relationship with Mr. Marc-Train to blossom. I was ready to move on given the time that had elapsed since my last relationship. Mr. Marc-Train had activated emotions in me that I never knew I had. This was not a rebound relationship, neither was it forced. Everything between us was as natural as our first encounter.

My mind should've been focused on the church services I attended. My mind should've been attentive to my relationship with God. My mind should've been a lot of places that it was not. It had been months with a free mind, a clear mind, and a mind that hadn't been abused or manipulated. My mind had been focused on pleasing God and listening to His direction. My mind had become stronger, but in my mind I was lonely. I knew God said that He would never leave me nor forsake me, and He hadn't. But I was lonely.

I was in Baltimore living my new life, but where had my spiritual life gone? I didn't feel the closeness to God like I used to. Those feelings had been replaced with a lust that was so strong and too powerful to fight off or ignore. Within my mind and my soul God is becoming second place. Everything about my existence was linked to Mr. Marc-Train. This Oreo cookie had a new life. I had new energy flowing around me. I had a new point of view and a strong desire for Mr. Marc-Train to be my new-life-covering.

CHAPTER 12

TRANSITION

Mr. Marc-Train and I started off right. We were respectful, God-fearing and a real blessing to each other. Initially innocent, peaceful and a pleasurable distraction we embarked upon untested pathways. Mr. Marc-Train would drop me off in the evening and the tender good night kisses were all we had until the next time we were together. I saw it in his eyes and he saw it in mine. We were headed down an unmanageable road. No one had to know, was my rationale. It felt good and I felt I deserved to have a moment in my life where there was nothing to feel but good.

    He was fighting and resisting all he could. All he had to do was walk out of the door but he stood still in front of me not making any movement. I knew what he was feeling because I felt the same way. All I had to do was open the door for him to leave, but I stood still in front of him not making any movement. We tried to be strong but our flesh won over our will and there was no turning back. It was dark and everyone was asleep. I heard his belt unbuckling and I was trying to get my mind to work. There was only one word to say. No. But I was lonely and yearning terribly for love. The last thing on my mind was no. We thought we had control over the situation, the kind of control strong enough to make things stop right before we crossed the line. That night I realized there was no such control between us.

Neither one of us could believe we had done what we had fought hard not to do. Holding our heads in shame, we clothed ourselves in a rush. As I got to the last button on my blouse I began to cry. All this time I had been abstinent, and just that quick I was abstinent no more. Mr. Marc-Train tried to console me, but all I needed was for him to leave. Ashamed and full of guilt we both say good night and he left. I ran up to my room embarrassed and fell to my knees asking God to forgive me. I closed my eyes tightly so that I could see nothing but darkness as I talked to God, but images of Mr. Marc-Train kept flashing across my mind. I couldn't pray. I felt like God was rejecting my communication to Him. I felt like God was looking down on me in disappointment and disgust. I threw the covers over my head and tried to go to sleep. Between feeling the invisible glares I imagined that were coming from God, and reliving the feeling of Mr. Marc-Train inside of me, I was perplexed and full of emotions that I didn't know what to do with.

The next day I didn't want to talk to him. Although he had been a wonderful friend to me and so far I enjoyed his company, I realized I couldn't let him get in between my relationship with God. I cried repentant tears on the altar the Sunday after our indiscretion; all the while afraid that someone would be able to see through me and know what we had done. Even still, it mattered less what people thought about me; what mattered to me was what God thought, and I thought and knew I had grieved Him.

Mr. Marc-Train called persistently insisting that we needed to sit down and talk. I agreed, but I didn't want to face him. I couldn't cope with looking at him knowing what we had done. As we spoke over the phone we both expressed remorse and acknowledged that we had gone too far. In the heat of the moment we allowed ourselves to indulge in ungodly behavior that we knew went against what we said we believed as Christians. I revealed to him my reverence for God and he conveyed his also.

New in the relationship we had already had intercourse, binding ourselves to one another spiritually. We inform each other of our medical history, test results and overall health, assuring there were no diseases or any other concerns to worry about. Yes, it was after the act, but we thought enough of each other to put it on the table as we thanked God for His mercy.

Over and over again we went through what we should have done and how things happened so quickly before we knew it. We agreed this was something that we needed not to engage in again. This was what our mouths were saying of course. Our bodies that were joined together for a short glimpse of time were eager for more. It wasn't enough. The timing and the setting didn't allow it to be a complete moment of pleasure. We didn't get to go as far as we could have. Lust is a very aggressive emotion that will leave the strongest man on earth feeling weaker than a helpless child. Even the most innocent of women cannot resist once placed in these circumstances.

The soul tie between he and I was more resilient than I had ever experienced, and I knew this was out of my range. Surprisingly he stepped up to the occasion, cleared his throat and put a stop to the conversation. He intensely explained to me that as the man in this relationship who feared God he had to take responsibility for what went wrong. He said he knew it was wrong just as I did. We had overwhelming urges that we gave into.

He hated that he didn't stop himself and was going to God on behalf of the both of us so that God wouldn't remain displeased with the way we behaved. In that moment I knew I loved him. As wrong as everything was, it felt good to hear him say those words to me. No, not good. I felt secure. I was sure that he would protect us. This would be our secret. We would keep it safe between us until we worked it out together.

We prayed together repented and accepted God's forgiveness while putting it behind us. However, it never left my mind, and every day after that we were around each other, I knew it never left his either.

*****

Michael didn't keep constant contact with us, and he used my family and friends to try and get information on our whereabouts. I was not in hiding nor was I a refugee and refused to live like one. Being far away from him I no longer feared for my life as much as I had when I was in Rochester, but I didn't let my guard down either. I knew I had to be careful. When it got back to me that he had hired private investigators to find us I was furious. He would rather spend money on an investigator instead of spending that money taking care of his son.

I was cut off from all access to any finances from Rochester and was left to fend for myself. Michael continued to say that I would be back, but as weeks went into months he got the picture – I was not coming back. He could keep the money, accounts, and property; I had my freedom and peace.

Michael sent a $100 bill for Zion and wrote on it in red marker, "To my son Zion, from Daddy." I made a photo copy of the money to show how I felt about the gesture. *Why would he send money to Zion supposedly to support him, and write all over it to lessen its value?* I was going to get mad, but I realized there was no reason. I didn't expect Michael to provide for Zion, so if the bank didn't accept his $100 bill then it was no loss to me. It would be a waste of his money, not mine. I saw his gift as outlandish. I didn't see the need for Michael to make a show of his support. I wanted him to do it. No fluff, no fanfare. Just do it. But he wouldn't, and I chose not to be a fool standing by waiting on him to do the right thing. I made my stance very clear to Michael when I said,

I am not the type of girl that is going to take you to court and make you provide for your child. I don't believe it should be forced. This should be something you are honored to do. I will not be a baby

Transition

mama calling and demanding money. You will not hear anything from me good or bad, because you and your money do not matter to me. It is not in me to cause grief in your life – you've caused enough in mine. So don't look for the unnecessary calls or surprise visits. No drama to stop you from moving on with whomever you choose. I have no reason to pick a fight or argument with your current love interest, I am sure they will have other women and your other baby mama to bicker with. There will be no begging, no pleading for help. I will make it without you; raise this boy to be a man without you; love, protect and provide for him without you. I will never say a bad word against you to your son and allow him to continue thinking of you as a hero –even if he thinks I am the bad guy. The truth always reveals itself, he will learn the real you on his own without me ever saying a word. He will be taught to love and respect you, but I will never have him asking for anything from you. If you do it, good for you, if you don't shame on you. But one thing's for sure, we will be just fine – you can roll that up and smoke it!

None of the conversations that Michael and I had were peaceful, but I continued to tolerate him so that his son could have access to him. I knew he despised me for moving on with my life. I knew he took the easy way out by blaming everything on me. With all the positive changes I had experienced since living in Baltimore, it didn't bother me at all that he thought I was the sole culprit of his horrible life. Thankfully his threats stopped, but the undertone of anger was still there, lurking in every word he spoke to me.

Knowing what Michael was fully capable of, I let Mr. Marc-Train know in the event that any drama arose in the future. He lovingly let me know that he was willing to deal with my crazy baby daddy just like I was willing to deal with his crazy baby mama.

I wanted desperately to have my own place, and Mr. Marc-Train and I had been discussing when and where I should move. I was still fairly unfamiliar with Baltimore, and appreciative of his taking the time to show me suitable neighborhoods. Baltimore City was unchartered territory for me. I was unaccustomed to its mass transit, busy highways and row houses, but I was adapting speedily with Mr. Marc-Train's help. It was fascinating for me to walk down one block that felt suburban, then walk a few blocks over in another direction and feel as though you've entered a war zone. Finding a place would not be easy, but I needed to find one. Tina and Chon were going through their own relationship issues, and I didn't want wear out my welcome.

I told Mr. Marc-Train about a house that the pastor wanted me to purchase. I went and took a look at the house, but I didn't want to buy it. The neighborhood was unsafe, and I had to consider my son. His father already had people tracking me down and I didn't want him to be able to prove in court that where we lived was too dangerous of an environment for his son. I had to be wise about any moves I made because they wouldn't only affect me, they would affect Zion as well.

Transition

The pastor concocted the bright idea of my purchasing the house so that another one of the young girls from the church could live there along with me. That would have been a good idea if we knew each other, but some of the things that I had heard and learned made me very cautious about living with anyone.

I knew the pastor wanted me to own a home, but I was not ready. I wanted to own my home and raise my son like my mother and father raised their children, but it didn't seem like the right time. I wanted to rent an apartment temporarily and see if Baltimore was where I would plant my feet for a while. I didn't want to have purchased a home, and then the Lord leads me to move to another state. What if my husband finds me and wants to move me someplace else? That would leave me trying to sell property that didn't appear promising in the first place. I reasoned that I would rather not be tied to high maintenance real estate, and it was definitely not a place I would want to live in for a long period of time.

Mr. Marc-Train told me to pray about it and whatever the Lord tells me to do, that's what I should do. This man is like a dream come true. He is not trying to tell me what do, nor is he telling me how bad my decisions are. He tells me to go to God, who has the answers, and do whatever He tells me to do. If he was after me to merely sleep with me, he would have encouraged me to hurry and buy the first house I saw so that he would have a place to visit me; a place where he and I could be alone without any disruptions or anyone ever knowing.

Transition

I was sure that I didn't want the house in Baltimore and I decided to let the pastor and the owners know that I appreciated the offer, but respectfully declined. I did not want to live on the west side of town nor did I desire to live that deep in Baltimore City. As badly as I wanted to move from where I was, I decided to wait and find a nice apartment and start renting in a safe community. Besides, if I got married my husband may already have a beautiful home prepared for me and my son, or maybe he will buy me the house of my dreams. Whatever the case would be, I would not be persuaded into doing anything I was not 100 percent sure of doing.

I was settling into Baltimore, but there had been no closure to my life in Rochester. I was in the midst of getting my life together in Baltimore, but Rochester kept haunting me. When my credit was pulled during the process of purchasing a house, my credit report showed that someone had been using my social security number under different names. My credit score had gone down because of identity theft. I couldn't say for certain but I thought Michael may have had something to do with that. It was not beneath him to make my life as miserable as possible. Unfortunately for me there was no way to prove that the transactions were done without my approval. There was also no way to get my credit score immediately restored either. I had to accept the situation for what it was and move on.

One thing I was thankful for is that it caused me to expand my faith by reading more of the Bible. I came across a few scriptures that stuck in my mind. When it came down to that evil, manipulative man in Rochester, one that comes to heart is Galatians 6:7, "Be not deceived, God is not mocked: for whatsoever a man soweth that shall he also reap."

    I knew I would have to face him again one day. I couldn't be afraid to go back to Rochester and visit when I was ready. If I never went back, that would make Michael think that he still had control over me even though I was two states away. My spiritual birthday was approaching and I wanted to be home for the next Women's Retreat to celebrate. Too many people talk to one another in Rochester for me to go up there and it not be broadcasted so I chose to defuse things before I got there. Zion hadn't been asking to see his dad, but I knew he would love to see him if he got the chance.

    I had mixed feelings about attending the Women's Retreat because it would be my first time coming home since I left but I decided to go anyway. It was good to be back amongst my church family and friends, but at the same time I knew I had to be cautious. Even though I left Rochester on bad terms with Michael, I knew he wouldn't harm Zion so I agreed to let him come to the hotel where the retreat was so he could visit with Zion. We made the agreement that he would have Zion back to me before it was time for me to leave for Baltimore. This was difficult for me because there was no guarantee that he would bring my son back.

    When I saw him he looked at me with utter disgust. I knew he hated me, and at one point I hated him too, but all I wanted was peace. I kissed Zion goodbye and told him to have a good time with his father.

Enjoying the retreat was my way of distracting my mind from wondering what Zion was doing and where he could possibly be. I didn't want him to be around another woman that is going to mistreat him or be nasty to him because of me. I thought about that and I realized, his father loved him, even if he didn't want to take full responsibility for him, he still loved him. I chose to believe that the love he had for his son would keep him from allowing anything bad to happen to Zion while they were together.

The retreat turned out to be just what I needed; the praying, praising, crying, and rejoicing gave me great relief and encouragement to go on. I thought about the relationship I had developed with Mr. Marc-Train and knew that I had to correct my behaviors. God wasn't pleased and neither was I. No matter how much I loved this man, no matter how thankful I was that he was in my life, I had to do things right so that our relationship would last forever.

Everyone was there and happy to hear that God was blessing me. I was glad to see He had been good to them too. I was so caught up and distracted with the retreat that I didn't notice I hadn't heard from Michael or Zion.

Don't panic was my first thought. *The devil will make horrible thoughts come into your mind and if you are not careful it will drive you crazy,* I tell myself. I called to see if everything was alright and I got no answer. I took it as Michael being himself and refusing to talk to me as if I were disrupting precious moments with his son. After dinner and trying to relax at the retreat I couldn't help but wonder where they were. I talked to Mr. Marc-Train and he told me that I needed to calm down and not get myself uptight. I asked him how he would feel if he was in my situation and what would he do, and he told me to ask myself that same question and put myself in Michael's position. Instead of him just taking my side and agreeing with me, he challenged me to be more objective before jumping to conclusions. I was glad I talked to him and felt that everything was going to be alright.

I knew deep down that Michael wouldn't let anything happen to Zion. He is the boy's father for God's sake. But not letting something happen to him and never returning him to me were two different things. Michael was certainly cruel enough to do the latter. Time for them to return is approaching and I haven't heard from him yet.

I paced back and forth through the hallways of the hotel wondering if I should make some calls and get my old acquaintances to search for Zion. I was getting angrier by the minute and was preparing myself to go for blood over my son. I was civil enough to allow Michael to see Zion, even after all he had done to me and this was what I get in return? How dare he take advantage of my kindness again? I couldn't wait any longer. It was time I made a few phone calls. I wanted him to regret ever attempting to break our agreement.

Some of the women at the retreat who knew my situation began to pray. They encouraged me to calm down. I sat in the lobby thinking about the phone calls I wanted to make. I thought about what I was there for and who I was surrounded by. I didn't need to call for the cavalry; I had the Lord on my side. Who could be against me when He was for me? I begin to pray, *Lord wherever they are please allow my son to return back to me. Protect them God so that they both make it back from wherever they are and I will forever give you praise.*

Michael finally returned. I was so eager to get Zion out of his arms that I almost snatched him. I saw how much Michael missed his son and the pain in his eyes and it softened my heart. I was used to the way he treated me, I was accustomed to him being evil and doing evil and crazy things, so much so that I didn't think about the hurt or the pain he was going through not being able to see his son. He asked me if we could discuss visitations and I agreed. Glad to have my son back, I was ready to get on the road and head back to my new place of residence – Baltimore, Maryland.

*****

Mr. Marc-Train dove into our relationship and was moving strong. I was pleased that he loved to love me and wanted things to progress. He wanted to meet my family in NY. It was cold in Maryland, which meant it was freezing in NY. I had no desire to drive to Rochester during the winter season. Nevertheless I was happy he requested to meet my mom and the rest of my family. My pastor wanted to meet him before we left, so we made plans to eat dinner at the church's restaurant called Heaven's Gate Eatery on W. North Avenue in Baltimore. Pastor is very protective of me and is not really interested in Mr. Marc-Train being a part of my life so this meeting is a bit nerve racking for all parties involved.

My pastor wanted to make sure that I had enough money for gas and that my car would run okay. Mr. Marc-Train stood beside me and let him know that I was well taken care of. Mr. Marc-Train respected my pastor and was glad that he was protective of me. He told me it says a lot about me that the pastor was that curious and concerned. He said I was someone worth loving, and highly valued in the eyes of many. I hadn't heard words like that about myself in ages, and this time around they were sincere and beautifully spoken.

Mr. Marc-Train and Zion have formed a bond with each other, and Zion loves hanging out with him. I was still uneasy about another man around Zion, and Mr. Marc-Train understood that. He told to me he wished his son's mom was the same way and didn't bring random guys around his son. He said he wanted to meet Michael when we got to Rochester. I didn't think that was a good idea. I didn't need Michael enraged and violent towards him so I shut that door as soon as it opened.

He explained from the perspective of a father that he would want to know the man that his son was around; to put his mind at ease. He would want to look the man eye to eye so that they both have an understanding and a respect for one another. In other words, he didn't want any problems.

The ride to Rochester from Baltimore was a 6 hour long trip. The entire time Mr. Marc-Train and I talked and talked some more. We gave each other input on our plans for the future, and we both were excited to hear how we saw our future together. My family embraced Mr. Marc-Train as if they had known him for years. He fit in perfectly with us. He wore a broad smile alerting me that he was pleased to meet the family he might one day being a part of. My mother and sisters have a way of making anyone feel like family. He welcomed the invitation and considered himself family from that point on. I wasn't comfortable letting Mr. Marc-Train meet Michael just yet, so I decided to talk with him on my own before dropping off our son.

Michael said that he wanted to talk to me about visitation, moving beyond our tumultuous relationship and raising Zion the best we could despite the distance between us and I felt it was best that we had that conversation in private.

When I got to his place, I refused to go up to his apartment and chose to stand in the doorway at the bottom of the steps instead. He shut the door and insisted that I go upstairs. I told him no and whatever he had to say to me he could say it standing right where we were. He kept pleading with me to go upstairs, and reluctantly I did. He shut his apartment door and we sat down on his couch. I looked around and was amazed that he had left things the same way they were when we lived together. It brought back many memories good and bad. I couldn't help but bring up one of the last times that I was here to Michael. He smirked as he recounted the night I came to his house with our son while he was entertaining a woman. He regretted having my number in his phone on speed dial which resulted in that evening's turn of events. He thought it was funny, but the look on my face showed him I did not.

I reminded him of the time before that when I was pregnant with his son. I took him back to how he dragged me throughout the apartment furious because I had come home unannounced. I knew it had been years since any of this had occurred and maybe I should have forgotten about it but I needed him to tell me if there was someone in the apartment with him that day. I never saw anyone else. I never heard another voice, but I know I saw two shadows on the wall. For years I tried to make myself believe that it was clothes on a hanger or an object's shadow that I had mistaken for another person, but I knew better than that.

Finally, Michael told me the truth. He opened his mouth and for a change he decided to be honest. He explained to me that it was true he felt he wasn't getting enough sexual attention from me back then while I was sick and pregnant. He admitted that there was someone in the apartment on that evening. They were in the midst of watching a porn tape and attempting to perform the acts they were viewing when I came home unexpected. Michael described how he frantically grabbed the girl and ran into the bedroom walk-in closet so that I couldn't see them. He didn't realize that although I was out of direct view of them, I could see their shadows. While I banged on the door and became more agitated with the situation, he had to explain to the female he was with, that I was going to attack her if she didn't hide. He told her that he was sorry for doing this to her, but he couldn't allow me to catch the two of them. He closed the door to the closet and pushed open the drop ceiling. He lifted the naked girl up into the ceiling and pushed the drop ceiling back in place. He then came out to confront me and carried on as if he were there by himself.

I knew I wasn't crazy or seeing things. He did have someone there. He was cheating on me (as he had done many times before). He said he loved me too much for me to have seen what he was doing and that was why he was so angry at me. He told me that if he had opened the door and allowed me into the apartment, his life would have changed forever for the worse. Michael said that if I saw who was there with him he was afraid that I would try to kill the both of them. I asked one last question already knowing the answer – who was with him? Michael held his head down as if he were ashamed. He looked at the floor contemplating whether he should give me this piece of information or not. After taking some moments to gather himself, he looked up at me. He looked me straight in my eyes and told me it was Virginity-girl.

I knew it already, but I needed to hear him say it. I needed to hear it come from him so that I could lay this issue to rest in my heart and my mind. On that day he confirmed so many things about our relationship, the most important being that he was not the one God intended for me to marry. I was not sad, but rather thankful. I was not hurt, I was relieved. I was not angry, I was free.

    As he tried to bring up happy times between us I listened with an attentive ear. The statement I heard Oprah make on her show - "When someone tells you and shows you who they are, believe them," came to mind. That snapped me out of my reminiscent moment. I realized this visit was not a smart move and I needed to get out of his apartment as quickly and safely as possible. Michael wanted to hug me and kiss on me and I wouldn't let him. He asked me was my new man treating me right as if I was in a relationship that was all about sex. He wanted to know if this guy knew how to make me feel good and continued taunting me with his childishness and ignorant statements. My phone kept ringing and I wouldn't answer because I knew it was Mr. Marc-Train on the other end. I pushed Michael off of me and told him there was nothing to talk about. He wanted me to come to the apartment because he thought that he could manipulate me as he had done in the past.

    As I hurried down the steps, he followed to stop me. He grabbed me from behind pinning his body close to mine and told me he loved me in my ear. I wiggled out of his clutch and he asked me to give us another try. I told him we were better off just being Zion's parents. He reached out to grab my breast and came towards me as if I was going to accept his advances. I opened the apartment door told him that I would be sending Zion over later and left. I could feel him staring at me as I got into the car and I pulled off.

    I knew Mr. Marc-Train was going to be upset with me, but I didn't realize how upset he would be. Unfamiliarity with this city and not knowing where I was made for a dangerous mixture and he was its helpless victim. He didn't appreciate me not answering the phone and thought something happened to me. I had never seen him upset, and I felt awful knowing that I was the cause. How would he have felt if something had happened to me while he was up here with me? He told my pastor that he would take care of me. How could explain letting me go to an irrational man's place all alone? I acknowledged my actions as unwise and I hoped he could forgive me.

*****

    Mr. Marc-Train was a good friend to me. He talked to me and we discussed different topics as close friends, not as people that were dating and trying to impress one another. That was my most cherished characteristic of his. He was a man, a father; he was separated from his son just like Michael. It never occurred to me that the things going through Michael's head were some of the same things as a man that would be going through Mr. Marc-Train's head as well.

    He knew I had to see Michael alone, and he was praying the entire time that I didn't fall for him all over again. He was worried that he would lose me if Michael was able to brainwash me into thinking that he had changed. I guess it was a test for us all. It was a test for Michael to see if I was really done with him, it was a test of trust for Mr. Marc-Train, and it was a test of heart for me. I needed to show Mr. Marc-Train that my heart was with him and that is where I wanted it to remain.

It was getting late and we wanted to attend Friday evening church service. My church family was so happy to see me that they requested a sermonic solo. This was my first time singing in front of Mr. Marc-Train and I was nervous. I knew he wasn't happy with me and I could only pray to God that he let it go so that we could move on. I sang my heart out to God wanting to let God know that I appreciated all that He had done for me and especially for sending Mr. Marc-Train my way. After service I proudly introduced him to everyone and as my former pastor's wife shook his hand she said, "Thank you for putting this smile on Lillian's face, she looks like she is glowing with happiness." Oh yes I was. He made me happy and brought joy into my heart.

After saying our farewells we head back to the city. He had planned to stay in a hotel, and I was going to stay with my mom. Although the plan was to stay at my mothers, I found myself in the hotel room with him. I made excuse after excuse, trying to justify it in my head. I began to talk about the service we attended, and in agreement with me he said the service was nice. We discussed the message preached that night. Mr. Marc-Train told me he didn't want to be a hypocrite; one way in church and living something totally different when he leaves. We both talk about how we want to do what is right and must do more to focus on what God has planned for our lives.

He was impressed with my New York church family and how much love and concern they had for me. He said he wasn't surprised that people loved me that way. He knew how he felt about me and hadn't known me as long as they had. He grabbed my hand and pulled me to him telling me how thankful and grateful he was to have met me. He kissed me and told me how refreshing it was to know that I was not a woman that talked church, but that I lived the life of a Christian woman. He told me about the women he had come in contact with that portrayed themselves as saved women, but they weren't. He whispered that he had never met anyone like me and I returned the gesture. He hugged me tightly as though he would never let me go. With every compliment and discussion of gratitude he would kiss me; every kiss becoming longer and more passionate.

I was a Christian woman, and there I was in a hotel room with a man I was physically attracted to. I was a Christian woman, and all I wanted at that moment was for this man to have his way with me. I was a Christian woman, and still I wanted to feel more than a passionate kiss. I wanted to experience what if felt like after the kiss and long after the hug in its entirety. I wanted him to ask me to stay with him, make love to him, enjoying every minute and going beyond where we had gone before. I was the picture of contrasting emotions, the poster-child for divergent activity.

Transition

I was a Christian woman and without delay I wanted him to caress my body, tenderly touching me and feeling every inch of me. I wanted him to look me in my eyes and allow the passion between us to take us where we both wanted to go. I wanted him to gently lay me down on the bed and begin to undress me. I wanted him to show me that he could please me in any way I desired. I wanted him to know that I could please him too. I wanted him to take his time because there is no rush. I wanted the moment to last forever.

I was a Christian woman. *What would either of us gain from these wants? What would we see if we crossed this road together?* He would see in depth what was hiding under the inexpensive clothing I wore. I would see just how muscular he was. He would see that I didn't have a perfect body; I still had the muffin-top I hadn't lost after having my son. I would see his hidden childhood scar and the hair on his chest, arms and legs.

We would have just left from a church service as two young people who loved the Lord, but then would have to say we were fornicators. We would have to say that no matter how spiritually strong we looked, we were weak. We would have crossed the line and gone into territories only married people were supposed to go. We needed to stay on track and stay focused. We needed to concentrate on doing the right things. We needed to remember that I was a Christian woman and he was a Christian man. We needed to repent and ask God to forgive us of our very thoughts and actions.

Transition

We needed to stop trying to fool ourselves and admit we didn't have control over the situation like we say we do. We needed to go home.

    We enjoyed our time in Rochester and now it was time to go. Before we could get on the road, the snow began to fall. Mr. Marc-Train not being from this area was very worried about how thick and hard the snow was coming down. He wanted to get back on the road as quickly as possible. We went to Michael's place to pick up Zion and to prove my love and commitment to Mr. Marc-Train I made sure he got out of the car so that I could introduce the two of them. They both were very cordial with each other and I was glad that was over. On the road Mr. Marc-Train held onto my hand, and as he drove he whispered to me that he wanted to spend the rest of his life with me.

    Is this really real? When am I going to wake up from this romantic dream? This is going fast and there are no brakes to slow this love train down. My mother loved him and didn't have one negative thing to say about him. I loved him and have yet to see a negative thing about him. Michael wasn't happy that I had moved on, but he didn't disrespect Mr. Marc-Train and that said a lot as well. Mr. Marc-Train got the blessing he was looking for from my mother, and now all that was left to do is make it official. I was thankful to God for making my dreams come true. The prayer I made was answered and I was well on my way to becoming Mrs. Marc-Train. This was meant to be and all I could do was pray that God allowed it to be so.

Transition

The last thing I was expecting to have by the end of this year was a man in my corner that I was deeply in love with. It felt so strange having such a physically powerful relationship with someone I had known only for what seemed like just a short time. We had already spent birthdays and holidays together and with each occasion there was a memorable celebration. I was expecting my independent woman phase to be a lot longer than it was.

I learned that there were no rules or time set for love. Falling in love would come when you least expect it. Never in my wildest dreams could I have imagined the man I would be in love with and ready to spend the rest of my life with would meet me on a train from D.C. Never would I have thought that he and I would be such close friends. I didn't love this man for his status or what he could do for me. He didn't love me out of sympathy nor was he looking for a charity project. We loved each other with our hearts, and felt deeply that we are both worthy of all the love and happiness we could receive and give to one another.

I was in transition.

What does that mean to an Oreo cookie? Transition is the process or a period of changing from one state or condition to another. I had unquestionably changed from one geological state and certainly changed from one condition to another. No longer was I worried about Michael, especially since he had met Mr. Marc-Train. I would not fear going to New York anymore because I had made it through the year without any of Michael's threats on my life

Transition

manifesting. New York and all the drama that came with it was finally over, I was now in Maryland. I had transitioned and this was my new state; an Oreo cookie in the state and condition of being loved and being in love.

My heart was open and exposed and full of joy and great expectations but because of our flesh, and lack of self-control I had disappointed and left my true covering. With transition there are usually modifications, changes, and evolutions of sorts, shifting and altering of deep and abysmal places. During this time things may be lost, found, opened, closed, gained, given, taken, made or destroyed. In the midst of my liberating transitioning I had to ask myself, did I walk from under my covering?

CHAPTER 13

DECEPTION

Do I choose church or being with my man? Why can't I have both? If he would come to church with me I could...

As soon as we got back from Rochester Mr. Marc-Train had to go away for work, which meant I wouldn't hear from him for a while. I kept myself occupied by being in church all the time and hanging with my new church family. The pastor's children had become my big brother and sisters. My new big brother nicknamed Mr. Marc-Train 'The Ghost' because no one from the church ever really saw him. I assured them that he existed; he just hadn't made his way to church yet. I in turn nickname my big brother 'Deacon Cash Money' because he always had a wad of cash in his pocket.

Mr. Marc-Train had dealt with my family back home in Rochester, but there was another level of acceptance he would need to go through in Baltimore. My pastor's son - Deacon Cash Money, and his wife Dion humorously ask me questions about him. As my big brother Deacon Cash wanted to interrogate Mr. Marc-Train, but I was not ready for that. He wanted to know what his intentions were regarding me and if Mr. Marc-Train was truly serious. Deacon Cash Money had plenty to say about Baltimore men, and how I had to be careful. He kept reminding me that I didn't want another 'Piano Man' experience to occur, ending very badly.

When I first moved to Baltimore, I enjoyed talking and hanging out with someone I'll call 'Piano Man'. As I would with any guy that took an interest in me, I questioned and sought God to show me if this was a man I could spend the rest of my life with. We talked on the phone often and I even went over to his apartment a few times. His parents were quite hospitable and everything seemed to be going pretty well. I was visiting Piano Man's apartment one day as we sat in his bedroom listening to gospel music on his computer. Suddenly there was a noise that came from the outside hallway and then the apartment door opened. I was startled and Piano Man alarmed as well jumped up to see who was coming into his place. He motioned for me to stay quiet as he left me alone in the bedroom. I was nervous not knowing if someone was attempting to break into his apartment or if it was an old acquaintance that still had a key to his place. When I heard him speak calmly to his dad I was relieved that it wasn't an unwanted intruder like a burglar or an ex-girlfriend.

I liked Piano Man's dad a lot. He always looks out for me and my son, walking us to our car after evening service was over, making sure we were safe. When I arrived to Baltimore, he inquired of my parents often and would make small talk with me so that I didn't feel left out as a new member in a new city and a new church. He was a nice man to be around.

I got up to go out and say hello to him, but then I paused. How would this look? I am a saved, single woman, alone with a man at his house, and I am coming out of his bedroom. If I had come out with Piano Man to see who was coming into the apartment that would have been better, but I had been in his bedroom by myself for a while and all of a sudden it felt as though I was hiding. I thought I'd better stay put until he leaves.

> Note to self: The next time someone invites you over to their apartment, stay in a common area just in case a burglar, an ex-girlfriend, or their father stops by for a random visit.

The longer I think about it and stay in the room, the worse the situation is going to look. At last Piano Man says Sis. Lillie is here and on that queue I went out and greeted his dad. I felt ashamed even though we weren't doing anything wrong. I didn't want his father to look at me differently because of what it looked like I may have been doing with his son. On that day I learned I had to be wiser with my decision making. The Bible tells us to stay away from the very appearance of evil, and I had no business alone with him in his apartment especially in his bedroom. I was not that kind of girl and I hoped his father didn't think that I was because of this.

Weeks passed, and we were in revival at our church. I began to fast and pray as instructed by our pastor. I asked the Lord to speak to my heart, and He let me know that He brought me down to Baltimore for a purpose. I wasn't entirely sure what the purpose was, but I felt God's displeasure with my attempt to carry out His plan for my life without Him. I was too eager to be in a relationship. Instead of waiting on God, I clung to the first church guy that showed interest. Instead of concentrating on God and putting him first, I allowed my time to be occupied by Piano Man. God wasn't pleased. I decided to cut back on the communication between us.

Piano Man wasn't ready to break things off. He automatically assumed I was interested in someone else. It's true. I was interested in someone else, and that someone else was God. He had taken care of me this far, and I didn't want to let Him down. No matter how much I didn't want to, I had to end things with Piano Man. I didn't want him to feel that I was leading him on knowing that our relationship was not God's plan for me.

It wasn't until he proposed to me one Sunday after service while walking me to my car that I knew it was too late. Things had gone too far. I turned him down and said no. I knew he would probably hate me for the rest of his life, and I didn't blame him. I was to blame for thinking God needed my help to join me with my lifetime mate. Nevertheless, I didn't expect all the negativity, lies and silent treatment that came from this mistake. There were no deep secrets, no intimacy, no sex, nor inappropriate behaviors between me and him. Just a relationship that I decided wasn't for me.

Surprisingly, many good friendships were lost from our breakup. *Lesson learned. Lord you lead and I will follow.* Deacon Cash Money wanted to make sure those events stayed fresh in my mind since he thought I was avoiding introducing Mr. Marc-Train to my church family. He had no clue how far things had gone between Mr. Marc-Train and I, and I wanted to keep it that way.

Since moving to Baltimore everyone had been kind. I believed people were doing things for me and with me because they genuinely cared for me as a single mom new to the area and to the church. Knowing that I had no family around and I was starting from scratch, my church family embraced my son and I, showing us we were not alone. Everyone receiving us as family was, I considered, the Godly thing to do. It hurt when it became clear that some didn't have my best interest in mind.

I realized that everyone doesn't accept you for who you are and sometimes people do things, even kind things with ulterior motives. Some people showed me I wasn't as welcome as I thought I was. I began noticing that some things were being done to me and for me to influence me to be against others. If I didn't follow or accept the urging or guidance certain members sensed I should, I was shunned. Not being from here, and not knowing who to trust and who not to trust became discouraging and disheartening. I had been through a lot in church but this was a new and intimidating experience for me. I knew I needed help navigating these unchartered waters.

Deception

Times like these would merit a call to my mom. This time I didn't want to call her and tell her all the drama that was going on because I didn't want to worry her. Dion and my mother were very close, and because my mother trusted her, I believed that I could too. Every now and then I picked Dion up for church. Zion loved when I did because she treated him extra special. She and I always had the best conversations when we rode together. Simple things like us both being from the state of NY and our birthdays being in the same month, we used as things to link us together.

I didn't know until I moved to Baltimore that Dion and my mother were as close as they were. My mom would always talk about the pastor and his family, but they were of no interest to me back then. Dion had Lupus like mom's sister - my Aunt Lela, and mom has a special love for Dion like a daughter. When my birthday came she bought Dion and me gifts – actually, she purchased us the same thing! Dion got a collectors baby doll just like me. We would laugh about it because I would always say she was stealing my mom. She would correct me and say she was gaining a wonderful sister.

I guess that was why she and I were able to trust one another and get along so well. I couldn't understand why she would call and write to my mother all the way up to Rochester when she had her own mother, mother-in-law and other church woman to connect with. She explained that there was something about my mom that joined them together and mom would say the same thing about her. For whatever reason, there were things she was more comfortable sharing with mom more than with anyone else. All I could do was be proud that my mom had been there for her. I couldn't imagine being our age and having the condition she had. Dion made me appreciate my life no matter how screwed up things had become. She really blew my mind when she said hearing what I have been through made her appreciate her situation in life as well. We both were thankful that we had my Mommy to support us through it all.

Dion was easy to talk to; very laid back, she always had something nice to say. I felt comfortable talking to her about my transition to Baltimore and the difficulties that came along with it. It wasn't until I began telling her that sometimes I felt displaced or as though no one understood me that we really began to bond. She told me how she felt the same way sometimes. We agreed that many times people would mistake things that you say as being rude because of cultural differences. Being from New York, we had a different way of communicating. Sentences didn't end with the word "hear?" like they did (in Baltimore). We didn't call everyone Sweetie or Babe either. Just because we didn't have certain mannerisms didn't mean we were rude. Where we came from telling it like it is didn't necessarily mean that we were telling you off. Telling it like it is meant just that; describing things from our perspective. We laughed about how 'Baltimorians' say "zinc" instead of sink, "hot dug" instead of hot dog; "Muh-va" instead of mother. We would go down the list of so many different sayings and words.

*****

Deception

Being the single parent at the church felt awkward. Plans to do fun things were made but I got left out because I had a child. With Dion being sick all the time she felt the same way, as if the hand that life dealt us caused us to be shorted when it came to having fun. Life in Baltimore was different in countless ways. I shopped at Kmart instead of department stores in the malls. My clothes weren't name brand, and buying Coach Purses were out of the question. My finances were vastly different than before. I had to live in a different salary bracket.

I was a newly independent woman so asking for help was not on my list of options. It was hard for me going from one extreme of being able to get whatever I wanted with my paycheck to now having to decide what I can do without until my next check. It was a big culture change and also very humbling. I saw the women and young ladies at church and work that seemed to be able to shop at will with no hesitation. My wardrobe was nowhere near as fancy as theirs. I decided to spend on my son and lack what I wanted to be able to take care of my responsibilities. This was the table I made for myself. Instead of complaining, I accepted it with God's help.

Dion reminisced about her college days when she was young and vibrant. It hadn't been long before when she had flowing, beautiful hair and was popular in her sorority. A full shaped woman back then she was usually dressed to the 9's. Now, instead of spending time combing her long, beautiful hair, she spent it watching her hair fall out, another terrible effect of Lupus. When I picked her up from the salon all she could do was say how much she didn't like the style because it showed just how thin and short her hair had become. Instead of her shopping for the latest fashions, she was a young woman shopping for wigs.

Her weight diminished before her eyes. No matter how hard she tried she couldn't gain weight. And while she would swell up at times, she didn't feel as sexy as she once felt. She would often tell me how much she appreciated me picking her up and taking her to the places she needed to go when she couldn't take herself. She, like me, didn't care to depend on others. She was used to doing things on her own. Like me, she was now in a position where she needed grace, mercy and the favor of God. We had more in common than we thought. I could see that it was hard living with Lupus. I didn't want her to feel like I was doing her a favor by helping out a little here and there. I was looking out for her like I know she would have looked out for me had I been in her shoes.

We were both recent college graduates with a promising life ahead of us. Life happened and things turned so quickly we both had to ask ourselves how in the world we got where we were. She had just married Deacon Cash Money and they should have been making baby plans and thinking about enlarging their family, but instead they spent countless nights in the hospital because she was sick. I had the prettiest home in Rochester. Everyone loved to come over to and hang out at my house. Now I was staying in a room in someone else's home. I had a closet full of clothes, furniture, and a family all around.

Now my wardrobe consisted of what I was able to fit in the trunk of my car.

No, our situations were not exactly the same. But she and I both agreed that God had His own special way of humbling His children. We were both so appreciative of each other. It was priceless having someone to talk to that could relate.

As I helped her into her house, watching her cat watch me as we take it slow going up the steps, I began to thank God for her life. Even in her most painful moments, she was there to lend an ear to my struggles. I was not known for making new friends, but I was glad she extended herself as a friend and sister to me genuinely. She didn't attempt to seek out my personal business, but shared hers first. We would usually end our chats by testifying that we didn't know how good we had it until we heard someone else's story.

To hear her say that I had encouraged her and had made her thankful for my life was truly amazing because when I leave her presence I feel the same way about her. I couldn't wait to get to Mr. Marc-Train to let him know just how much I appreciated him and was thankful for him being a part of my life too.

Mr. Marc-Train and I typically talked to each other all day long while at work, but lately I haven't been hearing from him like normal. He doesn't say much about his job, but I know it is in D.C. and he keeps it very confidential. I know he said he had to go away for work and I wouldn't hear from him for some time, but now I was getting worried. Finally he called me and told me that he had been out sick because the sudden snow and cold weather caused him drastic pain in his back. He told me his mom had been taking care of him and that he was going to be alright.

More bad news came when he told me that he still had to travel for his job. I began to wonder what his trips were all about. He finally came to see me. I was giddy with excitement. It had been a while since we saw each other. We went down in the basement to be alone for a while and watch television. As the television glared in the background he sat me on his lap and said there was something he had to tell me. I was a little nervous because he seemed serious. I didn't know what he was getting ready to say to me, and I didn't want to guess either so I told him to just say it. He told me he worked for the government. The reason why he would go in and out of town all the time is because he does covert work. *An agent. Really? I know I look young and all, but I was not born yesterday.* He told me that he needed to tell me because things were really getting serious between us and he wanted to know if I would be able to handle being the wife of a man that had to live a double life.

Everything this man has said to me up to this point was true. He had never given me a reason to believe he was a liar, but because of my past, it was difficult for me to fully trust and believe in men. He had shown up to my house without his vehicle so I needed to drive him to Penn Station. He begged me to be patient with him because he wanted our relationship to work. I expressed my concern of not knowing where he would be and when I would see him again. He promised me that whatever he could tell me he would.

    With one hand holding mine and his other hand on my face, he looked me in my eyes and told me he loved me and he wanted to spend the rest of his life with me. He asked me again if this was something I could handle. I told him I loved him too, and I would be there when he returned. Surprisingly I was glad when he got out of the car, walked into the train station and I returned home.

    I couldn't believe the man of my dreams that God sent to me was an agent for the government. How? And furthermore, why in the world would God do that? He was going to be gone for a few days, and I began thinking this may be just what we need to distance us so that we didn't make the mistake we had made before. Maybe this was God's way of keeping us on track so we wouldn't be tempted to fornicate.

    Nevertheless, I found myself looking down at my cell phone and the house phone just waiting for him to call. When he was gone I prayed and read my Bible, all the while getting closer to God so that He would bless me. Not talking to him all the time is tough, but because I truly care for him, I wait.

    I was overjoyed when he called and said he was home. We made plans to see each other and I could hardly wait. A lot of time had passed yet he and I were growing strong. I was searching diligently for a home of my own so I could give Tina and Chon their space back. They had been gracious to me and my son for longer than

I had planned. For some reason, Mr. Marc-Train's behavior seemed to be changing. I didn't understand why nor could I explain it, but I sensed there was a change. When he came around he was constantly hugging and kissing me as if it was his last time being with me.

Afraid that he was going to leave and not come back I began to inquire what was wrong. He told me his job was very dangerous. He wanted to give me his lieutenant's contact information. He sat me down and explained that if anything ever happened to him Zion and I would be set for the rest of our lives. He named me as a beneficiary, and his job would provide every need I would ever have.

I looked at him in awe and could not believe that he was telling me this. I needed for him to understand that I didn't want to spend the rest of my life without him. Money meant nothing if he was not here with me. I refused to believe that God would send my soul mate for us to remain together for only a short period of time – we hadn't even married yet and he was already preparing for his demise. This was very disheartening and hard to accept, but the fact that he was being responsible enough to prepare for me and my son's future made me love him even the more.

He always talked about his mom. He loved her for being supportive of him. He said he told his mom that he was afraid his job would run me away from him, but he was glad when I told him that I was willing to be understanding. I couldn't wait to meet his mom as she is an important pillar in his life. I hoped she would like me and accept me as my family accepted him. Mr. Marc-Train was always working so it was challenging to arrange a meeting with his mom.

I felt it was important to meet her. That would let me know he was serious. I didn't pressure him about it. I decided to wait. One thing I learned was to never force anything to go where it may not need to go. I was happy and I wanted to stay that way. *When the time comes I will meet her.*

Mr. Marc-Train always had surprises and tricks up his sleeves. He called me and told me that I needed to find a babysitter because in a few days he wanted to take me out. He said that this was a very important date and I could not stand him up no matter what. I called Tina and told her so that we could make child care arrangements for Zion. We were both excited because we knew what was going to happen. This was the proposal date. I was overjoyed. This would seal the deal. *But wait, I haven't met his mom yet.* Tina said maybe his mother would be there, which made me wonder if he had contacted my mom for her to be there too. We were thinking too much and going way too deep. We had overwhelmed ourselves and the date hadn't even happened yet.

The morning of our date I was super excited to get to work. I wanted the day to hurry and go by so that I could get to my date. I made sure I looked good and arranged for my ride to the train station. Mr. Marc-Train arranged for me to catch the train to D.C. and meet him there. When I got to work I realized I had left my cell phone at home so there would be no way for him to reach me when I left my job. After work I got a ride to Penn Station and caught the train to D.C. as planned. I was able to ask a passerby if I could use their phone and I called him to tell him I was waiting in the station. I could tell I had ruined his plans, but he was still as sweet as could be to me on the line. He told me someone would be in to pick me up. Shortly after our phone call I saw a woman looking around and when our eyes met I knew it was her. It was his mom. She gave me a big hug and told me Mr. Marc-Train was outside waiting for us.

I was so happy to see him and finally meet his mom. Such a wonderful and inspiring woman she was. This was a wonderful surprise, but I was looking forward to the ring. I didn't eat all day long with great expectations of this evening being one I would never forget. I began listening to them talking and she kept saying we're going to be late. He was doing all he could to get through the D.C. traffic and I was extremely apologetic. It was my fault we were behind because I had left my cell phone at home. I was praying under my breath Lord please don't let me ruin my engagement date night.

Finally we arrived – but I had no clue where it was that we had arrived to. We got out of the car and he said to me, "Baby we have to walk and we have to walk fast." His mother asked me was I excited and I said, "Yes, but I wish I knew where we were going and what we were doing." She smiled as Mr. Marc-Train told me I would see momentarily and we continued walking. There were lots of cars and I started to see a lot of people. I began to wonder where exactly he was planning on proposing to me. As we walked up the stairs to a huge building I heard people saying the show was getting ready to start. *A show? Really?!*

My surprise turned out to be the HOPEVILLE TOUR with Kirk Franklin, Donnie McClurkin and Yolanda Adams. It was a great surprise. It would have been an even greater surprise if I hadn't worked myself up thinking he was going to propose to me. I was a bit disappointed, but I loved the concert. I enjoyed sitting between him and his mother as if we were a happy little family. That was, after all, what I wanted and I prayed it was what God had in store for me.

Welp, since I am not getting engaged tonight, I sure hope we stop and get something to eat after this concert. I haven't eaten all day and now that the excitement had ebbed, my stomach is singing louder than Donnie McClurkin.

The first time that you meet the mother of the person you love, you don't expect it to be at a gospel concert, but I was so glad he got us together. She was just as short as I was and looked far too young to be his mom. When I professed my undying love for her son she was moved with happiness, and I was glad she had given me her stamp of approval. There was nothing left for us to do but get married now. *So where is my ring?* I settled for a tasty meal after the concert and hoped for the ring at another time.

I was in no rush, but I silently wished the waiting didn't take so long. Day after day, week after week I was waiting for him to pop the question. In every surprise bouquet of flowers he sent to my job, every restaurant we went out to, and every encounter we had I was waiting. I made sure my nails were done and my hands were fully moisturized in preparation of what was to come. I had been proposed to a few times already, but I knew that when this one happened it would be the best proposal ever.

Lately Mr. Marc-Train had been acting as if there was something he had to say to me, but it was not a proposal. Every time we got together he said we needed to talk, but we never got around to what he wanted to discuss. I didn't know what it was that he wanted to tell me, but it seemed to be bothering him and he needed to get it off of his chest.

I understood his situation. When you have a child, dealing with the other parent can be hard and I was willing to deal with anything he might be going through personally. I could imagine his son's mother being upset that he spent so much of his time with me and my son when he could be spending it alone with his own son.

I told him about the church having a big event down at the restaurant and that the pastor had asked me to come and help out. I typically kept certain days open for Mr. Marc-Train and me to have quality time together and for me to be with my son. It was getting more and more difficult to do this while living in someone else's home, but I didn't feel the need to find an apartment now especially since I would be getting married soon. If I moved too fast we would have to get another place together, and there would be the lease and moving all over again. I decided to wait for my proposal.

Deception

Mr. Marc-Train came by to see me anyway and I saw the look on his face again. As he came up to my room he and Zion were playing, but he seemed preoccupied. I sent Zion out of the room for a moment and asked him what is going on. He looked at me and again said I want to talk to you about something. Before he could start talking Zion ran back in the room between us and we continued playing and enjoying one another as if nothing was wrong until Zion fell off to sleep.

Mr. Marc-Train was glad that I was going down to help the church. He looked at me and smiled as he reached in to me holding my face kissing me. He told me how much he loved me and how much of a good woman I was. I told him I couldn't wait to become Mrs. Marc-Train so that he could tell me these things over and over again. Since Zion was sleeping we laid next to each other holding each other feeling the passion between us. Time was moving so quickly, and we both knew the emotions in the room were rising by the second. I had to get ready to go, but he wanted to talk. I wanted to show him that I was supportive of him and was willing to sit and talk, but instead he told me that we could talk about it later.

I walked him down the stairs and we stood in the living room hugging and kissing. I didn't want him to leave and I wanted to stay too, but I knew I had some place to be. I could tell he wanted to stay by the way he couldn't take his hands off of me. As I was enjoying every minute, there was a knock at the door. The doorway had a long thin window off to the side with sheer white curtains in them. I saw the silhouette of a female and assumed it was one of Tina's friends or the next door neighbor.

I was surprised when Mr. Marc-Train let me go as he pulled the curtain back, looked out the window and said to me hold on a minute. I was unsure what was happening as he opened the door. He reached for the screen door I heard him say "What's up slim?" *Slim? Who is Slim and why is she on my best friend's porch?* He shut the door behind him and I went to the door to open it. Something told me to leave the door shut and I did. I stood there and waited. I heard her ask him who he was with. He told her I was a friend. My heart dropped as I could clearly see where this was going.

Okay so obviously this is his baby momma who has tracked him down and wants to start some drama because he doesn't want anything else to do with her. He hasn't been with her and now she is mad because he has moved on. Right? They begin a deep dialog with one another. Angrily she asked him if I knew who she was and he told her that I didn't know anything and she needed to leave. She then asks him if he loved me and he told her, "Yes, yes I love her with all of my heart." He went on to tell her again that I was unaware of what was going on and she needed to leave so that he could talk to me. She asked why she needed to leave and stood her ground saying she wasn't going anywhere. Furious she wondered what made him think he could just come over here and be with another woman and demanded to know how long he had been involved with me. He confessed to her that he had been in love with me for a while; that we had met months ago, and explained that he hadn't had a chance to talk to me about her. She asked if he was going to tell me, and he sharply told her not to worry about what he was going to tell me. I became alarmed when I heard him tell her that the news was going to be hard for me because I didn't know anything about it. She told him she didn't care how I was going to take any news and insisted he make his choice, whether it would be her or me.

My heart was beating fast as I heard him say, "I choose her. I am in love with this girl and there is nothing you can do about it. You need to leave because I don't want to hurt her." My heart almost felt like it was going to stop when I heard her reply, "Why are you so concerned about hurting her? I am your wife. Does she know that?"

Did I just hear this woman say that she was my future husband's wife? He doesn't have a wife – he has a baby mama! What is really going on? My heart was beating through my chest. Before I knew it I had opened the door. He looked at me and said, "Hey baby." I asked him if there was something that he wanted to tell me and she interrupted saying, "Tell her." As I laughed, she said, "Tell your little friend there ain't nothing funny." Keeping calm, I responded that clearly there was nothing funny, and I wanted to know what was going on. Mr. Marc-Train replied, "Don't worry Baby, I will tell you everything," to which I reply, "It sure doesn't look like you have been telling me everything so please will you enlighten me?" He replied, "Baby please, give me a chance to explain," he pleaded. His wife interrupts, "No you are leaving with me, so let's go!" He tells her, "I am not going anywhere with you. You need to leave." I'd had my fill with the entire scene and said, "Why don't the both of you leave and never come back."

I slammed the door in disbelief and couldn't move as I listened to them continue to go back and forth on the steps; him telling her to leave and her wanting him to leave with her. Every time she tells him to come home with her, he tells her he will not leave and that he loves me too much to hurt me. *Doesn't he know that I am already hurt?* This is crushing me piece by piece this Oreo cookie had been crushed to crumbs like grains of sand. Like a shattered piece of glass I was broken with the guarantee of never being the same again.

Mr. Marc-Train told this woman once again that he was not going to leave with her and that he wanted to spend the rest of his life with me. He told her how much he loved me and that he was not leaving until he talked to me and made sure I was alright. He told her one final time to leave and he would talk with her later. He wasn't going to leave, and she wasn't willing to leave without him, but she did. I opened the door and stared at him. With his head held down in shame he stood there looking like the liar that he was. I asked him who it was that had knocked on my door, as if I didn't know. He told me she was his ex.

I couldn't believe that he was willing to keep lying to me after knowing full well I knew who she was. I asked him again and begged him please not to lie to me and he disgracefully admitted that the

Deception

woman was his wife. Not his ex-girlfriend, not a current girlfriend, not a scorned baby mama, but his wife.

Thoughts of the first time we were together affectionately and passionately - albeit improper and wrong, came to my mind. I saw us together romantically loving one another and feeling guilty and ashamed because I knew it was fornication, crying out to God in repentance for forgiveness. All the while it wasn't fornication but adultery I was unknowingly committing. Gasping for breath I recalled opening up to Mr. Marc-Train during one of our long conversations, explaining to him that I could never have respect for my father's wife because any woman that would lay with a man that is married deserved no respect because she clearly doesn't respect herself. Well, well, well. Look at me. Here I am a part of an adulterous relationship. How could he do this to me? How could he cause me to be qualified for that category?

If I had known he was married I wouldn't have opened my mouth to have any type of conversation with him. If I had known he had a wife as soon as he attempted to pursue a relationship with me this Oreo cookie would have read him like only my Black side can. He would have been put directly on notice that I was the kind of Black woman that had no problem informing his wife and blowing his cover.

I had no tolerance for a man that felt it was okay to be unfaithful to his wife. I had taken a glance at her, and I wondered if she was pregnant. She didn't look pregnant, but there was just a vibe

I felt. I asked him if she was and he said no, and I was relieved. I desired to be his wife and to have a baby with him prior to all this. If she were pregnant *and* married to him that would have hurt me even more.

I gathered my belongings and got my son together to go down to the eatery – *I must get out of the house and away from him as quickly as I could.* I was numb and could not collect my thoughts. He grabbed me and hugged me, holding my face continuing to tell me that he loved me as I pushed him away loathing his presence and his touch. I wanted to be awakened from this dream-turned-nightmare. Furious, full of anger and hurt I was speechless. It was sickening me to my stomach to hear him call me Baby and say "Let me explain," It ripped my heart apart every time he said "Baby I love you, I am sorry." I felt myself becoming Oreo cookie crumbs falling to the floor every time he said, "I didn't mean to hurt you," But you did was all I could think… You did.

Why would he do something so cruel and life changing to a woman who has done nothing but befriend him, fall in love with him, and want to spend the rest of my life with him? As he stood there and tried to explain himself everything got fuzzy and I couldn't hear what he was saying. My vision had become blurry, and as I walked I felt like I was floating from place to place as though I was in a Spike Lee movie. I had nothing to say. I knew I needed to call this relationship to an end immediately. There was nothing that he could say to correct what he had done. The love that had developed and had grown into

Deception

something deep and strong had been demolished into irreparable fragments. All because he lied.

I got into my car to drive down to the eatery feeling dirty and rancid inside. So gullible and naïve I believed every word this man said to me. I believed in the fairytale he created with me. All my hopes and dreams for our future all came to an abrupt and unexpected end. Ashamed and fearful, knowing God is displeased with me I panic clueless as to what I should do because this couldn't possibly be what God had planned for my life. This couldn't be what God had for my future. Suddenly my ears were unplugged and I heard the *Fred Hammond Pages of Life I & II* tape playing in my radio. I gasped for air through each word as I tried to sing the song, *"Falling apart and tearing at the seams..."* My throat was so tight I felt like I couldn't get the words out, *"Tribulation lends a hand and squeezes all your hopes and dreams..."* I felt like I couldn't breathe. I wanted to give up, but started singing even louder, *"You say you retreat, you say you just can't win. Before you let your circumstance, tell you how the story ends..."*

How in the world could you say all things are working for me right now Fred? That was my question to my radio. I know God's ways are so beyond me, but this is worse than anything I could ever have imagined. I have never been this low. And the tape continued to play as if Fred was speaking to me saying *"I know you say you've got it bad right now, Let me say I know that feeling well. To make good plans for life and then watch them take a downward spin..."*

Deception

I tried my hardest to stop them, but the tears began to fall. I needed God to speak immediately end the pain I was drowning in. Just when I thought I had felt every hurt that any man could possibly put me through, here I was going through something new. I had been deceived. Deception is cruel and hurtful. I had been deceived into engaging in an unacceptable relationship that God Himself said He would judge. I must now ask for forgiveness and repentance for the wrong I had unknowingly committed. Tricked and scammed by a fraud, it was crushing to comprehend what we had was bogus and insincere. Dishonesty is a destroyer of relationships. Disappointed that my covering was a counterfeit, I mourned.

I rolled my window down to get some fresh air and to dry the tears that were falling from my eyes. As I drove down North Avenue I didn't care who was looking at me. I just kept yelling out the words to the song, *"Many days and nights I cried because I felt let down…"*

Today of all days was the biggest let down ever. *"But I won't always receive good but a praise in my heart will remain…"* I wanted to believe that I would be strong and that I could be strong. *"So with tears in your eyes know sometimes it might get rough…"* I couldn't sing any more so all that came out were screams and yells from my damaged heart; the heart devastated by an artificial and fictitious covering.

CHAPTER 14

FORGIVENESS

The only way I will ever get married or believe that a man is my husband will be for God himself to come down and tell me he is the one. No more believing in lies, no more assisting God as if He really needed my help. I was done and finished. I was beyond saying it. I was doing it. The pain I was in was palpable. I couldn't believe how much it was affecting my life. I didn't have anyone to talk to about this because the man I confided in and told my deepest secrets to was the one who hurt me. I refused all his calls. I ended any type of communication with him. I needed him to know and understand that Lillian Mary Nowlin was not raised to behave and engage in the foolishness he tricked me into.

Sunday finally came. I made it to church and once again I cried out on the altar. There I was in my choir robe, looking to heaven, lifeless and undeserving of the robe I was wearing. I felt unworthy to be a part of the church. I felt dirty. Putting my head down in shame, I couldn't close my eyes. They were fixated on my robe. *Did anyone know what I had done? Could they see through my robe, past my layers to the heart of a woman who had committed a*

Forgiveness

horrible sin against the God she said she loved? I was surrounded by a church full of righteous people dressed in their Sunday best; hats, suits, shiny shoes, people who had been saved much longer than me. People who would never fall the way I had fallen. There I was broken in pieces wearing a robe meant for saints. Surely they were stronger than me. Surely I was the only one on the altar who had been tricked into adultery. Surely they could see that I was guilty.

    I let God down again and for that I was ashamed. I told God that I belonged to Him and my desire was for Him to use me as He pleased. When I gave my life to the Lord I said the last thing I wanted to be was a hypocrite. If I wasn't going to be real for Him then there was no need for me to be in relationship with Him. The truth was I had cheated on God. Then I wondered why the very ones I cheated on Him with cheated on me. Despite my guilt I wanted to be forgiven. I wanted God's hand, His presence to heal my broken heart on that altar.

Precious Lord, take my hand
Lead me on, Let me stand
I am tired, I am weak I am worn
Through the storm, through the night
Lead me on to the light
Take my hand precious Lord, lead me home.

When my way grows drear precious Lord linger near
When my life is almost gone
Hear my cry, Hear my call
Hold my hand lest I fall
Take my hand precious Lord, lead me home.
When the darkness appears and the night draws near

Forgiveness

And the day is past and gone
At the river I stand
Guide my feet,
Hold my hand
Take my hand precious Lord, lead me home.

Forgiveness. That was what I needed from the Lord. I needed Him to forgive me for the route I had taken to the happiness I desired. It was easy for me to ask for forgiveness and expect it, but would I be able to forgive? Forgiveness. This is the act of pardoning someone for the mistake or wrongdoing committed against us. God does it for us all the time and here I am once again requesting a pardon, but the larger question that loomed over my head was could I give the same pardon I was requesting? Would I ever be able to forgive the past hurts of my life? I realized my life couldn't move forward until I did just that. Not only did I need to forgive recent hurt but all of the offences I had suffered up to this point in my life.

First things first. I needed God to know I was seeking His forgiveness. I had to get myself right with God. As I took one step at a time, by faith, I believed I would be able to move on from this. He had done it before and I believed God would help me again. I know the Lord will take my hand and lead me home. He will lead me into His presence where I will find peace and joy, and the love I long for. The more I seek God for His forgiveness He continues to put in my mind and in my heart the question: Will you forgive?

I opened my computer at work and noticed an email message. I didn't want to talk to Mr. Marc-Train, not even electronically. He

Forgiveness

didn't deserve any of my precious time. To me he no longer existed. He was simply a moment in time in my life that I must move on from. Yet I couldn't shake the strong urge God placed on my heart; the urge to forgive. *I can hardly forgive myself. How could I possibly forgive anyone else?* Every time I went to church and kneeled at the altar I was repentant. I asked God, please help me to let go of the anger and the hurt that I felt. I didn't know how I would or could ever forgive a man for doing something like this to me.

Every day I woke up and went to work I would think of what I had just been through. I drove home wondering if his wife would appear out of nowhere again. *How did she know about me, but I didn't know about her? How did she know where I lived?* This woman could be crazy for all I knew. I didn't know her name, and I didn't know where she lived. I didn't know anything about her but somehow she was able to find out about me. I wondered if she knew; if she believed that I really had no idea she existed. I wondered if she knew that if I had known about her, there would never have been a relationship between me and Mr. Marc-Train in the first place. I wondered if she would ever know how sorry I was and how much I regretted my part in his infidelity.

I needed answers, but didn't know how I would get them without communicating with Mr. Marc-Train. I went to work unable to concentrate with this on my mind. I found myself sitting at my desk teary eyed. As the days passed and things settled down, I realized just how much I loved him. I see his emails, hear his

Forgiveness

voicemails, read his instant messages, and I hurt. I hurt badly and I don't know how to move past this without understanding why this had to be. I needed to get away from all of this. I wanted to be with my mother –the only one that seemed to be able to help me comprehend what I had just experienced.

I was reluctant to tell her because I knew how sensitive the topic of a cheating husband was to her, but I needed to be around her. My mother hadn't been feeling well and I wanted to see her badly, but I didn't want her to see me hurting. I decided to go home to Rochester anyway check on my mom's health and to get things off my mind for a while.

While in Rochester my work cell phone rang and I answered. It was him. There was something about his soft and calming voice that made me stop in my tracks. I froze unable to speak or do anything. I heard him say, "I'm sorry. Baby please. Talk to me." I acknowledged that I heard him and he asked me could he come over so we could talk. I told him that I was in Rochester, and he instantly became upset. With a startled voice he asked me if I had moved back to Rochester because of what happened between us. I explained that my mom wasn't well and I needed to get away from everything. He asked me to please come home so that we could get together and talk. I did want the answers and he owed that to me, so I agreed to meet with him when I returned to Baltimore.

It had been a while since I talked to Mr. Marc-Train. Hearing his voice and listening to the concern he had for me made me realize

Forgiveness

the reason I was still hurting. It was simple really. I was still in love with him. I knew he was unavailable. I knew he was a liar. I knew he hurt me badly. And I still loved him. I was angry with myself, but I had to be honest and admit that the feelings were still there. No matter how bruised it was my heart was still connected to him.

*****

Mr. Marc-Train and I met. He sat me down and began pouring out his deepest, darkest secrets to me. I was not in the mood for foolishness. I wondered if I should believe anything that came out of his mouth. I looked into his eyes as he began to tell me about the woman who came to my home. He told me how he met her. Although they were in the church, they started a sexual relationship. He said he fell in love with her, and thought she loved him too. He found out later that she was dating someone else as well.

With disappointment shrouding him, he continued telling me that he stayed with her despite her actions. He said he still loved her and wanted to be with her. Everyone told him that she wasn't the one for him and that he should move on. As soon as he accepted everyone's advice and decided to break things off with her, she told him she was pregnant with his baby.

I was shocked at what he shared. If his story was true, it could have been a daytime Soap Opera. He told me that because he was in the church and determined to live a godly life, he proposed to her. He wanted to get married to do right by her and the baby. He said that his spiritual advisors, family and friends told him not to marry her just because she was pregnant, but he felt it was his duty and responsibility to do so. A few weeks into the marriage he came home and found an open condom wrapper in his bedroom and the toilet seat left up in the bathroom and he knew he hadn't left it that way.

With this evidence he became very suspicious. He was determined to get the truth. His wife of just a few weeks told him that she was still in love with her ex and had not ended her relationship with him. To make matters worse, she didn't know who the father of the baby was. As I sat across from him I saw the hurt on his face. I felt compassion for him as he told me how he wished he had listened to everyone that told him not to marry her.

Mr. Marc-Train said he felt he was doing the right thing by marrying her. He knew he should not have had sex with her. He shouldn't have gotten her pregnant before he they were married. A few months into the marriage and after finding out she was cheating, his wife had a miscarriage. The one and only reason that he married her was no longer there. She didn't want to be with Mr. Marc-Train and was not willing to end the relationship with her ex. Instead, she would force Mr. Marc-Train to stay with her so she could reap the benefits of being his wife.

He said her plan was to stay married to him and have him accept her unfaithfulness, but he was not willing to stay in the relationship another minute. As I took this all in, he told me that he decided his marriage was never real and they separated. He attempted to get the marriage annulled, to end the marriage as quickly as possible, but in the state of Maryland you must be separated for a year before there can be a divorce with no option for an annulment.

Going through the hurt and the pain of his failed marriage he attempted to go on with his life. He boarded the train after work leaving D.C. to come to Baltimore, when he noticed a woman with her little son. He was immediately attracted to her, but knew the situation that he was in. He gave her his number, but waited months before returning her call because he knew he had to handle business before engaging in a new relationship.

After falling quickly in love with emotions and feelings flowing so freely, he became afraid to tell me what he was going through because he didn't want to lose me. He knew he was wrong for not telling me, but he thought he would have been able to make things right before I would find out.

His family, friends and church support system did all they could to encourage him not to marry her because there was way too much drama in the relationship long before she became pregnant, but he would not listen to them. Embarrassed he tried all he could to make things work with her, but it was never going to work. She never really loved him. He regretted not paying attention to the arguments, unfaithfulness and all the other signs. As I listened to him I realized he had an, 'I can change you' mentality, and was determined to make a better person out of her by making her his wife.

So often many of us get involved with someone we know is toxic. Everything about the person tells you to run far, far away, but

Forgiveness

instead you stay. We accept their horrible behavior, hurtful mistreatment and abuse with hope and belief that one day the love you have shown will cause them to change for the better. There is some level of attraction present and so quickly you fall victim to a heartless evil person that is the total opposite of what you desired them to be. The truth of the matter is if God didn't ordain the relationship, nothing good will ever come from it. If the person that needs to change doesn't realize or agree to a change, nothing you do will change them either.

He told me how his wife's lover, who happened to be a police officer, resided in the same neighborhood as me and saw us together one day. He looked up the residence information finding out that the house was in the name of a male whom I must be married to or dating. She plotted to come over to the house to confront me and tell the man of the house I was cheating on him with her husband. All I could think about was what if Chon answered the door and this woman began with a rant of infidelities leaving Chon to believe that Tina was cheating on him? I became a little angry at the fact that she felt the need to try and tear down someone else's home after destroying her own. This explained why she wasn't as aggressive as a woman would be who just caught her husband red-handed with another woman. Although she didn't want him for herself, she didn't want him to be with anyone else either.

It kept playing in my head how on that day he had no problem telling her that he wanted to be with me and that he loved me and that

I meant the world to him. He told her over and over again how much he desired to spend the rest of his life with me. At the time I couldn't help but feel that under no circumstances was it okay to say these things to someone you have married and are supposed to be committed to. Now I understand why it was so easy for him to say these things to her and mean it. It was because he didn't love her and wanted nothing to do with her.

He looked me in my eyes and said, "If I had only waited..." He grabbed my hands and pulled me closer to him and said, "If I had listened to everyone trying to get me away from her I would not have been married when I met you. We would not be going through this right now. If I had waited for God to send you to me like He said He would - and He did, there would only be tears of joy right now and not the pain that we are feeling – If I had just waited." Tears came to my eyes and he held me. We sat together consoling one another for hours. Forgiven, but not forgotten.

Hearing all he had been through softened my heart, but it did not clear my mind. There was no denying one thing: his status remained the same. He was a married man and therefore unavailable to me. No matter how dysfunctional, faulty, and short-lived his marriage was, it was honorable to God, and therefore it was honorable to me.

I could say those words with my mind, but my heart hurt because my love for him was still there. I wished he had met me before he met his wife. I wished he hadn't married her and waited on

Forgiveness

me too. I wished I was his wife. He would never have to worry about finding condom wrappers, urine on the toilet or underwear that didn't belong to him. He would have had a woman that wanted nothing more than to love him for the rest of his life. He had that with me, but it didn't matter because he was a married man. He was not my husband.

With tears in my eyes I admit I still love him and I know he loves me too, but this is a love affair that cannot continue. Just when I have fallen so deep in love with the picture perfect man, my best friend, my son's role model, my gentle giant, the man who had my back, the only man I could ever talk to, a man who listens, a man that supported me without looking for anything in return; the one who held me and loved me when I felt I was so damaged I could never be loved again; just when we came together, something like this happened.

As I prayed to God I asked why. The more I read the Word and sought the Lord, I accepted that God would not allow this relationship to move any further because we didn't obey his commands. We both knew we were wrong by engaging in any kind of inappropriate relations before marriage, especially since we were saved. When you know right from wrong and still make the decision to do wrong you will have to suffer the consequences. All I could do was ask God to have mercy on me. I had to accept that we cursed our relationship the day we disobeyed God, thinking that all we had to do was repent later and everything would work out just fine.

I still loved him but knew I had to stay far away from him. He told me that he was in the process of getting the divorce and asked if I would wait for him. Knowing the full story, I understood that there was never a real marriage, but I can't pretend that he doesn't have a woman still walking around Baltimore with his last name. Being in the process of a divorce and finished with the divorce process are two different things.

I never saw myself being with someone who had been married anyway because of what my mother and father had gone through. It breaks my heart that something so genuine had to come to such an abrupt end. All my hopes and dreams with him had been terminated. That stigma of being with someone who is a divorcé was something I didn't want to deal with. Why would I wait was the question that popped into my head, and then my mind fell back to what he had said to me…"If I had only waited."

He called my mother to tell her what happened and told her all about his wife. I was glad he did because I knew how my mom felt about infidelity, and I knew whatever she said to me and him, it would encourage me not to entertain any desires to be around or with him. My mother would tell Mr. Marc-Train that what he did was wrong, and that there should be no thought of us ever being together. My mother would tell him that he should have been honest with me and that being deceitful and lying did not help the situation, but instead made things worse. She would tell him that his behavior

Forgiveness

caused him to miss out on being with her wonderful daughter. Yes, I believed she would say this to him and mean it too.

My mom actually did say all those things to him, but she was also filled with compassion for him. She was able to feel his sincerity and regret for not going about things the right way. She was able to hear the genuineness in his voice as he told her how much he loved me and desired to spend the rest of his life with me. She accepted his honesty and apology and told him that he would have to go before God to know what he should do next, and accept the consequences.

I didn't expect her to care so much for him, but she did. I didn't expect her to feel sorry for him, but she did. I didn't expect her to show love to him as if he was her son, but she did. Then she says, "Everyone makes mistakes and everyone makes bad decisions, but God is a forgiving God that makes no bad decisions and never makes mistakes. Mr. Marc-Train has a soul too, and God gives us all time to repent and a chance to make things right," she said.

Being the woman of God she is, she saw there was no need to condemn him for his indiscretion. Yelling and screaming at him would have been overkill. Instead she used this opportunity to witness to him and tell him God yet loves him; that God loves him more than he loves me. No, God doesn't make mistakes, and it was no mistake that he and I met the way we did and fell in love the way we did.

She didn't create a heaven or a hell to put him in, but simply loved him for who he was and let him know God will forgive those who are looking for true forgiveness. She helped me humble myself to see that it wasn't about me forgiving him, but more it was about God forgiving us both.

I want God to forgive me, and I must forgive Mr. Marc-Train – no matter how much it hurts. I didn't want him out of my life because he had been a true friend. I didn't want to lose him because he was the best thing to happen to me since I moved to Baltimore. More importantly, I didn't want God out of my life because He has been more than a true friend. I don't want to lose God because He was the best thing that happened to me…period. My relationship with God is more crucial to repair than the relationship with Mr. Marc-Train. He understood this and gave me space and time to heal as I turned to God for guidance.

Mr. Marc-Train's focus should have be on dealing with his marriage to a woman who he said didn't love him. I did not want to be a distraction to him, nor did I want to intentionally have any dealings with his dilemma. He told me all about his divorce and what the lawyers were telling him. I didn't understand why a divorce couldn't be as simple as signing a piece of paper and moving on. There were many delays and dramatics that I did not want to hear about. I wanted our friendship to remain, but I was not ready to hear about divorce proceedings and bank accounts and alimony.

I did all I could to remain a friend and listen to him vent about all the horrible things that this woman was doing to him, but each day it tore me up inside. He kept telling me to hold on, and that it wouldn't be long. He had a plan in mind that as soon as his divorce is final we would not waste any time and get married immediately.

Things seemed to be going pretty well as time passed. The smoke cleared and when I saw his face or heard his voice on the phone, I realized even more that I was still in love. I heard nothing but positive things from him about the divorce and slowly began to feel excitement for the future I thought was lost and gone away. He still made me smile. He still made my mind wander so far into him that I could daydream for hours. He still showed me that he had my back no matter what, and for that I was willing to wait.

*****

It was finally time for me to move and I was super excited. Living with my best friend and her husband was fine but it was time for Zion and me to have our own place. We had shared a room comfortably at Tina's and she had been good to us, but he was growing and it was time for me to branch out too. I moved into my own apartment and God blessed me like never before. With two bedrooms with a walk-in closet in the master, a large living room, and a full kitchen I was satisfied. I never went to the furniture store, yet I was moving into my place with my own bedroom set, my son with his own furniture set; we had a dining room table, and a kitchen nook. I was even gifted plates and silverware without paying a dime.

Tina and Chon were protective of me. Their level of concern and patience for me and my son was something I wouldn't forget. In the midst of working out their own lives and relationship they took the time to help me with mine. I would be forever grateful to them for their unhindered kindness.

Mr. Marc-Train was happy for me and I was overjoyed. Because I turned my focus back to God, I could see His blessings in my life again. I wanted badly to move and God blessed me to do so. I was thankful to Him for Chon and Tina. I don't think I would have made it in Baltimore if it weren't for them. They supported the fact that I needed my own, and it was time for me to have my own.

I had driven my poor car until the axel fell off of it, and then I had to park it in the alley behind Chon and Tina's house. One day the car was towed and I never saw it again. I wondered if it was the friendly neighborhood police officer that was sleeping with Mr. Marc-Train's wife who had my car towed to spite me because of the divorce proceedings that were taking place. It didn't matter because I was out of there, and now Officer Friendly and his lover would not know where I lived. I had peace and happiness in my new place and I didn't want any drama there.

Mr. Marc-Train would leave money with me so that I could catch a taxi to work every morning. He would sometimes get up early and pick me up to take me to work before he would go to his job. Not having a car is a horrible feeling because I had to ask people for rides everywhere I needed to go. I always wanted a Jetta so Mr. Marc-Train took me out to the Volkswagen dealership to see if I could get a car financed. I had been saving money for a while now and I prayed I would able to get the car of my dreams. The car dealer asked Mr.

Marc-Train if he would co-sign with me, but I told him no. This was something that I wanted to do on my own. He loved me enough and was willing to co-sign, but I wouldn't allow it.

    I went home disappointed because I couldn't get the car I wanted. I was hurt because I had co-signed on a car for Michael when we were together. My credit was destroyed because of that decision. I wished I had known then what a foolish choice I was making. Thankfully Mr. Marc-Train was supportive of me and encouraged me to continue saving money and paying my bills on time. He told me that my credit score would go up so that I would one day be able to purchase a car on my own. I loved him for that, no matter what was happening he stayed an encouragement to me and I did just what he said. I saved my money and paid my bills in hopes that I would one day buy my own car. I allowed Mr. Marc-Train to have access to my bank accounts and money because he wanted to help me better my spending and saving. I was reluctant to allow another man to have access of that magnitude to my bank accounts because I was taken advantage of in my last relationship, but not one time did Mr. Marc-Train ever show me that he wanted to take from me; he only to wanted give.

    Mr. Marc-Train was always giving to me. My bank account would say one amount one day, and the next moment the money would increase. There were never any withdrawals, but always deposits. The only thing he ever questioned was why I continued to give so much money to the church. He would calculate my tithes, offering and special offerings and would say that I was giving a bit much. I explained to him that God was the reason I had what I had. I couldn't ever cut back on my giving. He respected that and never asked about my church money again – in fact he would give me a little extra to add to it.

Mr. Marc-Train came by the apartment and said that he wanted to take my son and me out. I was feeling kind of down because I couldn't find a car to purchase and he wanted to cheer me up. We left out of the apartment and as he walked in front of me, he asked me what I thought about a car that was outside. It was a nice car, so that was all I would say about it.

He asked me if it were mine would I like it enough to drive it. I said I would love it, and with that being said, he handed me a set of keys and said, "It's yours." I was stunned. *What? How?!* It was a four door Hyundai Elantra with a cd player, automatic windows and a wood grained dashboard on the inside. I couldn't believe he had gone to the dealership and worked out a deal without me knowing. No, it wasn't the Jetta that I wanted, but it was a car.

The only time he ever withdrew money from my account, he took it to put a down payment on my first brand new car. The love this man had for me, going to this extreme to make me happy. We drove back to the dealership to complete some paperwork and I pulled off the lot in disbelief. He joked about me paying all that money to the church must have paid off because look at me now!

I was thankful for my new car and apartment. As I refocused on God, He continued to encourage me to keep seeking Him even more. God gets all the credit for my car and my apartment. My son had so much space to run around and play in our home, and I didn't have to worry about him destroying anyone else's property. We spent so much time together laughing and playing around every night then we would say our prayers together. I would lay him in *his* bed, then go into *my* room and get into *my* bed. We had come full circle. I was finally in my own home again, a place where we could create our own routines.

*****

The one thing about being in an apartment is that you share the building structure with other people. Sometimes the walls aren't thick enough and you can hear business that doesn't pertain to you. The young couple that lived upstairs from me would play loud music, curse and argue, and I could even smell weed seeping through into my place some late nights. I was so glad this young couple didn't have children because they made enough noise between the two of them.

Every night Mr. Marc-Train would call to say good night and tell me he loved me especially if he didn't get a chance to see me during the day. I knew his job was demanding so I didn't worry about where he was or what he was doing. I trusted that he was being honest but if he wasn't, there wasn't much I could say. After all, the truth was out; he was married and was going through a divorce. I considered myself no more than a friend to him.

Being his friend was tough because I wanted more. I was lonely and I wanted to have a companion. I would lie in my bed and pray for God to help keep my mind focused on Him while I waited. It was hard being alone after experiencing such an intensely affectionate connection with another human being. I pulled the covers close to me and prepared to cry myself to sleep. It seemed as if every time I wanted to have a pity party and cry my eyes out Mr. Marc-Train would show up or call. That night, he talked to me on the phone. I was mesmerized by his voice. I loved hearing him tell me the plans he had for our future. I loved hearing him talk about how much he missed me, how he missed kissing my soft lips. I hung up the phone tired, barely able to keep my eyes open and ready to dream about him and our future together.

Right when I drifted into a lulled sleep lost in the happiest dream of Mr. Marc-Train and me, noises began to disturb my wholesome thoughts. The couple upstairs from me didn't have any children, but they loved to have sex like they were trying to make some. Now wide awake, I listened to their entire session of baby-making. With every scream she made and every moan he released, it made me yearn more for my chance to love and feel what they were feeling. With every bang of their headboard against the wall I start to break down. Like clockwork, after every bang there was a moan, and after every moan came a scream, and another moan, and another scream, and another bang; bang-scream-moan, moan-scream-bang, until each one's pleasures were fulfilled or until one wore the other out and then… silence.

With my head in my pillow, I could hardly think straight. There was no prayer that I could pray with deep thought-out words to be eloquent in my speech when speaking to God at that moment. All I could get out was, "God I need a Man!" Listening to my noisy neighbors rekindled a fire in me and I wanted that back in my life, but I wanted it the right way. The only way it would be right is if I was married. So I prayed, *Lord please rush this divorce so that this man can marry me and make me feel like I have never felt before…Amen!* Then I went to bed.

The next day Mr. Marc-Train called and told me that he was coming to see me after he got off work. I was so excited. After hearing what I heard from my neighbors the night before I would've been satisfied with a passionate kiss and a little touch n' feel right about then. When he spoke I heard something strange in his voice, but when I questioned him he said that he was alright. I was a little concerned and he said that he would talk to me later. I had learned not to get my hopes up and not assume anything anymore. I knew he had to meet with his lawyers that day, and all that I could think was that he was coming to tell me that the divorce is final, let's go get married. All day long I wondered and wished that he would just tell me over the phone what he had to say. I started wondering if he was going to tell me he decided not to divorce his wife because she got saved or something and now she was ready to be faithful to him. I had to stop thinking about it and wait to hear what he had to say.

He picked me up from work and seemed happy. *That's a good sign right?* That means whatever he had to tell me was good news not bad news. I needed to know what it was. I needed him to tell me. We got together and he told me that when he saw his wife today at the lawyer's office he noticed her stomach. Immediately my heart began to pound praying that he didn't say what I thought he was going to say. He hadn't seen her in a while but today he was able to see and know for sure she's pregnant. *How much worse can this get?*

I asked was it his and he said he didn't know. I couldn't get upset because she held the title of wife, not me. It didn't matter that I wanted to be his wife and she didn't, the reality was she was having a baby and it may be his.

It seemed crazy to me that the one who wanted to spend the rest of her life with Mr. Marc-Train and have his babies wasn't in the position or holding the title to be or do either. This is the reason why a woman or a man should never wait around for someone to get a divorce. You never know how the rollercoaster is going to end. I was speechless, and simultaneously distraught. I hoped that the baby wasn't his, but if it was there was nothing I could say about the matter.

He wanted to ease my mind and explained to me that after he filed for divorce she acted as if she was willing to give the marriage one last try. She claimed that when this brief union took place she became pregnant. With all the things that had taken place in the past, it sounded like she was conspiring to lock down a position where she would always have some involvement in Mr. Marc-Trains life.

I was not going to sit around and wait for a blood test to find out if it was his baby or not. I chose to believe that it was. That was the easiest way for me to deal with the situation. Mr. Marc-Train saw me drifting away and pleaded for me to be patient with him. I thought about all the times we shared with each other, the love and moments of pure happiness. I didn't want to lose that and neither did he. I poured out my deepest hurts to him and had shown him just how damaged this Oreo cookie was, and he never backed away from me. He drew closer and closer to me as if God placed him in my life to accept me for who I was; blemishes and all. I asked God for someone who was going to love me for me, and God placed him in my life to accept all of me. If he was here ready and willing to accept all of me, there should be no problem with me accepting all of him as well. Neither one of us had a perfect, clean-cut past, but we both desired to have a loving future together with God in the middle of it all.

*****

Lately I've been having the worst headaches. I didn't know what to do about it. My head hurt so much at times that I couldn't get out of bed. I had gone for prayer at church and even took medicine (which I hardly ever did), but the headaches would not go away. Mr. Marc-Train took me to the doctor, and after doing a CAT scan of my head, the doctor tells me that I have developed a mass on my brain that needed to be removed. *Lord what more do I have to go through in this life?* At that point I was tired and I needed God to give me a clear picture as to where He was leading me. I was feeling discouraged and beat down, and there is no more fight left in me. Just when I was ready to throw in the towel the preacher said in his message, "The battle is not yours, it's the Lord's."

    I rested on those words and surrendered totally to God. Whatever happened would happen. No matter what, my faith and trust would be in the Lord. My mother flew into Baltimore to be with me for the surgery and that put me at ease. I knew between her and Mr. Marc-Train taking care of me, my son and I would be just fine. I didn't doubt that I would make it through the painful experience but lying in the hospital awaiting surgery, I was nervous. I admit I was conflicted because I was taught not to doubt or be afraid, but I was. I knew the mass didn't belong on my brain. Right before I went under the anesthesia I remember knowing that everything would be alright. I awoke to a brain with no mass on it. Nobody but God took me through that ordeal. I am forever thankful.

    Mr. Marc-Train took me to my follow up appointment and the doctor gave me a clean bill of health. He asked Mr. Marc-Train if he was my husband, and Mr. Marc-Train replied, "I plan to make her my wife sooner than she thinks." I knew he loved me for sure, in sickness and in health, till death do us part. *I'm ready, but only if God says so.*

    In expressing how much I loved and cared for him to his mother, he also expressed his love for me to my mom, and I knew there could be more to this relationship. But after all I have gone through I no longer assume anything. I decided to leave it all up to God to literally come down from heaven and say that my husband was ready for me. Until God did this I was fully committed to Him and Him alone. He had already blessed me with life, health and strength, and to accomplish so much in only a few years. I owed God everything.

Through all my life's journey one thing I realized was that God had always been there looking out for this Oreo cookie. From childhood to womanhood God had been the only reliable and steady source in my life. Even when I strayed He waited for my return. When I cried, He dried my tears. When in danger, He was my protection. When torn to pieces, He was the mender of my broken heart. When I was weak, He made me strong. When I was sick, it was God that healed me.

God is everything to me. When my mind was stayed on Him, He really did keep me in perfect peace. He was unswerving, unfailing and steady. I knew I could depend on him. The question was, could He depend on me? My answer: yes God, you can. Whatever I needed to do, however it needed to be done, I was going to live this life of mine for Christ. I wanted to be a witness to all that what I have with Him is not religion, it is a relationship.

I felt blessed for this restoration in Christ. At last it was clear to me that it was through God that all my blessings flowed so I must realign myself with Him to receive all that He had in store for me.

Forgiveness

After all that the Lord had spared me from and brought me through, my soul finally, truly loved Jesus. I was finally, honestly able to say that Jesus was my soul mate. I thanked Him for helping me to forgive, for being the forgiver of my soul, and for always being my covering, even when I didn't deserve Him.

Chapter 15

A Storm

The closer I get to God the better I feel about myself. There wasn't any other relationship that I needed but the one I had with Jesus. It was this relationship that boosted my confidence to be all God planned for me to be. With every church service I attended, every fast I participated in, every song that I sang, every scripture I read, I felt God's presence and I knew He loved me. This was the love I'd yearned for, searched and cried for; and it was with my Savior all along. Truthfully, I still wanted to be married to Mr. Marc-Train, and I prayed that it was in God's will for my life, but finally I was content with Jesus alone.

Mr. Marc-Train began to act strange and I didn't understand why. When he came around he asked me about my church, but he never made time to attend church with me. He asked if anyone was flirting with me, I assured him that no one had my attention but him. I wondered what made him uncomfortable with my church all of a sudden, as his behavior shifted from strange to bizarre. When I asked him what was wrong all he said was that he'd been having reoccurring dreams and wanted to know if I still loved him.

A Storm

He said his commander told him it was impossible to have a healthy relationship and stay in his current line of work. He began to feel insecure and wondered if he would have to choose between me and his job. I tried to set his mind at rest by reminding him that I had waited all this time, and had no intentions of dropping out now.

Mr. Marc-Train's job was becoming more and more challenging and it was hard not seeing him as much as I would have liked. Even when he was not around he still tried to take care of me and my son. Hiding money behind the peanut butter jar in my kitchen cabinet was one of his infamous acts of kindness. A half opened cabinet was his telltale sign that he had stopped by while I was out. He knew he didn't need to leave money for us, but he did, explaining that it was a little spending money so I won't bother the money I had been saving in the bank. He would call to make sure that I had everything that I needed, and if I didn't, he made sure that I did.

I didn't like to hear him talk about the plans he had in place in the event of his untimely demise. I didn't want to think about him dying. He told me that my son and I will be taken care of and his mom and commander would know what to do if it ever came to that. *I don't know when he is going to get it through his head that I don't want his money, all I want is him - alive.*

Every time we made plans to be together he ended up having to work and it was starting to make me feel a little lonely. I would come home from work to see that he had stopped by. I silently wished his job's schedule would allow him to be with me after my

A Storm

work hours. Now I understood what his commander was talking about, but when you love someone the way that I loved him a replacement wouldn't do.

*****

Michael wanted to spend some quality time with Zion in Rochester. It had been a while and I wasn't sure if this was something that I wanted to do. Because I love my son and wanted the best for him I allowed it. He was excited to be back in Rochester. Michael was supposed to bring him back to the church Sunday night but I hadn't seen or heard from them. I felt the anointing and power of God moving in the service and I began to worship and give God praise. Tears flowed from my eyes, and I couldn't understand why. Service was over, and I felt refreshed and renewed, but I still hadn't heard from Michael and wanted to know where he was with Zion.

I made it home to my apartment and as I lay my head down I began to think about all the things God has brought me through in my life and I cried myself to sleep with tears of joy. My cell phone rang waking me up, and it was Michael. Half asleep I tried to get myself together as I listened to him tell me that they had been in a car accident and they were in a hospital in Pennsylvania. The car was totaled, but everyone that was in the car was alright.

Without panicking I put my clothes on and called my Pastor to tell him what happened as I left to make the drive to Pennsylvania to get my son. Before I knew what I had done, I was on interstate 695 heading towards highway 83 to go to PA. I left a message for Mr.

A Storm

Marc-Train, but I couldn't wait on anyone and was adamant about getting to my son. When I got to the hospital, I was overjoyed when Zion came running to me. Michael had his oldest son's mom with him, she was slightly injured and being examined in the emergency room. Something told me to stay there and show support instead of taking my son and leaving, so I did.

Once she was released I asked Michael what they were going to do and he said they were going to stay at a hotel because someone was coming to get them in the morning. I offered to drive them to the hotel and they accepted the offer. After they got out of the car I began thanking God all the way home as I realized it was at the time I was praising God in church that they were in the accident. I was crazy enough to believe that it was my praise that kept my son and the rest of the passengers in the car safe from harm. Taking them to the nearest hotel was the icing on the cake to show Michael that the Christ in me would always shine in the good and the bad times. That was the feeling that I felt when I knew I was finally over it!

The holidays were coming and Mr. Marc-Train hinted to me that this may be my best Christmas yet. I learned not to get excited about a proposal because the disappointment takes a while to get over. If it happened, it happened, but if it didn't I wouldn't be hurt this time. I was no longer waiting on a marriage proposal; I was now waiting on God to show Himself. Love was in the air and it was a beautiful winter season. I had to admit the closer it got to Christmas the more excited I became. I was anxious to see what would take place, and with that unrest God led me to do more praying and more fasting. I was obedient to His urge, and my son and I began praying together every morning and every night more than we would usually. My son even wanted to take the lead in the prayers holding my hands and giving God thanks. When my son tells me that he is thankful Jesus gave him the best mommy in the world, my heart is overwhelmed. Prayer is the gift that keeps on giving.

I did my best and gave my son all that he needed, and I wanted to show him that it was not of my doing that we were blessed, but it was God looking out for us. This has been a very tough journey, and there have been times that I wanted to throw in the towel and give up. But it was in the thick of those tough times that God strengthened me and equipped me with everything I needed to be an overcomer and not a victim. I wanted my son to see the strength in me and recognize that he too could make it against all odds no matter what was said or done to him in his life.

With tears in my eyes I lay in my bed once again and cried myself to sleep knowing that no matter how strong I was, my son still needed a father in his life to teach him what I could not. As I lay in my bed, I began to feel the blanket lifted up to cover my shoulders. My eyes were closed and I was doing everything in my power to open them, but they wouldn't open. I felt the sheets and blanket being tucked on both sides of me. My natural mind began to think maybe this was Mr. Marc-Train who had just gotten off from work and wanted to check on me, but I knew better. The feeling was one that I had felt many times, but never like this. Spiritually I knew it was the presence of God tucking me into my bed like a father would do his child. He was showing me that I was not alone and that He heard my prayers and saw my tears.

This experience was breathtaking, and I wanted to sit up and open my eyes but there was a force stopping me. I tried to move my legs and my feet, but no matter how many times my mind said to move, by body would not. For God to show me that He loved me like this was more than amazing, and when I was able to open my eyes all I could do was lie there and smile. It wasn't for me to see God, but to feel His presence and know that He was there.

*****

Christmas had come and gone with no ring and no proposal, but a smile was on my face. I was happy because I knew God was up to something. Mr. Marc-Train was still working a lot and my son and I were content at home enjoying every gift that God had given us. The weather had been quite frigid, alluding to a tough winter.

The New Year was here and I continued to fast and pray with my son and anoint him every morning before we left our apartment. I believed that it was my year and that all I desired and needed for my life God was going to make happen.

I missed my Mr. Marc-Train, and I couldn't wait for his schedule to slow down some so that he could be around more. I didn't question why he had to work so much, and honestly in a way I thought it was a blessing. As long as he was at work that meant that we aren't alone being tempted to do things we knew we ought not to do. I told him that I was waiting until my name was Mrs. Marc-Train. We both agreed we loved the sound of that. To hear him express his love for me always made me melt on the inside.

Expressing to me that I was a breath of fresh air after all that he had to go through made me glad that I was waiting to spend the rest of my life with him. He didn't have to ask me to be patient with him, but he did and I did – because I knew he deserved to be happy just as much as I did, and he wanted that happiness to be shared with me.

I came home from work only to find out that something terrible had happened. The church was in mourning, and the phone was ringing off the hook. My body became numb when I heard the news that my sister in Christ, Dion, had passed away. There were many conflicting stories: she had a heart attack, it was a stroke, or she drifted away in her sleep.

I was in total disbelief because she and I were not only close, but close in age. *That could have been me.* She was gone and unable to see or speak to her family again. I immediately called my mother because she loved Dion. Knowing that she would be upset at the news, I took my time and told her what happened. Dion was like a daughter to her. Something about Dion's death did something to me that I couldn't explain. She never got to have children, she was so sick and always in so much pain that she couldn't enjoy life like she wanted to and now she was gone. I couldn't imagine what her

A Storm

husband was going through. He went out of town with his father and wasn't there when she passed away. Just the thought was breaking my heart; knowing he wasn't there to say goodbye to his wife. They were married for almost 5 years, and she was gone, just like that.

Death. No one knows when our time will be, but we know that at some point our time on earth will be up. Hearing the sad news caused me to feel great sympathy for the first family of my church. The Pastor, his wife, son and daughter – I couldn't begin to imagine how they were feeling. After the deaths of my former church leader, Pastor Jones, my grandmother and then my cousin Tony all in close succession, I no longer wanted anything to do with funerals or grieving. Dion's was an unexpected death. I didn't know how to process losing her so abruptly with no warning.

I kept my distance from it all knowing that I was not ready to face the reality of life's end for someone so vibrant and full of life. It didn't feel right for people so young to have to experience that kind of pain that early in life. I called Mr. Marc-Train to tell him about the death of my sister in the Lord, and my tears wouldn't stop flowing. Crying from the depth my heart, I attempted to tell Mr. Marc-Train that Dion's death was hurting me indescribably.

Mr. Marc-Train was silent on the phone as he listened to me weep, expressing my deepest emotions regarding death. Dion's death helped me to see that I didn't want to live without Mr. Marc-Train. Her death caused me to acknowledge that I didn't know how much time I had left on this earth. I didn't know how long Mr. Marc-Train

A Storm

had either, and with his job being as hectic as he said it was, I wondered what if something happened to him before we could get married.

The more I thought about Dion the more I cried grievously and selfishly because I had lost my sister in the Lord and didn't want to lose Mr. Marc-Train. In all of my crying I realized Mr. Marc-Train hadn't said a word. I became curious because he always knew what to say to me to encourage me in any situation, but this time he was silent.

I paused to give him a chance to say something and I waited to hear his voice – the voice that soothed my worry every time he spoke. But I heard nothing. I looked down at my phone and abruptly said, "Hello?" After a short pause, he simply whispers, "Lillian, I love you Baby." I could hear in his voice that he was troubled, and I knew he was just as worried about losing me as I was about losing him.

He asked me if I believed that he loved me and I said yes. He asked me to promise never to forget that he loved me, and wiping tears from my eyes I ask him how I could ever forget that. I heard a sound of relief in his voice and he told me that he had to go, but promised to come by to see me later. When he came over he held me as if this was going to be his last time holding me and he didn't want to let me go. I embraced him as well no longer able to take any moment we shared for granted.

*****

A Storm

It was embarrassing to hear how women had advertised themselves to a man that had just lost his wife. Dion had only been gone for a little while, but apparently women were calling and putting their bid in to fill the void. Pastor made it humorous as he told the church about the advances his son received from different women, their mothers and grandmothers trying to grab the spot as the new wife. He was like a brother to me, and I found it ill-mannered and desperate of the women who carried on that way but it was somewhat amusing to hear about the advances and phone calls he received; a simple event silly enough to turn the corners of our mouths up - if only slightly, in the midst of terrible pain.

After listening to the Pastor comment on all the phone calls, Tina and I plotted to prank call him ourselves, if only to help find humor in the devastating situation which my friend found himself in. We thought about pretending to be one of the concerned women Pastor mentioned. I thought it would be funny and would get him to laugh for a change, but we decided against it. It was a bad idea and neither of us could find humor in it after a while. Instead Tina and I shared a laugh which slowly turned to reflection on the loss of a beloved sister.

Everyone was talking about how they had gone out to the Pastor's house, the food they brought there for the bereaved family and all the visitors that they'd had. I couldn't find the vigor to go nor could I find the energy to call. My mother kept telling me that if I didn't visit I should at least call to see if they needed anything, but

A Storm

she knew I was not skilled in dealing with situations involving death. I preferred to stay as far away as possible and grieve in my own way.

At last I gathered enough nerve call my Pastor. I cooked some food and sent it over with my friend Tina, and told him I was thinking of them. He asked why I hadn't visited, and I diverted the question so I wouldn't have to answer for not coming over. They had always treated me like family, and I suppose I should have been there in their time of need, but I was not well suited to be in the midst of their grieving.

I asked Pastor how his son was doing, and instead of him telling me he handed him the phone. I was stunned. I had no idea what to say to a man who had just lost his wife. I let him know that my mom and I were praying for him and tried to get off the phone as quickly as I could.

Mr. Marc-Train came over and I told him that I had spoken to my Pastor and his grieving son to offer my condolences for their loss. He seemed uneasy about my conversation with Pastor. Mr. Marc-Train asked me how the pastor's son was handling everything and asked what we discussed over the phone. I told him how nervous and edgy I was talking to the pastor's son. I said that I hurried embarrassingly through the conversation, hanging up the phone so abruptly I couldn't tell how he was feeling. To make matter worse I felt bad about rushing off.

Mr. Marc-Train asked me again if I believed that he loved me and that he wanted to spend the rest of his life with me. I told him I

A Storm

believed it with all of my heart, and I was ready. He grabbed my face to gently kiss me, and as our lips touched my son began to cough terribly. He hadn't been feeling well and I needed to give him more medicine.

I took him to the doctor, and they prescribed antibiotics, only to give me the wrong dosage amount causing me to over medicate him with each dose. Everyone around me is saying that death comes in threes. My mind is racing and I prayed for God to heal my son and protect Mr. Marc-Train.

For Dion's funeral my mother travelled down to Baltimore with Deacon and Mother Washington which happened to be my Pastor's uncle and aunt. I was so happy to see her and glad that she was able to come to the funeral. Death had a way of making us appreciate all of our loved ones, wanting to be in their presence as much as possible.

It was the middle of winter and freezing cold in Baltimore. The snow was coming down and sometimes it felt as though I was still in Rochester. With the drastic weather changes, my son's health worsened. His asthma flared terribly and he was constantly on medical treatment. He had become an old hand at preparing his breathing machine and arranging the treatment all by himself. Days later I had to take him to the ER because he had an ear infection.

I wasn't getting any rest and through my tiredness, I became weary. I had no help in my home to give me a break while caring for

A Storm

Zion, so I put him in the bed with me and cried out to the Lord to help us and heal my son.

Mr. Marc-Train had been doing his best to be around more, but there was always something going on. I had been fasting and praying, and I felt God was with me so I knew something was getting ready to happen. Not to mention, ever since Dion's death Mr. Marc-Train acted as if he had a deadline to meet and time was running out for him. I kept reassuring him that I was not planning on going anywhere. I only saw my future with him - the best friend a woman could ever have. I was glad he didn't take our relationship for granted, at the same time I knew there were things he needed to take care of so I decided not to pressure him; I would wait to see what God had to say about the matter.

It was Thursday night, February 6, 2003 and I had just gotten off from work. Mr. Marc-Train was off from work as well and we planned to get together at my house later that evening. The news had given a bad weather forecast, and with my son not feeling the greatest I decided that I was not going to attend church and go home instead. I went by the church, left my offering and went home to wait for Mr. Marc-Train. I got my son ready for bed and I was a bit tired myself. Mr. Marc-Train hadn't arrived or called, and I didn't know what had happened to him.

The later it got, the more the snow fell and it looked like the meteorologist was correct about the snowstorm. I looked out of my kitchen window staring at the snow as it fell looking for Mr. Marc-

A Storm

Train. I called his phone. No answer. After a while his phone began to go directly to the voicemail. I prayed that he was alright and that nothing had happened to him. Oddly I was not worried, remaining calm and in a peaceful place.

I didn't rush to go to bed, because I already knew my job would be closed after the accumulation of snow. *These Baltimorians wouldn't last one winter day in Rochester*. I couldn't believe that the city would close down because of a little flurry. However, to my surprise, this time wasn't a flurry; it was a full-fledged storm. *I will be home relaxing in the morning, and that's exactly what I need.* I decided to talk to my mom on the phone since Mr. Marc-Train wasn't there to keep me company.

In the middle of the discussion with my mom my phone beeped and I had a call waiting. The number looked familiar so I did a double take. It was Pastor's son, the Deacon calling. Without clicking over I tell my mother who it was. She laughed as I say to her I bet he's calling to get on my case for not going to church tonight. I clicked over to his call and just as I thought, he asked me why I didn't stay for service when I dropped my offering off. I had plenty of excuses from my son not feeling well to the weather, but being honest it was also because I was hoping that I would get to see Mr. Marc-Train for at least a few minutes tonight before it got late.

Over the line, he told me there was something he needed to talk to me about. He wanted to know if I was still up so that we could have a discussion. I felt bad for my big brother with all he had been

A Storm

through and he was still a faithful servant in the church. I said to him it was fine for him to stop over and with that, he was on his way. I clicked back over to mom and she asked how he was doing since it had only been a few days since he buried his wife. I told her that he was on his way over probably to ask me to help with a memorial service for Dion or something with the church.

As I put my son in the bed there was a knock at my door. I kissed my son on the forehead and there was a moment of excitement that rushed through me. I had waited so long for Mr. Marc-Train to arrive and finally he was at my door. When I opened the door to my surprise it wasn't Mr. Marc-Train, but Deacon at the door. I let him in and we sat down at my dining room table. I could see in his face that he was there to be serious and not joking as we all would normally do with each other.

As I sat down at the table things began to feel a bit unclear. I looked at Deacon and began hearing words come out of his mouth. There was a delay in my comprehension because there was anticipation for one conversation, but this talk was going in a totally different direction. An indescribable feeling came over me as he said to me, "I know that you are dating someone. I realize that you are in a relationship. But, God showed me that you are to be my wife. And I want to know if you could love me enough…to be…my wife."

So this is what an outer body experience feels like?

I heard what he was saying with his mouth but my mind was saying, *WHAT?!? Don't you know I am in love with Mr. Marc-Train?*

A Storm

I have been waiting for him to fulfill my hearts de- ... Before I could complete processing an entire thought in my mind I heard a voice that sounded exactly like me say, "Yes," confident and sure, with no hesitation or pause. I said, "Yes."

Bewildered I tried to understand what was happening. My mind was racing a mile a minute, and the Lord brought back to my memory the statement I firmly stood by, *I'm not getting married unless God Himself comes down and says this is my husband.*

I could not believe what had just happened. This was my close friend. We hadn't dated. I didn't even think of him *that* way. There was no attraction or desire between us. *How did this happen? What if Mr. Marc-Train comes to the door right now? What will I say, what will I do?* As these thoughts ran through my mind, he looked me in my eyes and said, "God is doing this. Before I came over I prayed, and I told the Lord if there was any hesitation in your response at all I would know that this was not what He wanted me to do. You didn't hesitate. That confirms that this was God leading me to you. You are my wife."

Even a woman who has been dating the love of her life, and who has waited a long time for him to propose would in excitement possibly fumble in her words while saying yes; but there was no stutter or delay with me. Only, "Yes." Just as if God knew that I would have hesitated, He came down and took over speaking through me with confidence to show that He is God and He was in control of the situation. I knew this man's wife – she was my sister in the Lord

A Storm

and had just passed less than two weeks ago. I knew I looked at him as a big brother and not as a potential lover. How did that *Yes* come out of my mouth with such poise and certainty; void of doubt?

God reminded me that these were the words I uttered when I surrendered my life to Him years ago, *Yes Lord*. I told the Lord I was His and I wanted to be used by Him because I owed Him my life, and He was taking me up on my word. Not my will but His will be done with my life.

I looked out the corner of my eye and I saw a little body moving and hiding behind his bedroom doorway. Still unclear as to what just happened, I looked at my son as Deacon said, "If I am going to marry you and you are going to be my wife that means your son will be my son. I will love him and treat him as my son, and raise him as if he was my biological child. I will be his father and do all I can to teach and groom him to become a Godly man, but you will have to allow me to be his father as we discipline him together."

God replayed in my mind all the prayers I had sent up to Him requesting help with the raising of my son. My appeals to God for my son to have more than a father figure, but a true father in his life that would love him, and prepare him for upcoming challenges as only a man could, under the fear and admonition of God. In every dream, in every fantasy and in every future plan I had, that was what I desired. But the dream was never with my big brother, it was with Mr. Marc-Train.

A Storm

My son was looking at us with a huge smile on his face. He hadn't been feeling well, but suddenly he didn't look sick at all; he looked happy. He was grinning from one ear to the other as if he was the man of the house shaking his head from side to side giving his stamp of approval on what had taken place. For the next few hours Deacon, (who I began calling by his first name, Kenny) and I sat at my table getting to know each other and discussing our future together. With the both of us completely shocked at what God was doing we kept saying that we were in 'Shock Trauma'.

Because we could clearly feel that this was the hand of the Lord moving in our lives we began to openly imagine how our union would bless many; two young people that were truly living for God, on fire and ready to witness to the world. So many lives would be changed because of our obedience. So many would be inspired and encouraged, and together we could go out and gather souls for Christ. With the both of us being anointed and equipped with God given gifts we saw ministry being birthed right in the middle of my apartment.

The more we talked the more we accepted God's plan for our lives, but would our loved ones, friends and family be as accepting? I knew Mr. Marc-Train was planning to come over, but he never showed nor did he call. Now I must figure out how in the world I was going to tell the man I had been in love with for years that I was getting married to someone else. After all this time waiting patiently, enduring all the ups and downs of our relationship and now I was going to marry my big brother.

A Storm

How could he and why would he accept this news without becoming angry? What if he wanted to fight Kenny for my love? Kenny being very supportive was willing to be with me so we could tell him together, but I felt this was something I needed to do on my own. As Kenny left he hugged me and it no longer felt like a brotherly hug. We agreed that we would talk every day and not have a prolonged engagement. He wanted to get married right away, but I was still in shock and unsure how I wanted to navigate through everything. Before I did anything or made any plans, I must speak with Mr. Marc-Train.

It was Friday and Mr. Marc-Train still hadn't called or come by. I prayed that he was alright and at the same time I thanked God I had time to figure out what I was going to say when I finally did speak to him. How could I let go of all the memories and the relationship we developed? Our bond had gone far beyond that of a typical boyfriend and girlfriend – he was my best friend, my love; my heart belonged to him. We matured into a union that had planned for a future and now all our plans were completely altered.

There was no easy way to say it to him, and I could not believe I was even thinking about going through with it. He would surely think I was crazy when I tell him God was leading Kenny and me to get married. He would surely think I had lost my mind, agreeing to marry someone I considered a big brother.

Telling my mother was what I decided to do first, even before I talked to Mr. Marc-Train. Kenny and I had talked long enough and

A Storm

since I hadn't heard from Mr. Marc-Train, I had to call my mom. "Mommy, Mommy, Mommy. I don't know how to explain this and didn't expect it to take place, but Kenny and I are getting married," I said. After telling mom what Kenny said the Lord told him to do, without hesitation she was acceptant of the decision. She said to me that on the way to the funeral with Kenny's uncle and aunt, his aunt Ada said, "Wouldn't it be something if Kenny marries Lillie?" My mouth dropped to the floor as mom told me this. Why would anyone be thinking about me as his next wife when we hadn't had the funeral for his first wife?

Nevertheless, my mother's response to the news further persuaded me that accepting Kenny's proposal was the right thing to do. At no point was my mother upset, nor did she feel as if I was being taken advantage of or that this would be a rebound relationship. Mommy told me to prepare myself by praying and seeking the Lord because nothing was going to be easy.

That was what I needed; a real-talk moment with my mom. She didn't stop there, she took her time talking to me, and giving me insight so that I was somewhat prepared for what was up ahead.

My next call was to Tina. I didn't know what words to say to her, so I just blurted it out. Tina and Chon were away and I didn't care that I was disturbing them, because I needed to talk to my best girlfriend so that she knew before anyone else what was going on. When Tina automatically accepted the news and didn't think I was

A Storm

crazy, I began to wonder if there was something wrong with me that no one but me felt like this was moving way to fast.

Neither one of us could come up with what I should say to Mr. Marc-Train, so instead of worrying, I remained relieved that he hadn't called. When my phone rang I expect it to be Mr. Marc-Train, but it wasn't. It was Kenny. I sensed that he was going through the same thing that I was going through. We both agreed that this was the Lord's doing and could feel His presence all in the midst of the situation, but because we are human we still wondered. To ease our troubled minds, we talked on the phone for hours and hours, using that time to get to know one another in a new way.

Friday came and went, and still no Mr. Marc-Train, but Saturday morning, two days later my phone rang. Finally Mr. Marc-Train was on the line. *What do I say? How do I begin?* I promised Kenny I wouldn't procrastinate and would tell him immediately so that there would be no confusion, but I felt like no matter when I told him it would be complicated. *If he had come as planned, if he had beat Kenny to the door, would this be a different story?* He could tell in my voice that there was something wrong. He told me to get my son and me together because he was on his way to us to pick us up and he had a surprise.

When I sat silent on the phone he said to me that he was sorry for not coming and not calling, but he was caught up. He asked me not to be upset with him and to get ready because he was on his way. He was not making it easy for me so instead of telling him, I kept

A Storm

asking why he didn't come, and why he didn't call. I deserved a phone call even if it was to say he was not coming, but also to make sure that I was okay during the horrible storm. All he could say to me was that he loved me and he was sorry, please forgive me and get ready.

I was waiting on God to give me the right words to say, but He hadn't yet. I didn't want to blurt things out like I did with my mom or Tina so I was begging God to form the right words in my mouth. I waited and still didn't know what to say. Then Mr. Marc-Train asked me what was wrong. I responded by saying I didn't think he needed to come over and that there was something I had to tell him. He got a little reserved and asks me why he shouldn't come over. He told me he had somewhere he wanted to take us and it was a surprise. I told him that I had a rehearsal to go to and I think it would be best if he didn't come.

Mr. Marc-Train being the smart guy that he was said to me that there was something more going on, and he wanted to know what I had to tell him. He apologized again and told me that he was wrong for not calling. He attempted to make the case that his mistake was no reason for him to not come and pick us up. He said I was taking things too far. He wanted me to stop being stubborn and get ready because he was in route and didn't want his surprise to be ruined.

Delaying no further, I opened my mouth and said God had shown someone that I was to be their wife. The silence on the phone was like no other. I wasn't sure if he was still there or not so I checked and said hello. He let me know that he was still there, and then he became silent again.

I felt obligated to tell him I loved him and that I wasn't stringing him along all this time, but he knew that already. I felt he deserved to hear me say that this was not my plan and I had no intentions to ever get involved with another man as long as he was in my life, but he was fully cognizant of that too. I felt he had to understand that my dream was to spend the rest of my life with him as I had never had a man make me as happy as he did, but he told me he was totally aware of that also. With tears in my eyes I wanted him to know that I didn't have all the answers and I didn't want the love he had for me all this time to turn into hate, and he calmly assured me that would never happen.

Now I was trying to understand why he hadn't flipped out, but at the same time I was thinking he was in just as much shock as I was. After a brief pause he said, "It's Kenny isn't it," and I responded, "Yes." He continued, "Remember a few months ago when I told you I had a terrible dream? I didn't tell you what the dream was about, but I asked you had you been talking with any other guys. I asked you that because the Lord came to me in a dream and told me that He was displeased with the way I handled our relationship. He told me that because we did wrong, He was not going to allow us to have the future we desired. He showed me that you were going to marry another man...Kenny," he said.

A Storm

I was drenched in my tears and could hardly catch my breath. I thought the bad dreams were because of his job not God speaking to him about me. We both were wrong and sinned against God, and now we had been handed down our punishment, reaping what we had sown. He said, "I asked God to have mercy on us and allow me to make things right. I got in a hurry to get my lawyer to complete my divorce paperwork, and began planning our future together. I wanted to show God that if He gave me another chance I would not take for granted nor mishandle what He had given to me. I promised Him that I would take good care of you and do right by you for the rest of your life. With Kenny already being married I felt I had time to marry you and show God I was serious. When you called and told me that Dion had passed so suddenly, I knew my time was winding up. I guess I know now you really can't box with God –you will never win."

He talked to me on the phone until he showed up to my door. I should have known that he was still driving to the house instead of staying away as I had requested. I didn't want my son to see or hear what was going on, so we went into my bedroom to talk alone. We sat on the edge of the bed silent – I guess neither one of us really knew what to say. I knew there were some questions to be asked and waited for them to come. Was I sure I wanted to marry someone that had recently lost their wife? Did I really want to do this with a man I considered a big brother? Why would I jump right into a marriage without dating the person first? And lastly, did I think Mr. Marc-Train would just walk away from this relationship without giving it

A Storm

one final try and fight for the woman he loved with all of his heart? He decided not to fight knowing that he wasn't going to win.

He kissed me on my forehead and gave me the spare key to my apartment. We stood up and he hugged me, but the hug felt different. It felt as if he knew I belonged to someone else and he respected that. Mr. Marc-Train went out to talk to my son telling him to be a good boy, and that he expected him to grow up and be a great man. He gave him instructions to take care of me and make sure no one hurt me. I cried until there were no more tears for him to wipe from my face, and then he said goodbye.

A covenant is a solemn agreement; a vow or promise to assure something will happen or certainly be done. When this Oreo cookie said *Yes* to the Lord I entered into an agreement that I desired never to break. I gave my life to the Lord for Him to use me and He was doing just that. Not only did I make a promise to God, but He also made promises to me. The Word of God is full of promises that God never breaks. I had to realize that in order for God to make good on His promises, I had to stick firmly to mine. His promises were true and He made certain that they were fulfilled.

We all make plans for our future, and if we are making these plans we want them to be the best. We seek to have the finest, be the greatest and live a supreme life with the resources God has given to us. Everything isn't always what it seems and after a while reality will set in. The reality is we are not in control of our lives, God is in control. Reality is we think we know what is best for us, but only

A Storm

God knows best. We think we can manage time, but in God's time He will demonstrate He has the power over all things. It takes a storm of reality to see that in all our planning it means nothing if it's not the design God already has set for us. But after the storm, my covering was there to reveal His purpose for my life. My covering showed me that He would keep His promises and answer every prayer and desire set before Him if I was obedient and submitted and committed to His will.

Chapter 16

Engaged

Out of all the women in the world in pursuit of husband and a happily ever after, why did it feel like my journey had to be a unique thriller, filled with comedy, drama, tragedy, excitement and cliff hangers? Every morning I awoke I waited for someone to tell me my dream was over. The feeling was indescribable, and I anticipated something bad would happen at any moment. *Is this really happening to me?* As I go from day to day, questions filled my head leaving me to wonder if this was the craziest thing I had ever done in my life – agreeing to marry someone I had never been in a relationship with.

I was an Oreo cookie but I was nobody's virgin. I'd had a child out of wedlock and the father didn't respect or love me enough to marry me, so why would another man? My son's father and I dated for seven years, it was five years before we got engaged, so how could I believe that a man I never dated would marry me in a matter of weeks without getting to know me, never going out with me, and never having sex with me to make sure that I was who he wanted?

Would a man that has no children be willing to marry a woman with a child and potentially have baby-daddy drama? Would he really want to marry me if he knew how broken this Oreo cookie really was? How would he handle my past, the dark sides of me that not even my closest friends were acquainted with? Could he handle being with a woman who had been sexually and mentally abused? I knew Mr. Marc-Train was willing to accept me, but when Kenny found out just how damaged I was I wondered if he would be like Mr. Marc-Train and love me anyway. What man would commit to marrying a woman that had been in a serious relationship with someone else, with a strong possibility of her running back into the arms of the man she felt safe with, was familiar with, and had been in love with?

Rough around the edges tends to be my overall personality description. My past has caused me to build up barriers not easily infiltrated. I wasn't accustomed to trusting very many people - especially men. It took me a long while to get to the point where I trusted someone, and one wrong move would cause permanent exile from my circle whether male or a female.

Kenny didn't know that I couldn't have any more children. If he ever wanted to have a bigger family he wouldn't be able to, not with me. He also didn't know that I didn't want children, and only recently wished I could have a child with Mr. Marc-Train as part of my silly dreams. Kenny didn't know that I did not approve of my husband being a preacher. My experience showed me that by and large preachers were sought after by eager women craving status or position, and I felt most preachers were weak in that area constantly falling for their traps.

As a Pastor's son there was a great chance he would want to follow in his father's footsteps. He didn't know that I would be the wife that had no problem physically putting a woman in her place for attempting to violate my territory in any way. He knew that my mom and dad would come down to Baltimore when we were children, but he didn't know as a child I hated church. He knew I was now a member of his father's church, but wouldn't be there if it weren't for my mother's suggestion and the Lord then leading me there. He didn't know many things about me, and there was so much more to uncover once he began to pull back my layers. He only saw me at church and functions or youth gatherings. He knew very little; hardly anything personal regarding me. Yet he wanted to marry me.

There were so many women who desired to be Kenny's next wife. He chose me. Friends of his sister, daughters and granddaughters of women in different churches all began planning their propositioning not knowing he had already made his choice. There were women that were prettier than me, had no children, and who were more likely to be accepted as his wife, but I was chosen. Young ladies who were already filled with the Holy Ghost that had been waiting patiently on their Boaz; all skipped over for me including his ex-girlfriends from college and church who were ready to seize any opportunity to reignite an old flame. Instead two unfamiliar sticks will be put together to start a brand new fire.

Kenny was a widow with a college degree; a hard-working man with no children; he came from a good family; and most of all he was saved, sanctified and filled with the Holy Ghost. He had proven himself to be a good man by the way he took care of Dion. I had never seen Kenny in another woman's face or conducting himself inappropriately with anyone. At Dion's funeral there was a long standing ovation, applauding him for how he gently took care of his wife; being there in the hospital months at a time throughout the night sleeping on a sofa chair next to her bed in the hospital. So many spoke highly of him and how he looked after her.

He was acknowledged as an honorable young man choosing not to step out on his marriage even when weaker men would have done so in the midst of the pain he had endured. He didn't have anyone on the side but remained devoted to his wife and his marriage. He didn't file for a divorce or try to send her back to her mother and father. He didn't put the responsibility on his parents to take care of her, and he never would have thought to do so. He stayed with her; bought wigs for her, and always told her she was beautiful even as her weight, her hair, and her strength began to fade away because of Lupus. Any man that could endure sickness to that magnitude and come out standing, faithful, loving, and respectful is definitely a man any woman would want to marry. The question I had was; would he really want me?

My brother and sisters don't have much to say about Kenny and I getting married. I guess it was a bit much for all of us to swallow. My brother didn't even feel the need to question Kenny's intentions since he had already said that God told him to marry me. My family was in awe of the situation (as I was) fully aware that Kenny's wife had just died. I appreciated the concern some of my family members raised thinking that Kenny could be going through a grieving process, and was unintentionally using me as a rebound relationship. The suggestions that we wait and get to know each other before getting married were shot down when Kenny explained that there would be no long, drawn out engagement.

Kenny and I were so excited to tell people we thought would be happy for us about our union that we didn't consider those who wouldn't be. After telling my mother and siblings, it was Kenny's time to tell his family. District choir rehearsal caused us to be around some of his cousins that had always expressed an interest in me. I saw them differently, knowing shortly I would no longer be a woman they could consider dating because I would be married to their cousin. We would all be family.

I wondered how his sister would take the news that I was marrying her brother and becoming her big sister-in-law. Would she accept me as more than a sister in the Lord? Would she let me love her and get to know her better, or would she feel awkward having me as an in-law? Would she continue to treat me kindly, or try and get to know me better?

The storm caused service to be cancelled on Sunday, so Kenny and I were able to spend a little more time together outside of the church. Every chance Kenny got to come to my apartment and spend time with my son and I he did. Bringing *Stoko's* personal pan pizza's and honey barbeque wings to eat we would sit together and plan our wedding. This kept my mind off of Mr. Marc-Train and kept me focused on getting to know Kenny better and become comfortable with everything that was taking place.

Once the weather let up and we had church service, Kenny went into his father's office to speak with him as his Pastor. He told him what God had instructed him to do. Needless to say, his father wasn't completely sure about Kenny's decision. It was no surprise to me that his father would have this reaction because I had a child. I had heard his father on numerous occasions speak about being careful of marring someone with children because you will have to deal with the other parent as well. I knew he didn't want his own son to have to experience this.

His father expressed great concern because I was a member of the church, and once some of the other members found out, I might not be able to handle their response. As his Pastor and father, Kenny's dad indicated with great and critical disappointment his opposition to our marriage. Kenny made it clear to his father that the choice was already made, and no one would be able to change the decision God had put in place. His father had to accept God's will over his own and pray for us that we would be able to handle what was up ahead.

Everyone continued to show Kenny support during the loss of his wife even going as far as encouraging him during the church services telling him to hang in there because God was going to lead him to find a new wife, not knowing how true those words were; I was already there. I was unaware that Kenny had spoken with his father when I went up to the altar for prayer. Pastor laid hands on me, but I didn't hear him pray which was unusual. I knew the dynamics of our surroundings were going to change once it was made know to everyone that Kenny and I were getting married, but I had no idea how challenging life would become.

Kenny took his mother to *Best Buy* in between services to purchase a stereo system for an upcoming event. He took this one-on-one time with his mother as an opportunity to tell her what God had directed him to do. Of course his mother was jolted by our announcement as any mother would be under the circumstances. This was not what she expected. Naturally she was concerned about her son's wellbeing.

In every decision God made for my life He had never steered me wrong. There had been times when I felt all alone in these decisions. I had to remind myself that God would never leave me. People might make you feel as though you are making the worse choice of your life when you follow God, especially when it looks like what you are doing doesn't make sense. They don't understand what God is doing and the truth is we don't either, but we choose to follow the plan God has for us and not our own.

Engaged

To the natural eye it looked as if we were making a reckless decision, but from our spiritual sight it took faith and trust to see that God had everything under control. Daily I prayed that I would continue to see with my spiritual eyes and not allow my natural eyes to doubt God and His astounding ways.

*****

Valentine's Day had arrived and Kenny was in charge of a special dinner at the church's eatery. Valentine's Day is *the* holiday for love and love was definitely in the air. Kenny and I were spending a lot of time bonding with each other and he with my son. Although I was still in shock trauma, I began to get used to the fact that I would be his wife. My fiancé purchased me a cute jean outfit and a Louis Vuitton hand bag for our first Valentine's Day, and finally I received an engagement ring. It all became more real as time passed. My days continued with no communication with Mr. Marc-Train. He had been keeping his distance but my mind would sometimes wonder how he was dealing with everything.

When Mr. Marc-Train and I talked he told me that he was trying to accept the decision I made. He expressed his concern for me moving too fast, and wanted to make sure that I wasn't being forced. Even after ending our relationship he still cared for me and loved me. He was busy altering his life to adapt to us not being together. I couldn't understand what all there was for him to alter until he told me he had purchased a home for us. When he called me after the storm and was on his way over with his big surprise, the surprise turned out to be that he bought a house for us to move into. He was anticipating proposing to me on Valentine's Day when he received his divorce papers so that we could live out our future as planned.

Unfortunately eight days earlier Kenny showed up with a different plan in mind. Could I now change my mind and run back to Mr. Marc-Train, now that everything was in order and he was ready for me? My natural eye would say yes and run to him in a heartbeat, but my spiritual eye persuaded me to remain in God's will and not to be distracted or deceived into believing I knew better than God who I should spend the rest of my life with. The chance to walk away and resume my happy relationship with Mr. Marc-Train was present. I chose to stick with God's plan over my own.

With all the things that Mr. Marc-Train and I had gone through I expected him to fight for me. Not physically go blow for blow with Kenny, but at least put up some type of resistance. If he really desired for me to be his wife, why didn't he show me? At the time I wanted Mr. Marc-Train to show me that he still loved me even though we both knew that it was over. I knew neither one of us wanted to let our relationship go, but it was bigger than us. I couldn't act off of emotions alone. I had to be obedient to what the Lord said.

I had a soul tie with Mr. Marc-Train that had to be denounced. I needed to release all feelings and free myself from the bond we had. The connection that we had could no longer exist and the only way to untie it was by seeking God.

I didn't want to be in a relationship with one man while thinking about another. I could not give myself to Kenny 100 percent if I hadn't let go of the link between Mr. Marc-Train and I. Mr. Marc-Train wasn't willing to assist me in disentangling the connection so I had to do all I could to free myself from it all. No more phone calls, no more emails, no more instant messages. He could no longer come to my home or show up at my job. I didn't need to call him for anything and he didn't need to call me.

Saying I was going to erase his number from my phone didn't mean anything. This man had been in my life for years and I knew his number by memory. I would not fool myself or play games as if deleting his number would mean that I had no way of contacting him. Self-control would have to stop me from dialing his number. It was no longer my duty to worry about what assignment his job had placed him on or if he was safe or not. He no longer needed to co-manage my bank account or be concerned about my money getting low.

God spoke to me and directed me to be honest with Kenny about the way that I felt. If we were going to be married I needed to be able to tell him whatever I felt having no secrets and never being deceitful. I had to remove Mr. Marc-Train's things from my home and keep him out of my life.

Pastor spoke a message about the battle of Joshua at Jericho and it was as if God was speaking to me directly. Jericho had been conquered and the people were given instructions to destroy the entire city and everything in it except for Rahab and her family.

Engaged

Everything in the city was considered accursed; therefore no one was to take anything for themselves. Achan, one of the men of the tribe of Judah, decided to take a garment and some silver and gold for himself and hid it under his tent. When Joshua went up to battle again they lost and he couldn't understand why if God was with them. When God told him what Achan did, Joshua had to kill Achan and his entire family.

I applied this story to my current life and recognized that holding on to any part of Mr. Marc-Train would be against God's will. I couldn't hold on to my past and expect God to bless me and my marriage. I didn't want to be the reason that our marriage didn't work out after God had chosen us to be together. Letting go of the ungodly soul tie was not an option, it was a command.

*****

Kenny made it known that he was not only receiving a wife from God to provide for, protect and love, but also a son. Not knowing much about Michael, Kenny wanted to make a few things clear from the beginning. I called Michael to let him know that I was getting married. He immediately assumed that I was getting married to Mr. Marc-Train. I explained to him that it was not Mr. Marc-Train, but rather the man God had specifically designed and prepared for me to be with for the rest of my life.

Kenny took this opportunity to introduce himself and be transparent with Michael. He told Michael that he was going to love and take care of Zion as if he were his own. He went further to tell

Michael that his father had raised him to be a man. He was taught that a real man took care of his own home and looked to no other man for handouts. He informed Michael that under his roof and in his home he was the provider so Michael's money or resources were no good to him. There would be only one head of our household, and Kenny let Michael know that position was filled by a very capable man and that no two men could run the show.

He let Michael know that he was aware I had never sued for child support. With him becoming my husband he no longer had a need to fear that I would change my mind. He didn't need to worry about how his son was going to be provided for because Kenny put it plain and simple; He had it taken care of. He continued explaining that his point was not for him to neglect his son, but to understand that as a man he wasn't going to force him to do anything. He even suggested that Michael save his money to pay for Zion's college tuition. Kenny told Michael he could buy and do whatever he pleased for Zion, but as far as supporting this home – our home, his money was useless and not necessary and would not be accepted.

I expected Michael to respond pleasantly and consent to what Kenny expressed. Kenny had given him a get-out-of-jail-free card, and he had never been close to being in jail. Kenny made it clear that he was giving Michael liberty. As my husband, Kenny would be the man responsible for fathering Zion, while Michael could attribute at will, with no penalties or strings attached. Kenny had taken on full responsibility as if he was the one who had gotten me pregnant.

Engaged

Instead Michael was angry. He realized that Kenny wasn't going to get into verbal or physical confrontations with him. He saw that there wasn't going to be any rude or disruptive phone calls being made to him for any reason.

He realized that Kenny was in agreement with me and wasn't going to make his life miserable by dragging him into a courthouse. He realized that Kenny had left the ball in his court to see if Michael truly wanted to provide for his own son. Michael recognized that I was happy and that made him angry. Not only was I happy, but the life that he was determined to never let me have I was finally getting. Michael realized that any chance of him repairing anything with me had ended.

Pastor had Kenny and I stand during an evening service. He announced to our church that Kenny and I were getting married, and I felt a cold breeze in the building. I thought it was a sign of relief that we were finally getting our relationship out into the open. After service we received a lot of congratulatory hugs and well wishes, and I was thankful that the church family was pleased with God's choice of a wife for Kenny and more importantly they were grateful to God for sending me a good husband and father for me and my son.

Being at this church as a single mom I always received compliments about the way I took care of my child and my desire to live for God. Many came to me and made me feel unashamed for having a baby out of wedlock and would encourage me that God would send me the wonderful husband that I deserved. The prayers they said they sent up for me had been answered, so certainly there was nothing but joy and gladness for God putting Kenny and me together. Yes we were an unlikely couple because we were like brother and sister who were never attracted to one another, but who would really sit back and say God has made a mistake?

As quickly as the news was told within the church, it was all over the internet and emails even quicker. The news had gone all over the country even to New York were Kenny's former mother-in-law was still grieving. It was then I realized the cold breeze I thought was a relief was actually fury and resentment. When Pastor spoke with us he warned us that there would be comments made and we needed to prepare ourselves through prayer to be able to manage the bumpy road ahead. When young women who I looked to as sisters in Christ began to openly express how opposed they were of the decision God made for me and Kenny, I had to keep in mind what our Pastor warned us of. When older seasoned women who I looked to as mothers and role models went to Kenny and said that I was nothing like Dion showing they were not in favor of this marriage, I had to accept the disappointment. It wasn't until the women had a meeting that I realized many were not pleased and felt there was more to Kenny and I being together than it was. I couldn't believe the words coming out of the mouths of some women. I couldn't believe I was actually still sitting in the meeting and not walking out. So many accusatory statements, but no one had asked me anything to find out the truth. It was easier to make things up than to accept the truth. I was willing and ready to answer truthfully but no questions were ever asked. People continued to assume what they wanted to assume and believe.

Hurt by the actions of some church members, I couldn't understand how I had gone from a respectable single mom, on fire for the Lord, to being a whore who hunted Kenny down as if he was prey. People always want to see you do good, but not if it seems to be better than them. I had turned from the young lady so many were willing to help, to a woman no one wanted to be involved with or assist in the planning of my wedding. Before I was so anointed and gifted, but now I was a gold digger looking to be a part of the "First Family". I was once good enough to be the young lady a mother's son was interested in, but now because I was marrying Kenny instead I had become the scum of the earth. I was the young lady other young women confided in and asked for advice when they were upset about relationships gone badly, but now instead of being talked to I was being talked about. My name had been dragged through the mud and I was confused as to who was supportive of me and who was not. Too confused to try and figure out who's who, I distanced myself and waited for everyone to show who they really were.

I was once popular with the little children because they loved to play with me and my son, but it caught me off guard to see grownups now forcing their children to keep away from my son and me. My son wasn't involved in this decision, but he felt the negative vibes from it. We didn't have any family in Baltimore so there were few children for him to play with, and the little group of friends that he did have suddenly were unavailable to play. This fueled anger in me because he was my child – a four year old little boy who had no idea what was going on and should not have been punished. Things had gone way too far and my child was being negatively affected. Anyone that has a child understands a mother's fury when it comes to their child being mistreated.

My mind went back to the innuendos made around me as a child about my father and mother. Mean-spirited adults would make comments about my father that clearly were inappropriate for me to hear. If the statements were true or not wasn't the matter, the point is a child shouldn't be exposed to this type of behavior. Knowing what I had to go through as a child I was on guard for my own child so that he wouldn't have to endure the same things I did, especially since the comments made about me weren't true. My sudden change in behavior shielding myself and my child from people and environments now caused individuals to be even more upset. It wasn't looked at as me trying to protect my child from two-faced people; it was deemed that I thought I was better than others because I was marrying the Pastor's son. Apparently I thought of myself as a VIP and I didn't hang with the common folk anymore. The truth was I hadn't changed at all, but the more I tried to be myself, the worse people talked.

Rumors spread quickly that Kenny and I had been in a sexual relationship, and we were involved with each other before Dion passed away. Just when I thought things couldn't get any worse, the rumors were passed on to Dion's family who obviously weren't expecting to hear anything of the sort. It was just weeks ago that Kenny was being praised at Dion's funeral for being such a good husband, and now some of the same people who gave the standing ovation were slandering him. He compared it to the story of Jesus coming through Jerusalem on a donkey as everyone cried out, "Hosanna! Hosanna!" and the very next week the same people shouted out, "Crucify him!"

 This news was not easily accepted by Dion's mother who was still grieving. Still hurting from the untimely death of her daughter, she was receiving phone calls and listening to untruths about her former son-in-law. She believed everything that was told to her and was against Kenny and me getting married. These untruths could have easily been disputed if they weren't coming from different negative sources right within the church. Members of the church calling her made the lies more believable. After all, what reason would a church member have to blatantly tell lies? There had to be some truth to this, right? None of the information being disseminated was true, yet Kenny and I had to sit back and watch as our names and reputations were on trial. We had to accept that every church member wasn't a saint and there is a difference. There were some who wanted to believe the accusations so badly that they refused to accept the truth – that God joined us together.

Engaged

Having a fiancé and actually planning a wedding was a time in every woman's life that should be filled with excitement and happiness. As I embarked on this new phase in my life, those around me who knew me should have been there to celebrate with me. Brides are supposed to get suggestions and ideas for the wedding along with offers for assistance. Everyone would be waiting for the wedding day, doing whatever they could to make sure the wedding day was a success. The bride would begin planning her dream wedding that she has imagined since childhood.

Every commercial on television and every song on the radio reminded the bride of her upcoming nuptials. She goes from store to store and website to website wanting to make sure she didn't forget anything because this was the biggest day of her life. She wrote ideas and plans down in pencil so that she could erase and change things when a new idea came to mind. Everyone she came in contact with knew she was getting married and could see the glow on her face. The bride-to-be was overjoyed with everyone being happy for her, and could hardly sleep some nights because of all the excitement. To grasp that this is not the way it would be for me was hurtful. It broke my heart to see individuals who strategically set out to do and say whatever they could to make this time in my life far from a glorious moment.

Kenny wanted some of the younger girls to be a part of our wedding because he considered them to be his little sisters. They were always around he and Dion and he wanted them to continue to feel included and not feel left out. Hearing one of the young girls say she didn't want to have anything to do with the wedding and didn't want to hear about it or partake in it offended Kenny terribly. Everyone's expectations of each other were not being met causing a lot of bitter words to be said and vicious actions to occur.

I kept hearing people say that God wasn't in the midst of confusion, so our engagement and marriage was not of God. I took this statement to be one of the most ignorant things I had heard during the entire ordeal. The confusion was in the lies being told. The confusion was in the mean-spirited behavior and hateful comments made. Our engagement and marriage was of God, I was a witness to that, but the confusion came from people, not from God, and He was definitely not in the midst of that.

I was built to be tough. After going through all that I had gone through in my life, I had no choice but to be tough. Throughout the ages, the church was a place for all to run to for safety, so no one expected to feel mistreated and injured while there, but sometimes it happened. The hurt affected you worse however, when you were caught off guard; not anticipating the harm.

I sat with Kenny at my apartment and he held me as I began to cry. I told him maybe he should go back to God and find someone else. The evil that had been directed towards me was attempting to bring up a very shady side of me that no one at our church or in Baltimore had ever seen or would be able to handle. It was my automatic defense mechanism that was coming into play, and now I trusted no one.

Just the thought of someone I looked up to and respected so highly saying to Kenny, "She is NOTHING like Dion", as if I didn't meet their standards was upsetting to say the least. Hearing our Pastor tell Kenny to stay away from my apartment because people had been driving by my place seeing his car in the parking lot late at night was even more wounding. I found this appalling as I remembered how difficult it was for anyone to come and pick me up for church when I didn't have a car. The silence in the car as I got a ride home some nights felt so awkward that sometimes I would miss church so that I wouldn't have to go through it.

Where I lived was so out of the way then but now it was a popular route to take. Not only that but one would just happen to notice- out of all the cars in the parking lot that Kenny's car was one of them. Yes he was at my place, yes we did eat late night dinners together, and yes we did watch movies, talk, and attempt to get to know one another better. His car being at my house didn't mean that we were having sex. We weren't. But we understood we needed to shun from the appearance of impropriety.

No one ever asked me if I was I having sex with Kenny. No one ever asked me what he was doing at my house. No one ever pulled me to the side and told me of the accusations to offer me any type of advice to clear my name. I heard about people going to the Pastor and to his wife, but not one time did anyone ever come to me.

Maybe if someone would've approached me correctly and told me what it was about me that was leading everyone to believe the lies, I could clear things up, but that didn't happen. I got silence.

I felt so alone not having a woman to talk to about this time of my life. I learned early that my family did not need to know all that was taking place at the time it happened. My mother would call me and ask how certain people were doing and I would want to tell her how they had been treating Kenny and I. Instead I said they were doing fine and to pray for them. I had to swallow hurt and move on making sure I did not render evil for evil. Kenny hugged me tighter as I demanded to know why he had gotten me into this. He gently replied to me that the same ones that were saying negative things now would be saying something different after a while; we just had to hold on.

Kenny stood over me as my covering and wanted to protect me from all of the darts and arrows being thrown at me to cause me great detriment. He did all he could to protect me even as he was hurting. That was the moment when I felt God placing the love in my heart for him that a wife has for her husband. No matter how much my natural-self wanted to give up, my spiritual-self dominated. Giving up was not an option. Knowing that he would stand up for me, defend and protect me, made me feel safe in his arms – the arms God prepared for me to rest in.

Kenny was being strong for me, but wounded himself he needed encouragement as well. The Lord led him to call Elder

Donald Farmer from Memphis, Tennessee. Elder Farmer was an Evangelist who came to Baltimore every year to do a tent revival. He was there for Kenny when Dion died, and Kenny wanted Elder Farmer to hear from him that he was getting married again. Before Kenny could say anything, Elder Farmer put Kenny's mind at ease and before Kenny could speak he said, "The Lord told me that you were going to get married, and He told me who you were going to get married to," Elder Farmer explained. "He told me not to call you and tell you anything but to wait for your call so that I can be a confirmation. You are going to marry the young lady who has the little boy, and had the headaches the last time I was there. God has spoken, and this is your wife." Amazed Kenny and I reverenced God for this unique affirmation of His divine will for our marriage. We never would have thought that God was going to use Elder Farmer as His mouthpiece to validate His plans, but He did and it was indisputable that we must carry on.

  This arrangement was put in place long before Kenny or I ever knew of it. God ordained our marriage and called it into fruition never looking or wanting mans approval because He is God and His plan will be fulfilled. With that being said, Kenny and I could no longer dwell in any pity or harp on any disapproving behaviors being carried out by church folk, friends or family. As the scripture says, "If God be for us, who can be against us?"

  God loved us enough to not only choose us for this distinctive journey, but to trust and believe that we wouldn't give up. If anyone was to search our hearts they would know that we never desired to do wrong and wouldn't do wrong out of fear of ruining what God was doing in our lives. With all the accusations being spread about it encouraged us more not to do anything erroneous. Making sure all the lies being told about us remained a lie inspired us more to live holy as God's Spirit made intersession for us.

We both agreed that our hearts were in God's hands and we weren't going to let anything stop us from carrying out God's purpose. This was inspiring as God breathed His Word upon us; leading us to the scripture and theme for our wedding "God's Will – Our Hearts Are in His Hands" Romans 8:27. According to Romans 8:27-39 reads,

And he that searcheth the hearts knoweth what is the mind of the Spirit, because he maketh intercession for the saints according to the will of God.

And we know that all things work together for good to them that love God, to them who are the called according to his purpose.

For whom he did foreknow, he also did predestinate to be conformed to the image of his Son, that he might be the firstborn among many brethren.

Moreover whom he did predestinate, them he also called: and whom he called, them he also justified: and whom he justified, them he also glorified.

What shall we then say to these things? If God be for us, who can be against us?

He that spared not his own Son, but delivered him up for us all, how shall he not with him also freely give us all things?

Who shall lay anything to the charge of God's elect? It is God that justifieth.

Who is he that condemneth? It is Christ that died, yea rather, that is risen again, who is even at the right hand of God, who also maketh intercession for us.

Who shall separate us from the love of Christ? Shall tribulation, or distress, or persecution, or famine, or nakedness, or peril, or sword?

As it is written, For thy sake we are killed all the day long; we are accounted as sheep for the slaughter.

Nay, in all these things we are more than conquerors through him that loved us.

For I am persuaded, that neither death, nor life, nor angels, nor principalities, nor powers, nor things present, nor things to come,

Nor height, nor depth, nor any other creature, shall be able to separate us from the love of God, which is in Christ Jesus our Lord.

It was the love of God that had us on this venture. It was not an escapade that we had created for ourselves, and it was not for man to condemn us for what God had commanded us to do. Praying together Kenny and I had to agree to let nothing separate us from the love we had for God because nothing could separate us from His love for us. No matter what anyone had to say, nothing could separate us. No matter what lies and persecution we had to endure, it would not separate us.

Every day we would be slaughtered over and over again with our names pulled through the mud, but we were conquerors through

Him that loved us. If Jesus could endure the cross, surely we could endure this journey God has placed before us.

We realized with our hearts in God's hands we were protected. Everything didn't go the way we desired, but it was all working together for our good because we loved Him and He loved us. It was God that had chosen us specifically for this walk according to His purpose. We weren't second or third choices, but we were predestinated and justified. The tragedies and triumphs that we endured prepared and equipped us for this moment. God didn't leave it up to man to choose who Kenny and I should spend the rest of our lives with. He was the decision maker, and He made His decision.

God didn't say that every day was going to be easy, or that everyone would support us, but He did promise to be with us. Nothing would separate us from His love or change His mind about the decision He made for us. We had to see that no matter what tribulation, distress or persecution we might endure, God's Word was final.

No matter how alone we felt or how beat up we were, God was not going to change His mind. No matter how many were in opposition through life or death, God was not going to change His mind. Because God didn't change His mind, we were winners no matter what it looked like. There was no arm long enough to box with God, no principalities, or powers, no things present, nor things to come. No height, nor depth, nor any other creature would stop our marriage from taking place.

All of my life this Oreo cookie had been training for fights. It was a natural reaction for me to go on the defense and allow my outside - my Black side to promote fear in anyone who attempted to cause me any harm. Having my son brought out an even tougher side of me. When I felt he was being mistreated or in some kind of danger, I almost slipped into my old stance. The last thing any sane person would want to do is mistreat my offspring. As Kenny and I sat together and expounded on the word of God I had tears in my eyes as we said we would not go eye for an eye with those who opposed us. Those that were attempting to harm us were the very ones we would pray for. Those that intentionally spoke ill of us, we would continue to love. While there would remain some that would never stop with the drama, we would promote peace. We knew we were on the winning side, so there was no need for us to fight. God promised He would fight for us if we remained still.

After God gave me Romans 8 to read, I came to understand that I no longer had to depend on either of my "sides" for a defense. I now had a man that was following orders from God and he wanted to protect me and shield me from any harm. He didn't want me to put up a defensive wall, instead he wanted me grab hold of him as he grabbed hold of God. Yes, the infamous late nights that we were together, we prayed for those who thought evil against us.

We comforted each other from the painful comments and coldness of hearts we endured. Kenny said to me that what God was doing in our lives was inimitable. When God did things this grand, it left one with the choice to want to be a part of it or choose to be against it. Down the line and for years to come many would regret being against a mighty move of God such as this. Many would be remorseful as they would have missed out on the opportunity to positively take part in a God ordained marriage of this magnitude.

Kenny was able to say the right things and do the right things to protect me throughout this entire period. Praying with me and for me he showed his strength, not just physically, but spiritually. Although I hated going through and feeling the way I felt about the people and the things they were saying and doing, it gave Kenny and I an opportunity to see God in each other.

If it weren't for some of the evil things people had done to us I would not have been able to see just how powerful my future husband was when he prayed. I would not have been able to see just how extraordinary he could be under pressure. We were getting married quickly and I would not have been able to witness how striking he could become in matters pertaining to my safety and the wellbeing of my child; our child.

Engaged. Yes, this was the man God had given me to and he was showing that he would do whatever God told him, guarding and shielding me as the precious jewel he was held accountable for. He was able to be a strong man because his trust was in God. We were engaged and he was able to be a first class gentleman because he believed God wouldn't give him a second class woman to love. He stood on the Word of God and the Word alone to show just how tremendous his faith in God truly was. He did that because he knew without a doubt that he was in God's hands. He wasn't trying to make a relationship with God to be my husband; his relationship with God was why God chose him to be my husband.

> `Note to self: Don't expect a man to be your covering until he has his covering in place.`

Thanks be to God my husband was already in His hands, fully equipped to be my new covering.

Chapter 17

The Wedding

It was about time I started being blissful about my blessing. It was time for me to be happy that I was getting married. It was time for me to have a glow of excitement on my face. Time to start dreaming about what colors the wedding would be, what flowers I would use, the songs that would be sung, the order of the service and where we would go for our honeymoon. I had to think about my wedding gown, what style it should be and how I was going to look in it. With less than two months to plan I had much ground to cover.

> Note to self: When a man really wants to do what God has told him to do, it will not take years for him to marry you. Money will not stop him, family will not stop him, and friends will not stop him. When he is certain he wants to marry you and is obedient to what God has told him to do there will be no hesitation or excuses.

Kenny had been pressuring me for a date so that we could send out invitations. When a man genuinely cares for you, he will do whatever he can not to prolong an engagement and lay to rest any

The Wedding

apprehension. When a man is ready there will be no game playing, only wedding bells ringing, and I kept hearing them in my head over and over again.

Kenny was ready to get married and finally so was I. For a long time I had been looking forward to my wedding. Now that the time had come I could hardly believe it was actually happening. This was my first time getting married and I wanted it to be the one and only time. I wanted everything to be perfect for this once in a lifetime event. Kenny and I had to get the wedding party together to choose who would be a part of our special day.

With all the drama that had taking place I told him that I preferred to have family only standing by my side. I didn't know who my real friends were in Baltimore. I would rather have people I knew for sure were happy for me in my wedding party over people who wanted to be in the mix just to know what was going on.

Kenny's sister Katina and of course my sisters Pamela and Melody along with Tina and Tisha were in my wedding. My favorite cousin Adrienne had to be in my wedding too, along with my big cousin Shan. All of these girls have been sisters to me and I loved them dearly. One thing was for sure, they all had my back. There was no question about that.

My laundry list of a bridal party left Kenny with work to do getting his Groomsmen together. He on the other hand had too many family members and chose to use his closest friends. Andre was his choice for the best man and Omar, Tarik, Diesel, and Devin were his

The Wedding

choices for the rest of the groomsmen. My God-daughters Jasmine and Kyana would be the junior bridesmaids, and handsome Kambry and Jalen would be the junior groomsmen. My niece Doobie was my flower girl, and my son Zion would be the ring bearer. Now that the wedding party was complete we could move on to the next step.

Everything was new to me. I had no idea what I was supposed to do. With no family in Baltimore to keep me on track and get things in motion like they should I began feeling overwhelmed. I wanted everything to be perfect. Apprehensively I sought out the wedding coordinator that Kenny suggested to me. Not knowing who I could trust during this time left me uneasy in asking anyone to do anything for me. But because this was important, I did it anyway.

I was relieved when the young lady agreed to be our wedding coordinator. Recently married herself she had even more insight on what steps to takes to make our day a success. Unfortunately, after no response to my emails and many unreturned phone calls, I began to think that this wedding coordinator was more of a wedding slayer. Back to square one. I was in utter disbelief, and couldn't chance asking anyone else to help me with the wedding not knowing if they too would have ulterior motives or simply be unavailable.

There were still ugly rumors spreading around and I had less and less people talking to me as we got closer to the wedding date. I didn't want to tell my mother or my family the bad news because I didn't want anyone being upset, but I had no one to talk to. Thank God for Sister Denise and Sister Clarise agreeing to decorate the

The Wedding

church for me and Ms. Robin from my job that was like a mother to me, agreed to take care of the wedding reception decorations. It was the family of the Bride who was responsible for planning the wedding. I found it was more than a challenge with my family so far from Baltimore and without a coordinator and a few weeks to plan.

Kenny and I drove up to Rochester and there was a Brumfield family gathering taking place at my aunt's new home. Being around my family with them seeing how happy I was rejuvenated me and I refused to allow myself to feel defeated. My family loved and supported me. It would be them that I would go to for wedding assistance. I knew all I had to do was ask and after that, I would not have to worry about another thing.

My superstar cousin Lelia agreed to sing "Faith" and my melodic cousin Crissy would sing "The Lord's Prayer". I knew God was working it all out. Thankfully there were several church members from my hometown willing to do whatever they could for our wedding as well. My two big sister's Michelle and Linda came to my rescue and a big smile came over my face. God was doing this and no one could stop it. Where it seemed as if a small few refused to lift a finger to help us, God had sent an army of women to help.

Michelle was coordinating the hostesses and Linda was allowing me to use the tiara she wore at her wedding for my something borrowed. Mother Pappins made all of the flowers for the wedding, Sister Harrell and Sister Ivy made the Bridesmaid's dresses. My Aunt Bobbette would make my wedding dress (this time I would

The Wedding

definitely get to wear it). Just like that I went from not knowing what I should do to checking things off my to-do list.

My brothers Elder Bradford and Elder Wynn would read the scriptures for the wedding and I had my church band from Rochester scheduled as our musicians. Kenny hears a Vanessa Bell Armstrong song on the radio called, "Then Came You" and insists that I sing it to him during the wedding. Everything was falling into place and the time was getting shorter and shorter. Soon I would be Mrs. Lillian Hunt. I liked the sound of that.

Because this was the Lord's doing and it was marvelous in our eyes, didn't mean that the devil would sit back and allow everything to run smoothly. One evening Kenny and I drove separately to a state church meeting and parked in the parking lot across the street from the church. When we came out of the service both of our cars had been towed. To get each car out of the impound lot was a total of $500. We needed that money for our wedding.

With no time to waste, Kenny began working day in and day out to make up the money we had lost so that I could have everything the way that I desired for the wedding. While he was out working diligently, he was pulled over by the police for not having on a seatbelt. When the officer ran his license they apprehended him and placed him in a paddy wagon. It seemed as if one horrible thing after another kept happening to discourage us, but we continued to go back to the scripture in Romans that was the theme for our wedding. We refused to allow anything to stop us. At the end of the day we had a

The Wedding

big laugh about the matter, acting as if Kenny was now a big-time-tough-guy who had actually spent time in jail. The reality was the devil knew that we were on the brink of a blessing and he used any ploy to distract us. Seeing that the devil didn't care how he vexed us we knew that we had to continue to fast and pray.

I always believed in the ritual that only a woman that is a virgin had the right to wear white on her wedding day. Many women, regardless of their status wore white gowns, and that was fine for them. I felt uncomfortable attempting to do that. I decided I wanted a platinum and navy blue wedding. After going from one fabric store to another all over Baltimore, I finally found the perfect fabric for my dress. I was so excited to buy the fabric and send it to my aunt to begin making my wedding dress.

The design of my dress along with the color would make it unique and stand out at the wedding. No, I would not be wearing white on my wedding day, but depending on how the light reflected off my dress, it looked a little white. The ladies wore my favorite color; navy blue and the men had navy blue tuxedo's as well. Kenny and I would be the only ones wearing platinum for the platinum wedding we were planning to have.

Since we had to go up to Rochester for our fittings, my bridal party planned a bridal shower for me up there. We had a bridal shower in Baltimore where a few women showed me love and brought gifts. We enjoyed sitting and eating together, however there is nothing like family. I was overjoyed that my family came through for me. There were so many women in attendance at my family bridal shower I couldn't begin to name them all. All of my aunts and my cousins and my friends and church family gathered together to celebrate with me. A first class bridal shower with all the fun and games also came with tears of joy. As I sat in front of the crowd of women and explained to them what had taken place in my life over the past few months many were amazed and even I realized that I was still in a bit of shock.

Knowing that God placed Kenny and me together and the confirmation of it all would never cease to blow my mind. As I sat there talking about the events that lead up to the present day, I pointed out that I was no different from any other woman who gathered there. I could identify with each of them; especially ones who were waiting on God to send their husband. Many times we see others getting married before us and wonder why we weren't chosen. We go to weddings or are in weddings all the while wishing we were the bride.

Every year single women attend bridal showers and play games and drive home with the idea of how they want their bridal shower to be and before now I was one of them. We had big plans. We didn't want bridal showers at our homes anymore. Oh no. It had to be classy at a banquet hall or a catered event. No more pot luck showers with cheese and crackers. We saw varying color schemes and imagined our wedding details down to the flowers.

The Wedding

We attended weddings with our significant other, holding on to him tight praying the idea of marriage came into his mind to propose for real this time. We hated hearing people say, "Ya'll next?" as an indictment of our relationship status, knowing neither of us had even started saving for an engagement ring. It broke our hearts when we were alone at the next wedding of the season because the first one was too much for him and he refused to attend another.

How crushing to hear that the man you love attended a wedding with you, heard the love story of a special couple, and then proposed to someone else. But that was the case for many single women. We acted as if we were patiently waiting for God to send our Boaz, but we were screaming on the inside. We stood with all the other single women trying to catch the bouquet ready to knock each other over or split our dress in two if necessary. We heard the different renditions of The Lord's Prayer and picked out who would be the best one to sing it during our nuptials. We compared one wedding to another from year to year keeping our minds occupied from realizing that another year had come and gone, and it still wasn't my turn yet.

What advice could I give? How did this happen for me and not any of the single women I knew? All I can say was, "Be happy." When it is your friend getting married, be happy. When it is your family member getting married; be happy. Be genuinely happy with and for whoever is experiencing such a joyous moment and don't allow jealousy or envy to overtake you. Why be happy? I simply said

The Wedding

be happy because I knew that I was going to marry Kenny and I had my own story to tell, For years I was happy for other people and now it was time for me to be happy. I was happy and it couldn't have happened any other way.

I had my own experiences to talk about. I had my own drama to remember. My story wasn't quite like any other's that had gone before me. My story was made just for me and it was worth the wait. I didn't have to pretend to be someone else or try to steal someone's happiness because I had my own. I was happy that it wasn't me in any of those other weddings I attended. I was happy I didn't force a marriage to later find myself pregnant and alone because he wasn't ready. I was happy I didn't go along with what others told me to do marrying someone just because we had a child together. I was happy I didn't take matters into my own hands and marry who I thought was Mr. Right to find out he was Mr. All Wrong. I was happy it wasn't my turn and I didn't get picked up by any other guy but the one God had predestined for me. So just be happy.

As my bridal shower came to a close we all gathered together outside in the parking lot and formed a circle. In the middle of the circle I stood as each woman sent up prayers to God on my behalf for a wonderful marriage. Tears formed in my eyes as these women young and older cried out to God with thanksgiving for all He had done for me. I wished I could bundle the happiness up and give it to every single woman to have and hold on to until it was their turn. My prayer was that God would send each woman the man that was made

The Wedding

purposely for her that would make her even happier than I was in that moment. That every desire they had be fulfilled according to God's purpose for their life.

    I asked God to give them patience to wait and not spoil their goods destroying the harvest He had prepared for their future. I asked that He give them wisdom and a discerning spirit to know when a wolf in sheep's clothing was nearby so that they would be protected from unnecessary hurt and not be deceived by unsavory men. I wanted them to be strong women resisting the urge to form ungodly soul ties or remain in abusive relationships. Be able to admit when they made a mistake and walk away from a bad relationship with their head held high instead of allowing their pride to have them pretend that the relationship was fine, staying miserable and allowing a man to use and waste their time and gifts to benefit him, all the while tearing her down.

    The wedding isn't about the ring and how many diamonds you can afford. It's not about who's in attendance, whether they come to signify or if they are there to sincerely celebrate with you. The wedding isn't about how many gifts you receive or how much money was in the cards. The wedding isn't about returning duplicate gifts to get money or exchange it for something else. The wedding isn't about everyone getting together to look nice and take a lot of pictures. The wedding isn't about single people wishing they were getting married, or married people reminiscing about their special day. The wedding isn't for family to get together and have a family reunion. The

The Wedding

wedding is about two people going before God and joining in a covenant. Making an oath that they will honor what God has given to a standard above none other.

They leave their mother's and father's and they cleave to one another never allowing anything or anyone to come between them. Never letting third party factors interfere with what God had joined together. The wedding, according to the Bible, is a ceremony between a man and a woman, and the two shall become one, no longer two separate individuals, but united together forever unto death.

Two components, unifying, developing a phenomenon that will never be replicated was what a marriage represented. A notable moment in the ceremony is when the father gave his daughter away to the man she would spend the rest of her life with. No matter how much I wanted to forgive and forget I always fell short on grace when it came to my dad. I felt like my life could have and would have been different if he had invested time in showing that he cared for me more than he cared for himself. I realized I strayed when I became uncovered because my natural covering wasn't in place as he should have been.

Any reservation that I had regarding marriage was because of my dad. I didn't want to end up hurting the way my mother hurt. I didn't want to end up alone and loving a man that wouldn't love me as my mother had to experience. Many daughters experience this and wonder how they can move on with their lives without the hurt of a

The Wedding

missing father affecting them. The truth is, no matter how strong or weak you are, you will be affected, and it takes a relationship with God for your past hurts to have a positive rather than a negative effect on your future.

All my life I was an Oreo cookie because my daddy gave me that name. On May 30th 2003, my name would change, releasing me from my dad. Daddy was where my covering began. If not for my dad being with my mom I would not be here. No matter what happened to make our father/daughter relationship horrible, he was still my dad. It was up to me to be the bigger person. On my wedding day I extended my arm to him to begin bridging the gap that had developed between us long ago. It fell on me to break the generational curses in our relationship and as always I called on the Lord for strength to do just that.

It was almost every little girls dream to have their daddy walk them down the aisle on their wedding day and give them away, and I wanted that too. Many wondered if he deserved to be in that spot since he walked away from being my father years ago. I said he did because he was still my father, and because giving me away would be an outward representation of my liberation from what went on before, to my long-awaited happily ever after.

*****

Leaving mother and father to start your own family is a huge step. As Kenny and I grew together we would be making history together. The Kenneth and Lillian Hunt family would have their own

The Wedding

traditions and rituals. We would create our own routines and create our own special moments. Our union would be a ministry, a living epistle read by many far and near. As we encountered events in our lives we would use each one as an opportunity to give God glory and be an example and encouragement to many. I may not be able to birth any children with Kenny but who knows, God has the final say on that as well. No longer would I be a Nowlin, my new last name would be Hunt. My license would need to change from a New York license to a Maryland license. I would become a resident of this state and no longer have the status as single mother. We would be a family of three excited and happy.

Two becoming one in every aspect of our lives, we leave nothing to be just his or all mine but now ours. All of our belongings were doubled with decisions to be made on what to keep and what to get rid of. Where would we live? The lease on my apartment was done in June, I had no desire to renew, and why would Kenny want to move into an apartment? Obviously there was no reason for me to renew since I was getting married and my future husband owned a house. Could I really live in the house that Kenny and his deceased wife resided in? With such a short timeframe before the wedding it isn't realistic to attempt to purchase a new home. Kenny and I realized that it would not be wise to purchase right away, so that leaves me consenting to stay in the home that was previously occupied by Kenny and Dion. No matter how much you say you are willing to do what God wants you to do in your life, some things just

The Wedding

cause you to look up in the sky in bewilderment. This was one of those things.

Who would want to live in a house that was previously the home the man you are marrying lived in with someone else – even if that person was deceased? There was only so much painting and redesigning that you could do to the house to change the décor, but changing the décor wouldn't change the address. Kenny brought my son and me over to his home to watch movies so that we could get familiar and comfortable with living there. No matter how comfortable he tried to make us, in the back of my mind I kept thinking that it was not going to work. Why should it work? Was it fair that I had to stay in this house knowing that Mr. Marc-Train purchased me my own home that would have been new to the both of us? The devil tried to plant negative seeds in my mind.

As comfortable as Kenny was trying to make us, would he be comfortable staying here with me surrounded by memories of what had taken place? Sleeping in the same bedroom and using the same bathroom, the more I thought about it, the more uneasy I felt. Dion had a cat that Kenny wanted to keep, but I was terribly afraid of cats. I needed to find a way to tell Kenny that this was not what I wanted so that we could come up with an interim plan while we looked for a new home.

God began to speak to my heart concerning my future husband. I keep hearing, *In my Father's house there are many mansions*. God always made provisions for me in my time of need. I have never been without a roof over my head. I never had to live on the street or in my car, because in my father's house there were many mansions. Although Kenny did what God told him to do, he was still grieving. Although he was excited about marrying me, the love he had for Dion wasn't forgotten, nor was it a distant memory.

The same way God prepared him to be the strong man in my life; He equipped me to be the entire woman Kenny required. God didn't give Kenny a woman that was going to be picky and complain. God gave Kenny a woman that knew how to survive under any circumstances. Kenny had a woman that didn't want him for what he had or didn't have. I was given to him by God to supply him with what he needed. He needed me, the woman created for him for this moment in time.

Me, the one God chose out of all the other women that had the desire and planned to be his wife. God chose me. Whatever it would take to be the helpmate I was destined to be, I must do it. My thoughts could not be on the simple minded things other women couldn't handle. I needed to rise to the occasion embracing the situation with confidence. Transforming my negative thinking into mature learning, the very essence of the home changed. As I began to value the ambiance, I discovered that I was there to empathize with what was before me, and identify with what will be.

My heart understood that Kenny needed me to be down for him no matter what. Kenny needed to see that I was willing to go with God's plan and not my own. For my engagement I didn't get a

The Wedding

huge diamond and a brand new home built from the ground, but I did get God coming down from heaven, hand picking the two of us to be together. God gave him to me, and I could not let God down because of the bizarreness of the circumstances. God created this path for us to take and He would be with us through it all. There were many rooms in the house and together we would change the design, we would do some painting, and put in new furniture, but most of all we would pray together, stay together and make this house our home.

We decided to marry on a Friday night changing the traditional day and time for weddings. I wanted an evening of elegance and romance and a great start to the holiday weekend. With many family members coming from Rochester, I wanted them to be able to get back home and still have some of their weekend left after showing up to support me. As my family arrived and the time was getting closer things became more and more real. I couldn't help but wonder when Mr. Marc-Train would come out of hiding and finally take a stand refusing to let his future be taken from him. I prayed he didn't wait until the wedding night to show up and disrupt the service. I never told him when we were getting married, but with all the commotion around the wedding, it wouldn't have been hard to find out. That didn't matter though, my heart was set on doing what God had for me to do, and that was marrying Kenny.

My flowers were beautiful and I could envision the church being decorated just the way I wanted. Mother Pappins was so gifted with making the floral arrangements, and I couldn't wait to see the

The Wedding

image in my mind become a reality. I wanted my wedding to be as common as any other wedding with the normal contributors putting forth an effort to make sure that it was a success. I had to accept that this wedding would be anything but common and embrace all the let-downs, disappointments and setbacks that occurred, understanding that it wouldn't be the end of the world if things didn't go exactly as planned.

*****

It's my wedding day and the sun is shining luminously. The morning felt like no other and I knew it was because my life was on the verge of being permanently altered from that day forward. What did it feel like to know I was about to become Mrs. Lillian Hunt? There were many thoughts running through my head. Kenny had shown me that he was willing to obey the instructions the Lord gave him, but what if after the wedding, when we were finally together alone to consummate our marriage I was not as pleasurable as he expected?

We had never been together before so neither of us knew what to expect. Spiritually my heart has pliable for him, but the physical attraction was still working into my mind. A part of me still saw him as my big brother and not my lover. What if he couldn't see past me being his sister in the Lord and didn't find me attractive?

It was easy to go with what we knew, but when we began to tread in the unknown fear set in. *I won't be afraid. I will be overjoyed today.* I couldn't wait to get into my dress and walk down the aisle. I

The Wedding

wanted to sing my heart out to Kenny and make him smile like never before. I wanted to show all the people who had nothing but negative things to say that they were wrong about us. *Who am I kidding? I am nervous.* I had no idea what things were going to look like or be like. All I knew was Kenny said he was with me on this and that God was leading us through it all. That was all I needed to know.

All my Bridesmaids were beautiful. The limo arrived to drive us to the church. My hair was done, and the tiara was in place. All that was left was for me to put on my dress and make it to the altar. When arriving to the church I saw people going in and I didn't want to start the wedding late, I wanted our wedding to start on time. I was so happy to see my grandma there with me while I got dressed. Being surrounded by my sisters and the rest of my wedding party put me in a very happy place. As we took pictures and I got dressed, my mom told me that she forgot the flower girls baskets and the groomsmen's boutonnieres. I was warned that on every wedding day there are minor disasters so I chose not to panic or overreact. My panicking and over reacting should have set in when I find out that the musicians that came all the way from Rochester decided to take a day trip to Washington D.C. not knowing that on a Friday afternoon of the holiday weekend traffic would be horrible, so they would miss my wedding. All the music rehearsed and the routine put in place for the wedding was ruined.

My father looked at me and told me I was beautiful, then asked me if I was ready. As the Fred Hammond track "Show Me

The Wedding

Your Face" from the album Pages of Life III began to play, the door opened, and my father and I entered the church while the guests rise from their seats to acknowledge my entrance. I looked over the church and saw the beautiful lilies on every pew with ribbons and lace making it look like I was walking down an aisle in the middle of a field of lilies. There were so many people there I couldn't believe how packed the church was. It seemed as if no one but my family was supportive of this wedding, but the church was full to its capacity with people from all over. As I held tight to my daddy and we got ready to walk down the aisle I couldn't help but greet those that had come to share with Kenny and I on our special day.

Instantly I looked through all the people standing and staring at me, and I caught eyes with my groom. I froze in time and it seemed like everything came to a halt as I looked at him from the back of the church waiting on me to make it to the altar. It was in that moment I felt God put the love and attraction a woman should have for her husband inside of me. For the first time, I didn't look at him and see a big brother. I was fully delighted with him, aroused by his presence and eager to become his wife. His name couldn't be Kenny anymore. To me he was now sexy KB. God waited until it was time for me to walk down the aisle and not a moment sooner to have me be fascinated by my husband, yearning to be with him as his wife on our honeymoon.

As I glared into KB's eyes I sang to him as if no one was in the church but him and me. The song sung by Vanessa Bell

The Wedding

Armstrong "Then Came You" from The Pinnacle Project flowed from my soul as I sang it to him for the first time. I meant every word as I looked him in his eyes and put the microphone up to my mouth and began to sing *"The satisfaction that comes my way, is a result of the debt Jesus paid"*. He swayed from side to side as I sang to him *"I've been searching, waiting for this day, somehow I knew things would turn out okay"*. Hearing the jazzy drum beat with the keyboard and base flowing I got into the song and let my man know, *"I needed an answer to all of my questions, it was you."*

Yes I will love you and honor the vows we made before all of our witnesses. My pregnant baby sister is getting ready to steal my thunder by passing out during my wedding, but she holds on for our "I do's" and finally I am Mrs. Lillian Mary Hunt. We did it. We went through with the plan God had for us. I couldn't help but wonder, *Is this the end or just the beginning?*

As the reception came to a close and KB and I address our guests, I noticed many there that were openly unhappy with the decision God had for KB and I. The Luther Barnes song in my heart rang out,

> *They said I wouldn't make it, they said I wouldn't be here today*
> *They said I'll never amount to anything.*
> *But I'm glad to say, that I'm on my way, and I'm growing more and more each day.*
> *Though I've been talked about, and oh I've been criticized,*
> *He's had to wipe many tears from my eyes,*
> *But I'm still holding on to his hands...*

The Wedding

As I grab a tighter hold to KB's hand, I was delighted that we made it through the evening and were now moving on to the next phase of our life. Off to the Bahamas to make our first baby. *I pray I can have children for this man and make all his dreams come true as he is doing for me.*

*****

A married woman, I was on my way to our honeymoon suite to make love for the first time the way God ordained for it to be. Excitement and butterflies filled my inner being. This former Oreo cookie was fluttering with anticipation of the satisfaction that was to come. Tired and exhausted neither of us wanted to let the other down. We didn't. On that night we got to know each other as husband and wife. Just when I thought I had experienced it all, and there was nothing new for me to learn, I became a wife. My husband took my body and demonstrated to me what it meant to have a true soul mate.

Gently and tenderly he showed me how much he appreciated God blessing him with me as his wife. So delicately from head to toe he familiarized himself with the one God entrusted him to be a husband to for the rest of his life. It was breathtaking. Everything was in perfect tune, playing out like a well-rehearsed orchestra. Each string when plucked made just the right sound.

Flawlessly each note was met with perfect synchronization. An original melody filled with love was composed on that night. A rhythm of heartbeats generated a series of verses developing a new

The Wedding

stanza. We invented our own poetry and crafted our irreplaceable plateau. A song was made and everlasting harmony created.

*****

Seasons. Season adds flavor and spice, but seasons are also periods in time. Reflecting back on my life, I realized that everything I endured prepared me for the moment I was experiencing. The good and the bad times alike were all mere seasons in time, and much like the seasonings you put in your food. We used seasonings to enhance the taste of foods that we prepared. There were mixtures of seasonings added here and there and we needed them. You never see someone sit and eat a bottle of pepper, but salt and pepper properly seasoned over your choice of food is a delight.

I wouldn't take nothing for the seasons I had to endure. It was because of those seasons that my life was beautifully flavored. Flavored and full of exciting activity. One escapade after another there were good times and happy times. Times I loved to reflect on and other times I wished no one else would ever have to go through. Lessons had been learned, and growth had occurred. Wisdom from God had been given, and second chances learned from. I made many choices in my life and horrible mistakes as well. I could not erase them because they made my story. They were not who I was, but what I had gone through.

My mother whispered that I would need to write down the experiences of my life that were to come. "Imagine those lives and hearts God will touch by the mention of your story," she said.

The Wedding

Somebody needed to hear the things we had gone through to let them know that they could make it through the current situation in their life and reach a blissful finale. So many things had taken place up to this point and now I was at a milestone. I was a mother, and a wife, fully living the Christian life. As a wedding gift my mother gave me a diary book and told me to write – The Diary of a Pastor's Daughter-In-Law.

The name Oreo cookie does not define who I am. The relationship between my father and me does not define who I am. Adolescent decisions; mistakes; single parenting; failed relationships; and even graduating from college receiving two degrees do not define who I am. What defines me is how well I rise after falling. I am who God says I am. It was His love for me that remained through every situation in my life. It was His wisdom that steered me out of tough situations. It was His all-knowing-ness that had and would continue to lead me to His expected end full of peace and prosperity. Having a man finally loving me given to me straight from God doesn't define who I am, but it does define who my God is.

No, a woman doesn't have to have a husband to feel complete and be successful in this life. I had to realize that it was never the relationship with any other man, but my relationship with God that mattered. Once complete and in place, He handed over my heart and my being into the hands of the one He felt capable to uphold the earthly obligation of being my head. As the highest form of

The Wedding

admiration and reverence I humbly submitted, showing God how much I valued and trusted His desires for my life.

No longer was I worried about the right man coming along and taking my breath away; he was already there. I didn't have to wait for my knight in shining armor to rescue me from danger; he was there. No more looking for the guy of my dreams that would cause me to smile even when I was hurting; he was there. My covering had arrived and he was doing what he was purposed to do - Cover Me.

Our coming together was not planned, but a beautiful mystery from God that we uncovered daily. My husband was the rare and distinctive man God prepared for me. He was mine and I was his. Together we completed and honored God's covenant. Now, my husband is The Covering.

Reflections

Reflections

REFLECTIONS